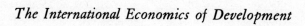

The International Economics of Development

The
International Economics
of Development

THEORY AND POLICY

A revised and expanded edition of *International Trade and Development*

Gerald M. Meier

Professor of International Economics
Stanford University

Harper & Row, Publishers

New York · Evanston · London

To David
—now also concerned

Parts of this book were previously published under the title,
INTERNATIONAL TRADE AND DEVELOPMENT by the author.

Contents

Preface to
The International Economics
of Development

I f the pace of development has been disappointingly slow, the same can certainly not be said about the outpouring of development literature which has grown so rapidly. This has been especially true for the subject matter of the international economics of development. In recent years, a number of significant contributions have been made to the subject; the relative importance of various issues has changed; and new problems have commanded attention—at both the theoretical and policy levels.

In this book I have attempted to recognize these changes by extensively revising and expanding chapters 1, 2, 3, 4, 7, and 8 of my earlier *International Trade and Development*. I have also added new chapters—5, 6, and 9—to make the discussion more comprehensive and immediate.

While *International Trade and Development* was concerned primarily with consolidating the analytical foundations of the subject,

The International Economics of Development incorporates more emphasis on policy questions. After two decades of experience with development planning, there is a need for a critical assessment of the effects of international trade and payments policies on development. And now the institution of the United Nations Conference on Trade and Development serves as a constant and challenging reminder of the interrelated problems of development planning and foreign economic policy.

Indeed, the major issue that underlies this entire book—namely, whether there is a conflict between the traditional "gains from trade" and the "gains from growth"—has become of increasing concern to economists engaged in the formulation and implementation of development programs. Whatever analytical clarity can be brought to this issue will surely contribute to a more effective guidance on the range of policy choices governing the balance of payments, inflow of foreign capital, commercial policy, and reform of international economic institutions.

In the realm of policy, I have sought to emphasize fundamental principles, and I have therefore limited the discussion essentially to the theory of policy. To have included quantitative analysis, or to have added country studies, would have made this a different kind of book. In order to define the major issues, I have wanted to keep the argument compact and fundamental; it will be sufficient for my objective if the present discussion suggests some basic questions to ask of the other empirical studies that now exist in this field.

I am indebted to Professors Jagdish Bhagwati, Ronald W. Jones, and Ronald I. McKinnon for their valued advice and comments. I am also grateful to the editors of the *University of Chicago Law Review* for permission to reprint some sections of Chapter 6, and to the editors of the *Stanford Law Review* for permission to reprint a part of Chapter 9. Some paragraphs from Chapters 7 and 9 appear in my paper on "Free Trade and Development Economics," in *Value, Capital and Growth—Essays in Honor of Sir John Hicks* (Edinburgh University Press, 1968).

G. M. M.

Stanford, California

Preface to
International Trade and Development

B y the very nature of its ambitious sweep, the subject of economic development is only too prone to diffuseness in its increasingly voluminous body of literature. There is a periodic need for studies that bring order to the various branches of the subject. This is especially true now for the international economics of development. Discussions of the connection between trade and development require greater analytical coherency; central issues must be clarified, and major insights consolidated. I have kept these objectives in mind in writing this book.

In so doing, I have found that the traditional theory of international trade, when suitably extended, provides the most useful analytical framework for bringing unity to a variety of observations on the trade problems of poor countries. I have not been convinced by the common criticism that theory in the classical tradition lacks relevance and realism for matters of development. On the contrary, the most pertinent statements about the relations between trade and development retain continuity with traditional trade theory. If its static assumptions are relaxed and additional variables introduced, traditional trade theory can still offer a powerful set of fundamental principles for illuminating development questions.

To this end, I have reconsidered from the standpoint of international development the main topics in the pure theory and monetary theory of international trade. Individual chapters analyze the changing structure of comparative costs in the course of development, the significance for poor countries of secular movements in their terms of trade, the relations between capital formation and the maintenance of balance of payments equilibrium, the developmental role of international capital movements, the use of commercial policy as a component of development programming, and the potential for transmitting development through foreign trade.

I am indebted to the John Simon Guggenheim Memorial Foundation for enabling me to consider portions of this study as a by-product of a larger project that I began while a Guggenheim Fellow. The hospitality of the Oxford University Institute of Statistics and my discussions with members of its staff and other Oxford economists are gratefully remembered. I have also benefited from the opportunity to lecture on an early draft of parts of this book at an Advanced Refresher Course in Economic Development held in Pakistan under the auspices of the International Economic Association and the Pakistan Economic Association.

I should also like to make explicit my special debt to Professors Gottfried Haberler, Harry Johnson, Hla Myint, and the late Ragnar Nurkse. Their writings have done much to enrich the subject matter of international trade and development, and no amount of footnoting could adequately indicate how strongly influenced I have been by their contributions. I also wish to recall my indebtedness to Professor J. R. Hicks, who first guided my interest in this subject.

Professors Bela Balassa, Gottfried Haberler, and Harry Johnson have been kind enough to read and to criticize most helpfully various parts of the manuscript; I have profited greatly from their suggestions. Needless to say, I alone remain responsible for any errors or negligences.

I am also appreciative for the secretarial services of Miss Catherine E. Cooney and for the financial aid extended by the Research Fund of Wesleyan University.

For permission to use portions of some earlier articles by the author, acknowledgments are due to the editors of the following journals: *Economia Internazionale, Oxford Economic Papers, Panjab University Economist,* and *Social and Economic Studies.*

G. M. M.

The opening of a foreign trade . . . sometimes works a sort of industrial revolution in a country whose resources were previously undeveloped . . .

—John Stuart Mill, *Principles of Political Economy*

The causes which determine the economic progress of nations belong to the study of international trade . . .

—Alfred Marshall, *Principles of Economics*

Underdevelopment economics is a vastly important subject, but it is not a formal or theoretical subject. It is a practical subject which must expect to call upon any branch of theory (including non-economic, for instance sociological, theory) which has any relevance to it. If there is any branch of economic theory which is especially relevant to it, it is the Theory of International Trade.

—Sir John Hicks, *Capital and Growth*

1
Introductory

1. The classical theory of international trade has shown a remarkable capacity to absorb modifications as required by advances in general economic theory and by the exigencies of public policy issues. Yet, in spite of its substantial evolution from Hume and Ricardo through Marshall, Edgeworth, and Taussig, to Professors Viner and Haberler, the traditional theory still remains an analysis of full static equilibrium with respect to domestic market assumptions, and is concerned most directly with rich advanced economies. In contrast, general economic theory has sought increasingly to incorporate long-period dynamic analysis, and the most pressing international economic problems now involve the acceleration of development in poor countries.

Followers of the classical tradition have long been uneasy about Professor Williams' criticism that "the relation of international trade to the development of new resources and productive forces is a more significant part of the explanation of the present status of nations, of incomes, prices, well-being, than is the cross-section value analysis of the classical economists, with its assumption of given quanta of productive factors, already existent and employed."[1]

More recently, Gunnar Myrdal has observed that "In the complex of tensions between the peoples in the underdeveloped countries, on the one hand, and the industrially advanced ones, on the other, there is an important intellectual element: a suspicion by people in the former countries that in their only recently challenged monopoly of advanced economic analysis, the economists in the latter countries have viewed matters too exclusively from the point of view of their own nations' circumstances and interests, which are not always those of the peoples in the underdeveloped countries."[2] According to Myrdal, "it should not surprise us that, on the whole, the literature is curiously devoid of attempts to relate the facts of international inequalities and the problems of underdevelopment and development to the theory of international trade."[3]

Even though Myrdal takes an extreme position in his condemnation of the "strange isolation of the theory of international trade from the facts of economic life,"[4] economists are still generally desirous that trade theory should have more to say about developmental problems. Many would subscribe to Professor Nurkse's more moderate statement: "The case for international specialization is firmly based on considerations of economic ef-

---

[1] J. H. Williams, "The Theory of International Trade Reconsidered," *Economic Journal*, June, 1929, p. 196.

[2] Gunnar Myrdal, *An International Economy*, Harper & Row, 1956, p. 222.

[3] Gunnar Myrdal, *Rich Lands and Poor*, Harper & Row, 1957, p. 153.

[4] *Ibid.*, p. 154.

ficiency. The world is not rich enough to be able to despise efficiency. The optimum pattern of specialization is governed by the principle of comparative advantage. This principle remains as valid today as it was in Ricardo's time. And yet there is some question whether it alone can give all the guidance needed by countries whose dominant and deliberate aim is economic development . . . If one asks what help it offers here and now to low-income countries in search of development, the answer is not altogether clear."[5]

Of greater practical importance than these individual statements is the fact that the institutionalization of the United Nations Conference on Trade and Development (UNCTAD) has now provided an organizational culmination for the trade complaints of less developed countries.[6] There is now a continual critical review of the operation of the international economy from the

[5] Ragnar Nurkse, "International Trade Theory and Development Policy," H. S. Ellis, ed., *Economic Development for Latin America*, St. Martin's Press, 1961, pp. 234, 235.

[6] UNCTAD was convened in 1964. At its first session in Geneva, 120 nations—including some 77 developing countries—discussed "solutions" to the problems of international trade and development. As a basis for these discussions, the Secretary-General of UNCTAD (Raúl Prebisch) stated that "On the international economic scene we are faced with new problems, new in kind, in some cases, and new because of the magnitude they have acquired, in others. We therefore need different attitudes from those prevailing in the past, and these attitudes should converge towards a new trade policy for economic development." Prebisch, *Towards a New Trade Policy for Development*, Report of the Secretary-General of UNCTAD, United Nations, 1964, p. 107.

UNCTAD has become an organ of the United Nations General Assembly, with the Trade and Development Board performing the functions of the Conference between sessions. The second session of UNCTAD will be held in New Delhi in 1968, and it has become clear that the controversial issues raised by UNCTAD now occupy a central position in international deliberations.

standpoint of its effectiveness in contributing to international development.

These criticisms, together with the widespread practice of development planning, make it apparent that the received body of trade theory needs amendment and extension. Although the classicists were attentive to the long-run growth of the domestic economy, they were content to analyze the international economy in essentially static terms. Classical and neoclassical writers did not completely ignore the developmental effects of international trade, but their allusions to developmental topics were quite subsidiary. Their statements on international development have been considered as merely in the nature of *obiter dicta* alongside what has become accepted as the main corpus of traditional trade theory.

For an examination of the poor countries in the international economy, traditional trade theory need not be completely supplanted; but it must be supplemented in a broader frame of reference and removed from the confines of full static equilibrium, as in classical analysis, and from the short period of the cycle, as in Keynesian analysis. It needs to pose a different set of questions. This study presents such an extension.

In adapting traditional theory to deal with phenomena of change, we shall use, in large part, the method of comparative statics. Although we shall refer as much as possible to the underlying dynamics of international development problems, we shall do so in a manner that is short of a truly dynamic analysis of the time-path of the process of change. It is, however, only too easy to make excessive claims for the use of dynamic analysis; dynamic model-building in this area remains a matter of aspiration rather than accomplishment.[7] Our more modest approach should

[7] Richard E. Caves, *Trade and Economic Structure*, Harvard Univ. Press, 1960, pp. 242–244. See also, Jagdish Bhagwati, "The Pure Theory of International Trade: A Survey," *Economic Journal*, March, 1964, pp. 48–

still carry us quite a way in clarifying the international economics of development, even though the desirability of applying a thorough dynamic analysis will be apparent for some of the issues we consider.

2. Our starting point is the simple recognition that at any given time the international economy will be composed of countries which have attained different levels of development as measured by per capita real income. Over a period of time the several countries will also experience differential rates of advance. Moreover, each country's pattern of internal development may vary, in accordance with particular leading and lagging sectors and different interconnections among the sectors.

Once these differences in the level, rate, and pattern of development are recognized, we must transform many of the "constants" in classical trade theory into variables. In the context of development, we can no longer allow resources to be fixed in supply, tastes constant, technical knowledge given, and imports equal to exports with no international capital movements. Such restrictive conditions preclude an analysis of the long-run evolution of international trade and ignore the very essence of the development process. If we are to analyze relationships between international trade and development, we must consider the effects of continual accumulation in productive factors, the evolu-

---

51; reprinted in *Surveys of Economic Theory*, Vol. II, *Growth and Development*, St. Martin's Press, 1965, pp. 203–206.

Although dynamic propositions in international trade and development still await full-scale systematic analysis, some interesting models have recently been suggested by H. Oniki and H. Uzawa, "Patterns of Trade and Investment in a Dynamic Model of International Trade," *Review of Economic Studies*, January, 1965, pp. 15–38; P. K. Bardhan, "Optimum Accumulation and International Trade," *Review of Economic Studies*, July, 1965, pp. 241–244.

tion of demand conditions, technical progress, and international capital movements. These changes affect international trade, and international trade, in turn, influences the development process. The international economics of development is concerned with these reciprocal relationships.

3. Such relationships have some relevance for every developing country, whether rich or poor, but they apply with particular force to poor countries. Although there have been studies of the effects of international trade on the maintenance of growth in rich countries, and of the impact of overseas development on the trade of industrial countries, there has been relatively little systematic consideration of the more urgent problem of the effects of trade on the acceleration of development in poor countries. In striving for simplicity, most of the theories of development have sacrificed relevance by abstracting from the international setting in which the national development of poor countries must occur.

The economy of a poor country can be characterized as being an "export economy" or a "dependent economy." These terms may be somewhat arbitrary, and the latter is needlessly emotive, but most of the poor countries do have a strong orientation towards foreign trade. This orientation appears in many ways: a high ratio of export production to total output in the cash sector of the economy, a concentrated structure of export production, a high marginal propensity to import, the inflow of long-term capital, the presence of foreign-owned enterprises, and even in the large share of government revenue derived from customs receipts. It is also an historical feature of the intersectoral pattern of production that export production has normally displayed the most rapid expansion and that the level of exports has tended to have more influence on aggregate demand than has private investment or government expenditure. The weight of exports in relation to total activity is especially great for the smaller nations.[8] And even though the ratio of foreign trade to national income is usually low in a predominantly subsistence economy before the pace of development accelerates, the ratio rises rapidly with development as foreign trade tends to grow faster than income in the early stages of development.[9] On both quantitative and qualitative grounds, it is therefore especially important to examine the development of poor countries in the context of their external environment.

4. In doing this, we shall focus on five basic problems:

a. If we determine how the structure of comparative advantage changes over time, we can then ask how the volume and composition of trade and the gains from trade undergo change. Traditional trade theory does not provide an immediate answer to this, insofar as it is restricted to the narrower questions of what commodities would be traded and what would be the gains from trade at a given moment. To extend this analysis to a developing economy we must consider how changes in factor supplies, technical progress, and changes in demand can transform the structure of comparative costs. We examine these developmental aspects of the pure theory of trade in Chapter 2, which introduces long-period changes into the theory of comparative costs, and in

---

[8] On the basis of data presented by Professor Kuznets, it is clear that the smaller the country, as measured by population, the larger is the ratio of exports or imports to total output, and that foreign trade is more important relative to total output for smaller rather than larger countries. Simon Kuznets, "Economic Growth of Small Nations," E. A. G. Robinson, ed., *The Economic Consequences of the Size of Nations*, St. Martin's Press, 1960, pp. 18–20.

[9] W. A. Lewis, *The Theory of Economic Growth*, Allen & Unwin, 1955, p. 342.

Chapter 3, which investigates the long-period determinants of the terms of trade.

b. In considering the monetary theory of trade, we should recognize that the international saving-investment mechanism is at the center of the international development process. We should, therefore, relate the problem of maintaining balance of payments equilibrium to the developmental problem of capital accumulation. Chapter 4 does this by analyzing the possible sources of conflict between the objectives of accelerating capital formation and preserving external balance.

c. Analysis of the international saving-investment problem also requires us to relate the inflow of foreign capital to the development process. The traditional theory of international capital movements focuses on the transfer problem and the mechanism of adjustment in the balance of payments. But the transfer of productive capital and its interconnection with the forces of development receive only slight attention. Chapter 5 attempts to remedy this deficiency by examining some developmental aspects of the inflow of public foreign capital and by considering the effects of a "development through aid" strategy. Chapter 6 focuses on problems of private foreign investment and appraises the benefits and costs of direct foreign investment in the context of a national development program.

d. Against the background of these modifications in traditional theory, we may then proceed to the overriding question of whether there is a conflict between the gains from trade and the gains from growth—whether the process of development is facilitated or handicapped through international trade. To what extent can the export sector transmit developmental forces to a poor country? Is free trade the optimal trade policy for stimulating development, or can development be more readily accelerated by the use of restrictive commercial policy? What has been the experience with policies that emphasize "development through import substitution"? What is the potential for "development through trade"? Chapters 7 and 8 attempt to answer such questions.

    e. Finally, we should consider the ways in which a reform of international economic institutions and a change in the "international rules of the game" might accelerate international development. The complaints of the less developed nations, as voiced at UNCTAD, against the General Agreement on Tariffs and Trade, International Monetary Fund, and commercial policies of advanced countries cannot be lightly dismissed. It is particularly important to assess the merits of the developing countries' demand for stabilization of their primary export prices, preferential trading arrangements, international monetary reform, and changes in the trade policies of industrialized countries. Chapter 9 examines these issues which are now very much a matter of international debate.

5. Each of these problems has attracted increasing attention in the recent literature on trade and development. The contributions remain, however, dispersed and rather fragmentary. The time has come to consolidate these contributions and extend them within the main corpus of international trade theory.

2

Comparative Costs

1. The pure theory of international trade has been most thoroughly refined in terms of static general equilibrium analysis. This analysis, with its emphasis on the relations between production and trade and its formulation of the doctrine of comparative costs, is a convenient starting point for our subsequent discussion.

To recall the leading principles of this analysis we may concentrate on the usual two-country, two-commodity, two-factor model.[1] This is the simplest possible model which contains the

---

[1] Gottfried Haberler, "Some Problems in the Pure Theory of International Trade," *Economic Journal*, June, 1950, pp. 223–240; James E. Meade, *A Geometry of International Trade*, Allen & Unwin, 1952, chaps. I-V; Kelvin Lancaster, "The Heckscher-Ohlin Trade Model: A Geometric Treatment," *Economica*, February, 1957, pp. 19–39; Richard E. Caves, *Trade and Economic Structure*, Harvard Univ. Press, 1960, chap. II; Jagdish Bhagwati, "The Pure Theory of International Trade," *Economic Journal*, March, 1964, pp. 1–84.

fundamental elements of the general equilibrium problem, but the major inferences drawn from it will, for the most part, be essentially the same as those of a multicountry, multicommodity, multifactor model.

Let the countries be E and G, the commodities X and Y, and the factors "labor" (L) and "capital" (C). We assume that (1) purely competitive conditions prevail in product and factor markets; (2) the production functions of X and Y are subject to constant returns to scale; (3) X is always the more "labor-intensive" industry, in the sense that, at the same relative prices for the factors in both industries, the ratio of total labor to total capital used in the production of X is greater than the corresponding ratio in the production of Y; and (4) in each country the factor supplies are fixed in total amount, and technical knowledge, consumer tastes, and the distribution of income between factors are all held constant. After summarizing the static analysis, we shall remove assumption (4) and introduce various long-period changes into our discussion.

2. Consider country E. In an Edgeworth-Bowley box diagram of production functions for country E (Fig. 1), the locus of the points of tangency of the two sets of isoquants forms an "efficiency locus" XY which represents optimal resource allocation for the production of X and Y with given supplies of L and C in country E. This follows from the fact that at each point of tangency the ratio between the marginal productivities of L and C (given by the slope of the isoquants) in the production of X is equal to the ratio between their marginal productivities in the production of Y. Production is then efficient in the sense that it is impossible to produce more of one commodity without reducing the output of the other.

By reading off the amounts of X and Y along the efficiency locus and translating these amounts to a plane such as in Fig. 2, we derive the "production frontier" (transformation curve or production-possibility curve) *MN*. This curve represents the maximum-possible combinations of *X* and *Y* that can be produced in country *E*. Its position follows from the conditions of factor supply and production functions indicated in Fig. 1. The slope of

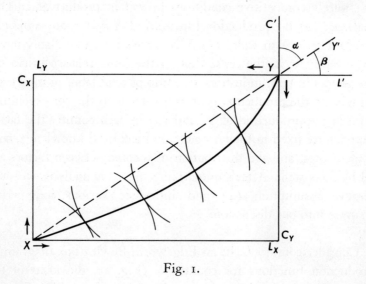

Fig. 1.

MN at any point denotes the ratio of the marginal opportunity costs of *X* and *Y*, the marginal opportunity cost of producing an additional unit of one commodity being measured by the necessary reduction in the output of the other. In Fig. 2, the production frontier is concave to the origin, indicating that the marginal opportunity cost of transforming one commodity into the other is increasing as more of the commodity is produced.[2]

[2] W. F. Stolper and P. A. Samuelson, "Protection and Real Wages," *Review of Economic Studies*, November, 1941, pp. 58–73; Caves, *op. cit.*, pp. 30–35. The production frontier is concave in Fig. 2, even though it

3. If we are now given the conditions of domestic demand, represented for simplicity by community indifference curves I_1 . . . I_4 in Fig. 2, we can determine the equilibrium position of country E before trade.[3] The domestic exchange ratio or its reciprocal, the price ratio, is given by the slope of RS in Fig. 2. Market equilibrium for the closed economy is then at P, the point of tangency between the production frontier and a community indifference curve. At P the following equilibrium conditions hold: In the factor markets, the ratio of the marginal product of labor to the marginal product of capital is the same in each occupation, and the price of each factor is equal to its marginal value product. In the commodity markets, the price ratio is equal to the marginal cost ratio (the slope of RS equals the slope of the production frontier at P). The price ratio is also equal to the marginal rate of substitution in consumption (as given by the slope of the

---

is assumed that constant returns to scale exist in the production of each commodity, because different factor proportions are used in the production of X and Y; if the production of one good expands, it must then use factors in a more costly combination. With constant returns in the production functions, the production frontier is concave to a degree depending on the elasticities of substitution.

If constant returns exist in the production of each good, and each production process uses factors in exactly the same ratio at any given factor-price ratio, the production frontier would be a straight line, indicating that the marginal opportunity cost of transforming one good into the other remained constant. If, however, the production functions were sufficiently strongly subject to increasing returns, the frontier would be convex to the origin, indicating that the marginal cost of X in terms of Y falls as more of X is produced.

[3] Community indifference curves are used merely as an heuristic device, not as an empirical construct or as a basis for conclusions about changes in economic welfare. See T. Scitovsky, "A Reconsideration of the Theory of Tariffs," *Review of Economic Studies*, Summer, 1942, pp. 93–95; P. A. Samuelson, "Social Indifference Curves," *Quarterly Journal of Economics*, February, 1956, pp. 1–22.

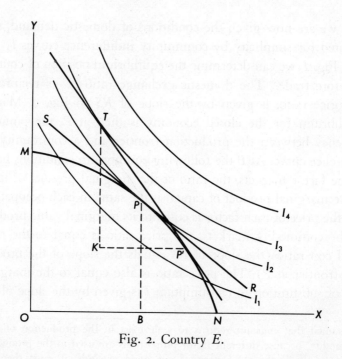

Fig. 2. Country E.

community indifference curve at *P*), and the consumption of each commodity is equal to its output (*OB* of *X* and *BP* of *Y*). Moreover, the position of market equilibrium is an optimum: it is on the production frontier, and the relative valuation of the products by consumers is equal to the relative costs of production to society (the marginal rate of substitution in consumption equals the marginal rate of transformation in production).

A similar analysis applies to country *G*. It may be assumed that the relative endowment of factors differs from that in *E*, and that *G*'s domestic price ratio is different from *E*'s in the absence of trade.

4. Let us now open the countries to trade, and allow an international price ratio—the terms of trade—to be established on the world market. When the terms of trade lie between the different domestic price ratios that exist in E and G in the absence of trade, both countries can gain through international specialization and trade. Each country will tend to specialize in the production of the commodity which it can produce relatively cheaply —namely, the commodity which is intensive in its relatively abundant factor—and will demand imports from the other country by supplying exports of this commodity in which it has a comparative advantage.[4] As the terms of trade vary, each country's "willingness to trade" will change according to its particular production possibilities and preference pattern. The country's "willingness to trade" can be represented by a Marshallian reciprocal demand curve, or an international trade offer curve. Once we derive each country's offer curve, we can determine the equilibrium terms of trade and the equilibrium volume of exports and imports for each country.

To derive the offer curve for country E, we interpret the terms of trade as a parameter and consider the reactions of E to variations in the terms of trade. If the terms of trade are identical

[4] Even if factor endowments were identical in both countries, demand conditions could be dissimilar and could cause the domestic price ratios to differ in the absence of trade, so that international trade would still be profitable. See Bertil Ohlin, *Interregional and International Trade*, Harvard Univ. Press, 1933, p. 16; W. W. Leontief, "The Use of Indifference Curves in the Analysis of Foreign Trade," *Quarterly Journal of Economics*, May, 1933, pp. 499–506.

If factor abundance is interpreted narrowly as meaning only "physical" abundance rather than "economic" abundance, it is possible that the influence of demand conditions may also give rise to an exceptional result: differences in tastes may be so great that a country may not export the product which uses relatively more of its abundant factor. See Stefan Valavanis-Vail, "Leontief's Scarce Factor Paradox," *Journal of Political Economy*, December, 1954, pp. 525–526; R. W. Jones, "Factor Proportions and the Heckscher-Ohlin Model," *Review of Economic Studies*, vol. 24 (1956–57), pp. 1–5; J. Bhagwati, "Protection, Real Wages and Real Incomes," *Economic Journal*, December, 1959, pp. 733–748.

with the domestic exchange ratio in E, namely the slope of RS (Fig. 2), E will continue to produce and consume the combination of X and Y indicated at P. If, however, the terms of trade diverge from the initial domestic price ratio, production and consumption will be altered, and the domestic production and consumption of each commodity will no longer be equal. The direction and degree of alteration will depend on the extent of the divergence of the international price ratio from the internal price ratio, the shape of the production frontier, and the preference pattern.

If the terms of trade line becomes steeper than the internal price line RS, a unit of X will exchange for more units of Y on the world market than on the home market; the country will accordingly specialize in the production of X in which it has a comparative advantage.[5] In contrast, if the terms of trade line becomes less steep than RS, a unit of Y will exchange for more units of X on the world market than on the home market, and the country will tend to specialize in the production of Y. Thus, in Fig. 2, when the terms of trade line is $P'T$, E specializes in the production of X, shifts production to the quantities represented by P', offers for export $P'K$ of X (the excess of domestic production over domestic consumption of X) in payment for imports of KT of Y (the excess of domestic consumption over domestic production of Y),[6] and consumes the quantities represented by T.

We may now derive country E's offer curve, EE' in Fig. 3,

[5] "Specialization" involves the production of more of the good whose world price has risen relatively, and less of the good whose price has been lowered relatively on the world market. In the present case, specialization in production is incomplete: the country concentrates relatively in X, but still produces both X and Y.

[6] We ignore transport costs. The price differences between countries before trade must, of course, be wider than transport costs in order to have trade be profitable.

by plotting in the first quadrant country E's offers of X for Y at the various terms of trade lines steeper than RS, such as $P'T$ in Fig. 2, and by plotting in the third quadrant E's offers of Y for X at the various terms of trade lines less steep than RS.[7]

By similar reasoning, we may derive country G's offer curve, GG', in Fig. 3. Only the first quadrant in which the offer curves intersect is of practical interest. If there is free trade, no transport costs and no surplus or deficit in the balance of trade, then the position of trade equilibrium will be at C, the point of intersection of the offer curves. This is a position of stable equilibrium.[8] The equilibrium terms of trade are equivalent to the slope of OC; the equilibrium volume of trade is OM of X or MC of Y; and E's exports are equal to G's imports. If in Fig. 2 the trading point T is an equilibrium trading position for country E, the point T must then lie on G's offer curve at C in Fig. 3, and OM (Fig. 3) equals $P'K$ (Fig. 2), and MC (Fig. 3) equals KT (Fig. 2). These

---

[7] In Fig. 3, $+ X_E$ and $- X_G$ denote exports of X from E and imports of X into G, respectively. Similarly, $+ Y_E$ and $- Y_G$ represent exports of Y from E and imports of Y into G, respectively.

[8] Cf. Alfred Marshall, *Money, Credit, and Commerce*, Macmillan Co., 1923, p. 341. A displacement of the terms of trade from equilibrium would set in motion forces inducing a return to that equilibrium. A change, for instance, in the terms of trade to the right of OC would create an excess demand for E's exports at the lower price, and the relative price of E's exports must then rise. A change to the left of OC would create an excess supply of E's exports at the higher price, and the relative price of E's exports must then fall.

The offer curves we have derived in Fig. 3 resemble, but are not identical with, the Marshallian reciprocal demand curves. Marshall assumed each country "to make up her exports into representative 'bales'; that is, bales each of which represents uniform aggregate investments of her labour and her capital." The Marshallian terms of trade are then factoral instead of commodity terms of trade. Conditions under which the commodity terms of trade will be equivalent to the double-factoral terms are discussed in Chapter 3, section 2.

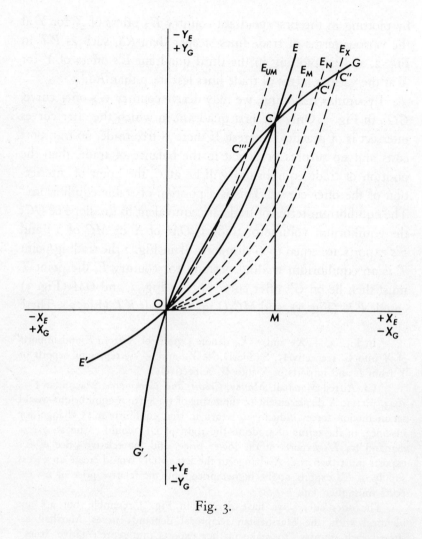

Fig. 3.

equilibrium conditions follow from (1) the rules of the purely competitive model that ensure tangency of the price ratio with the production frontier and the consumption indifference curve, and (2) in the case of free trade, the equality of the domestic and foreign prices which ensures that the imbalance between country *E*'s consumption and production is offset by matching imbalances from country *G* at the stated foreign prices.

In the remainder of the discussion, we shall let the equilibrium terms of trade line be *P'T* (Fig. 2), so that *E* finds it profitable to export the labor-intensive commodity *X*.

5. The contribution of international trade to economic welfare can now be readily recognized.[9] The equilibrium trading conditions, summarized in the previous section, fulfill the optimum conditions of resource allocation. In the absence of monopoly power, market imperfections, and externalities in consumption and production, the equilibrium conditions of free trade satisfy the necessary marginal conditions of a Paretian national optimum. Under the assumptions that we have made,[10] free trade produces the "first-best" solution which equates the marginal rate of transformation in domestic production (the marginal cost of exportables in terms of importables), marginal rate of transfor-

[9] Excellent summaries of the literature on the welfare effects of international trade are provided by Caves, *op. cit.*, chap. VIII; E. J. Mishan, "A Survey of Welfare Economics, 1939–1959," *Economic Journal*, June, 1960, pp. 197–265; Bhagwati, "The Pure Theory of International Trade," *op. cit.*, pp. 54–70.

Rigorous statements of the gains from trade are presented in M. C. Kemp, "The Gain from International Trade," *Economic Journal*, December, 1962, pp. 803–819; P. A. Samuelson, "The Gains from International Trade Once Again," *Ibid.*, pp. 820–829; J. Bhagwati, "Gains from Trade Once Again," *Economic Journal* (in press).

[10] When some of these assumptions are removed, so that the ratios of private money costs no longer reflect the social real cost ratios, the welfare results of free trade must be modified. We shall later allow for these qualifications when we consider in their own right a number of arguments for protection. See Chapter 7.

mation in foreign trade (price of exportables in terms of importables), and marginal rate of substitution in domestic consumption.

Without any increase in resources, or technological change, each country is able to enjoy a higher real income by specializing in production according to its comparative advantage and trading. Unless the terms of trade are identical to the rate at which X can be exchanged for Y at home, the country's access to a foreign market has a real income effect that is essentially the same as if there had been an outward shift in its production frontier.

If, in Fig. 2, country E's trading position were at some point on $P'T$ to the right and above the no-trade position P, a larger quantity of both X and Y would actually be gained. The country's trading position would then be clearly superior to its no-trade position. If, however, country E's equilibrium trading position is at T (above but to the left of P), then more Y but less X is available than at P. In this case, the collection of goods at T can be shown to be superior to that at the no-trade situation by a comparison of the quantity index numbers of the two situations. There is then still a potential increase in welfare, even if trade makes some individuals worse off, while making others better off; a redistribution of the larger product by resort to lump-sum taxes and subsidies could leave each individual as well or better off than he was before trade.

The increase in the level of satisfaction from trade will depend on the width of the gaps in the comparative advantages of the trading nations and on the differences in their relative demands. The gains from trade will therefore be greater when the less similar are demand conditions, factor proportions, and the technical coefficients of production for different commodities in the different countries. In other words, the greater the differences in the domestic price ratios and in the relative demands of the countries, the wider will be the range in which the international price ratio can diverge from the domestic ratio; the potential increase in satisfaction from the opening of trade will therefore be greater.[11]

The foregoing analysis refines the orthodox statement of the comparative cost doctrine in terms of modern general equilibrium theory. It also establishes explicitly the basis for offer curve analysis; the hitherto "unseen movements of the machinery" behind the offer curves, which were of such concern to Marshall and Edgeworth,[12] are now revealed to consist of production, income, and substitution effects as a new production point is taken up on the production frontier in response to a variation in the terms of trade. Finally, the analysis relates the gains from trade to modern welfare economics by emphasizing an efficient pattern of world production and the equality between relative prices and marginal rates of transformation in production and marginal rates of substitution in consumption.[13]

[11] Given its production frontier and preferences, a country will gain more satisfaction from trade, the larger is the price change from the no-trade position. But it should be noted that the gain from trade can not be measured simply by the price movement. See Chapter 3 for a discussion of why, in some cases, an improvement in a country's terms of trade may not be indicative of an improved welfare position.

[12] F. Y. Edgeworth, *Papers Relating to Political Economy*, Vol. II, Macmillan Co., 1925, p. 32.

[13] Much of this analysis could also be readily incorporated into the framework of linear programming; the international trade problem of determining optimal outputs by permitting price ratios to change can be interpreted as a particular case of "parametric programming." See Robert Dorfman, P. A. Samuelson, R. M. Solow, *Linear Programming and Economic Analysis*, McGraw-Hill, 1958, pp. 31–38, 41–45, 59–63, 117–121, 346–348; Helen Makower, *Activity Analysis*, Macmillan Co., 1957, chap. IX; T. M. Whitin, "Classical Theory, Graham's Theory, and Linear Programming in International Trade," *Quarterly Journal of Economics*, November, 1953, pp. 520–544; L. W. McKenzie, "On Equilibrium in Graham's Model of World Trade and Other Competitive Systems," *Econometrica*, April, 1954, pp. 142–161.

6. We can now extend the analysis to development problems by first interpreting a country's development in terms of outward shifts in its production frontier. These shifts can be traced to autonomous changes in factor supply and techniques of production. Each particular change will have a "production effect" (discussed in sections 7 and 8) and also a "consumption effect" (section 9); together these effects will cause shifts in a country's offer curve. The over-all strength of the combined production and consumption effects will determine the direction and extent of the shift in each country's offer curve, and thereby the changes in the volume and composition of trade that will result from particular types of factor accumulation and technological progress (section 10).[14]

7. We may first delimit the different types of production effects that will result from various types of factor growth. Introducing changes in the factor supplies of country E will mean that the dimensions of the box diagram in Fig. 1 are no longer fixed, but expand or contract according to whether the factors increase or decrease in supply. Only movements of the box into the quadrant northeast of Y (Fig. 1) are relevant to development problems, for only in this quadrant is the quantity of some or all factors increased without a diminution in others. Movement into any other quadrant involves a decumulation of capital or an absolute

---

[14] An earlier version of this analysis was given in the author's "Note on the Theory of Comparative Costs and Long Period Developments," *Economia Internazionale*, August, 1952, pp. 3–12. In its more extensive form, the present analysis owes much to J. R. Hicks, "An Inaugural Lecture," *Oxford Economic Papers*, June, 1953, pp. 117–125; H. G. Johnson, *International Trade and Economic Growth*, Allen & Unwin, 1958, chap. III; Johnson, "Economic Development and International Trade," *Pakistan Economic Journal*, December, 1959, pp. 47–71.

reduction in the labor force—not impossible, but certainly exceptional occurrences for a developing economy.

Accordingly, we may identify the following five types of factor accumulation and their respective production effects in country E:[15]

a. A movement along YY' (Fig. 1)—that is, the absolute amounts of the factors increase proportionately over a period so that the relative factor endowment remains the same at the end of the period as it was at the beginning. In terms of Fig. 2, the production frontier would then retain the same shape but would shift out proportionately for both commodities, since the original box diagram would simply be rescaled according to the proportionate increase in factor supplies. The effect on production, at constant product prices, will then be the same proportionate increase in the outputs of exportable and importable goods. This can be classified as a "neutral" production effect.[16]

b. A movement into region β (Fig. 1)—that is, labor increases proportionately more than does capital. The family of

---

[15] Although the analysis refers to country E, which exports the labor-intensive commodity, it is a simple matter of translation to recognize the opposite effects in G, which exports the capital-intensive commodity.

[16] The terminology "neutral," "export-biased," and "import-biased," is suggested by Hicks, *op. cit.*, pp. 127 ff.; also, Hicks, *Essays in World Economics*, Oxford Univ. Press, 1959, note B. Professor Johnson uses the terminology of "pro-trade-biased" instead of "export-biased," and "anti-trade-biased" instead of "import-biased"; Johnson, *International Trade and Economic Growth*, *op. cit.*, pp. 76–77. See also, J. Black and P. P. Streeten, "La balance Commerciale les termes de l'échange et la croissance économique," *Économie Appliquée*, April–September, 1957, pp. 299–322.

The difference in terminology is explained by Professor Hicks' concern with whether technical progress occurs in the exporting or import-competing industry, while Professor Johnson is interested in other kinds of changes as well, and the effects of different changes on the demand for imports (supply of exports).

Y-isoquants that originated previously at Y must now be shifted northeastwards to the new origin in region β. This will bring into tangency isoquants that originally neither touched nor intersected, thereby forming a new efficiency locus. The production frontier derived from the new efficiency locus will then lie beyond the initial frontier at all points, and the outward shift of the frontier will be proportionately greater in the direction of the labor-intensive commodity X at constant prices. A proportionately greater increase in the factor which is embodied most intensively in the exportable good X will thus result in the supply of exportables increasing in greater proportion than the supply of importables Y. This type of output expansion can be classified as "export-biased."

c. A movement into region α (Fig. 1)—that is, capital increases proportionately more than does labor. The origin of the isoquant map of Y will be shifted into region α, and a new efficiency locus will be formed. The new production frontier derived from this new efficiency locus will then lie beyond the initial frontier at all points, but at constant prices the outward shift of the frontier will be proportionately greater in the direction of the capital-intensive commodity Y. A proportionately greater increase in the factor which is embodied most intensively in the import-competing good (Y) will thus result in the domestic supply of importables increasing in greater proportion than the supply of exportables. This type of output expansion can be classified as "import-biased."

d. A movement along YL' (Fig. 1)—that is, there is an increase in the labor supply without any increase in the quantity of capital. The production effect of this increased labor supply will be to expand the supply of exportables (X) and reduce the domestic supply of importable goods (Y) at constant prices. This type of output expansion can be classified as "ultra-export-biased."

The proof of this production effect depends on the theorem, originally stated by T. M. Rybczynski,[17] that at constant relative prices of the two commodities, an increase in the supply of one factor, with the other factor constant, will result in an absolute expansion in production of the commodity using relatively much of the increased factor, but an absolute reduction in the production of the commodity using relatively little of this factor. In order to absorb the augmented factor at an unchanged price it is necessary to secure more of the other factor as well; this can be achieved only by freeing the other factor from the industry in which it is used intensively, resulting in a contraction of that industry. Stated more precisely, this result follows from the condition that if the ratio of product prices is to be kept constant, then it is also necessary that the ratio of factor prices should remain constant. This, in turn, requires maintenance of the labor: capital ratio that existed initially in each industry; an unchanged factor ratio will keep the relative marginal productivities of the factors constant, and relative factor prices will then remain constant. To maintain, however, a constant factor ratio in the industry which uses the extra factor intensively, it is necessary to free the other factor by contracting the industry which uses it intensively.

Since country *E* has an initial comparative advantage in the

[17] T. M. Rybczynski, "Factor Endowment and Relative Commodity Prices," *Economica*, November, 1955, pp. 336–341. For a mathematical proof of this proposition, see W. M. Corden, "Economic Expansion and International Trade: A Geometric Approach," *Oxford Economic Papers*, June, 1956, p. 227.

Rybczynski's theorem has been generalized to apply also under certain conditions to cases in which the proportionate rate of increase in the quantity of one factor is greater than that of the other factor. See Akihito Amano, "Factor Endowment and Relative Prices: A Generalization of Rybczynski's Theorem," *Economica*, November, 1963, pp. 413–414.

labor-intensive commodity X, an increase in labor supply without any capital accumulation will extend production in the direction of X. This will be accompanied by a transfer of both labor and capital from the capital-intensive industry Y to industry X. But capital will be released from the Y-industry in a greater quantity than is required to operate the released labor in the X-industry, and this surplus capital will then be available to work with the additional labor. The point on the new efficiency locus with the same labor:capital ratio in X and Y, and thereby the same exchange ratio between the factors as existed initially, will involve a larger output of X but a smaller output of Y. It follows that the new point of production on the new production frontier, corresponding to the initial price ratio of goods, will entail an absolute increase in the output of the exportable commodity X and an absolute reduction in the output of the importable commodity Y. Thus, an increase in labor without any increase in capital will have for country E a production effect that is ultra-export-biased.

e. A movement along YC' (Fig. 1)—that is, the quantity of capital increases without any increase in labor supply. By reasoning similar to that advanced above, the production effect of this capital accumulation will be an increase in the supply of the capital-intensive importable Y and a reduction in the supply of the labor-intensive exportable X. Such an output expansion which reduces the domestic production of exportables can be classified as ultra-import-biased.

The five types of production effects due to the different types of factor accumulation in country E can be summarized in simple geometric terms as in Fig. 4.[18] Let the terms of trade line

[18] Corden, *op. cit.*, pp. 223, 225; H. G. Johnson, *Money, Trade and Economic Growth*, Allen & Unwin, 1962, pp. 77–81; Bo Södersten, *A Study of Economic Growth and International Trade*, Almqvist & Wiksell, 1964, pp. 41–45.

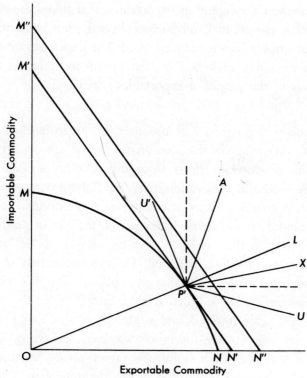

Fig. 4. Country *E*.

M″N″ be drawn parallel to and to the right of *M′N′*, indicating constant relative prices but expanded production. If the path of output expansion from *P′* is along the straight line *P′L*, the production effect is neutral; the supply of exportables (*X*) and the supply of importables (*Y*) increase in the same proportion. If the output expansion line rises to the right of *P′L*, such as *P′X*, the production effect is export-biased; the supply of exportables increases in greater proportion than the supply of importables. If the line rises to the left of *P′L*, such as *P′A*, the production effect is import-biased; the supply of importables increases in greater proportion than the supply of exportables. If it slopes negatively, such as $P'U$, the effect is ultra-export-biased; the domestic production of importables is reduced. And if it slopes negatively in the other direction, such as $P'U'$, the production effect is ultra-import-biased; the supply of exportables is reduced.

8. Technological progress will also alter the structure of comparative costs. Allowing for this, our analysis must now incorporate the various production effects from different types of innovations.[19] A technical innovation may be "labor-saving," in the sense that, at constant factor prices, it lowers the optimal ratio of labor to capital; at the initial factor prices, the cost of producing a given output is then reduced, and the supply of the "saved" factor labor is in effect increased. Or the innovation may be "capital-saving," in the sense that the optimal ratio of capital to labor is lowered at the original relative factor prices; the cost of production is again lowered, and a quantity of the "saved" factor capital is set free. Finally, the innovation may be "neutral," inasmuch as it is neither labor-saving nor capital-saving, but allows a reduction by the same proportion in the amounts of the two factors required to produce a given quantity of output; the optimal factor ratio is unaltered, but the output obtainable from a given combination of factors is increased.

[19] This problem has been clarified considerably by R. Findlay and H. Grubert, "Factor Intensities, Technological Progress, and the Terms of Trade," *Oxford Economic Papers*, February, 1959, pp. 111–121. A good summary of the effects of biased technical progress is presented in J. Bhagwati and H. G. Johnson, "Notes on Some Controversies in the Theory of International Trade," *Economic Journal*, March, 1960, p. 82. Also see, Johnson, "Effects of Changes in Comparative Costs as Influenced by Technical Change," R. F. Harrod and D. C. Hague, eds., *International Trade Theory in a Developing World*, Macmillan Co., 1963, pp. 97–105; Z. Hodjera, "Unbiased Productivity Growth and Increasing Costs," *Oxford Economic Papers*, November, 1963, pp. 244–265.

Considering these different types of innovations, we may now ask what type of bias in production will result, according to whether the innovation occurs in industry X or Y. In the following cases, we shall concentrate on country E and determine what will be the shift, at constant relative product prices, in the output of one of the commodities as a result of an innovation in the production of that commodity or the other commodity.

a. A neutral innovation: If this occurs in the labor-intensive industry X, the output of X would increase, and at the original relative factor prices its production costs would fall. To have the original product price ratio remain unchanged after this innovation, there must then be a shift in the factor price ratio. In this case, there would be an incentive for factors to move from industry Y to X, where the marginal productivities and factor earnings are higher. When this occurs, the price of labor rises, and the price of capital falls, since capital is used less intensively in X where the innovation has occurred. The relative costs of X and Y are thereby altered, and the initial product price ratio is restored. Thus, at constant relative product prices, the effect of neutral technical progress in the exportable commodity X is to expand the output of X and to contract the output of the importable commodity Y.[20] The production effect of a neutral innovation in the export industry is ultra-export-biased.

If, in contrast, the neutral innovation occurred in the production of the importable commodity Y, the production effect would be ultra-import-biased.

b. A labor-saving innovation: If this occurs in industry X, production costs in X will again be reduced, and a quantity of labor will be released. As in the preceding situation, the reduction in cost requires a shift of resources from Y to the innovating

---

[20] A rigorous proof of this proposition has been given by J. Bhagwati, "Growth, Terms of Trade, and Comparative Advantage," *Economia Internazionale*, August, 1959, pp. 412–414.

industry X. And, as in the case of an increase in the labor supply, the labor set free by the innovation in X must be absorbed by an expansion in the output of the exportable commodity X, which uses labor relatively intensively, and by a contraction in the production of importables Y. The production effect is therefore ultra-export-biased. Moreover, since in the present case technical progress saves the factor which is used relatively intensively in the production of the exportable commodity X, the production effect will be even more ultra-export-biased than if the innovation were neutral.

If, however, the labor-saving innovation occurs in the relatively capital-intensive import-competing industry Y, the production effect may be anywhere between the extremes of ultra-import-biased and ultra-export-biased. This range is possible because the innovation will not only reduce the unit cost of production in Y, thereby tending to increase the supply of importables Y, but will also release labor from Y, thereby tending to increase the supply of exportables X, since at constant factor prices the labor that is released from Y must be absorbed by an expansion of the labor-intensive industry X. The factor reallocations will tend to raise the cost of capital relative to labor and thus dampen the initial expansion of the import-competing industry and induce an expansion of exportables. Depending, however, on the respective strengths of the cost-reducing and factor-saving effects which operate in opposite directions, the production effect on balance may vary from being ultra-import-biased to being ultra-export-biased. If the innovation is only slightly labor-saving, the production effect will be ultra-import-biased. But if the innovation is so strongly saving of labor as to offset the substitution effect of cheaper labor, the production effect will be ultra-export-biased.

c. A capital-saving innovation: If the innovation is in the capital-intensive industry Y, then, by reasoning similar to that in the previous case of a labor-saving innovation in X, the supply of importables Y will increase at the expense of exportables X. The production effect will be ultra-import-biased.

If, however, the capital-saving innovation is in the labor-intensive export industry X, the production effect may vary from being ultra-export-biased to being ultra-import-biased, depending on how much capital is released by the innovation. Again, in this case, the cost-reducing effect of the innovation and the factor-saving effect work in opposite directions; according to the balance of these effects, the resultant production effect may vary from being ultra-export-biased to being ultra-import-biased.

9. We now know how different kinds of factor accumulation and technical progress will have various production effects. But we must also recognize the effects of these developmental changes on the pattern of consumption. To complete our analysis of the developing country's demand for imports, we must examine the various possible consumption effects and then note the combined effects of the changes in production and consumption.

Considering country E, we may first separate out the consumption effect of only an increase in real income if we assume that the preference system remains unchanged, and then recognize how, at constant relative commodity prices, a new consumption point will be reached as income increases.[21] In Fig. 5, let the initial terms of trade line $M'N'$ be tangential to a community indifference curve at T, the initial consumption point. If development now occurs, the consumption point will shift. Let the terms of trade line $M''N''$ then be drawn parallel to and to the right of $M'N'$, denoting unchanged relative prices but an increase in income after development occurs. If the income-elasticity

---

[21] We exclude the possibility that although national income may increase because of population growth, this may at the same time result in a lower income per head.

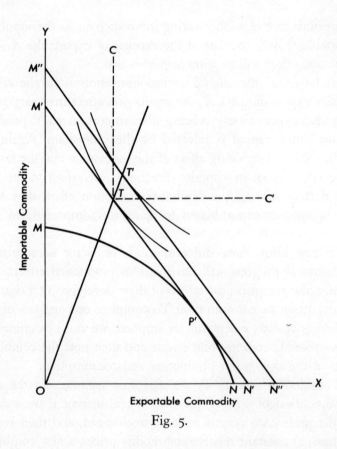

Fig. 5.

of demand for Y equals unity, and that for X also equals unity, the new consumption point is T' on the straight line income-consumption curve OTT' drawn through the origin; the ratio of $Y:X$ that would be purchased at initial prices is the same after an increase in income as originally. In this case, the expansion of income raises the demand for importables Y in the same proportion as it increases the demand for exportables X. The consumption effect can thus be termed "neutral."

Although a neutral income effect is possible, this will not generally be the case. Instead, the income-consumption curve will normally lie to one side or the other of OTT' beyond T. If the income-elasticity of demand for Y is greater than unity, and that for X is less than unity, the income-consumption curve lies to the left of TT' in the region CTT'; the ratio of $Y:X$ that would be purchased at initial prices is higher after the increase in income. When the growth of income thus raises the demand for importables Y in greater proportion than it increases the demand for exportables X, the consumption effect can be termed "export-biased"—that is, on the side of demand, development is biased *against* exportables. A consumption effect which is export-biased will require a relative increase in the supply of exports to pay for the greater proportional share of importables in total consumption. At this point, Professor Johnson's terminology of "pro-trade-bias" is useful in avoiding any confusion.

If, however, the income-elasticity of demand for Y is less than unity, and that for X is greater than unity, the income-consumption curve lies to the right of TT' in the region $C'TT'$; the ratio of $Y:X$ that would be purchased at initial prices is lower after the increase in income. When the growth of income thus raises the demand for importables Y in lesser proportion than it increases the demand for exportables X, the consumption effect can be termed "import-biased"—that is, on the side of demand, development is biased *against* imports.

The two possible consumption effects that remain may be described as "ultra-export-biased" when the demand for exportables falls absolutely as income rises, and "ultra-import-biased" when the demand for importables falls absolutely as income rises. These are, however, exceptional cases involving inferior goods, a situation of lower per capita income with population growth, or the possible effects of income redistribution; for simplicity, we exclude them from further consideration.

We must, however, allow for the possibility that development will alter the relative demand for commodities not only because income increases, but also because the preference system will be modified if tastes change or income is redistributed. Instead of considering an income-consumption line as based on an unchanged preference system, we must then refer to a "demand expansion line,"[22] which shows the combined result of changes in income and preferences on the relative demand for the commodities, at constant prices. If the particular demand expansion depends only on the income elasticity of demand—that is, tastes and the income distribution do not change—the demand expansion line corresponds to an income-consumption line. If, however, the different types of factor growth or technical change also result in different patterns of demand, the demand expansion line will diverge from a given income-consumption line. A change in tastes in favor of commodity X, for example, or a redistribution of income in favor of that factor which has higher average and marginal propensities to consume X than has the other factor, would cause the demand expansion line in Fig. 5 to be to the right of a given income-consumption curve. Conversely, changes in tastes and income distribution which would favor the consumption of Y as compared with X would cause the demand expansion line to be to the left of a given income-consumption curve.

10. We can now proceed to incorporate the various production and consumption effects into the offer curve analysis of traditional trade theory. Having considered separately the production and consumption shifts associated with development, we can next combine the various production and consumption effects to determine their over-all bias and their total effect on the developing country's demand for imports. To derive this total effect, we must weigh the change in the domestic supply of importables, as

[22] Corden, *op. cit.*, p. 225.

given by the production effect, against the change in demand for importables, as given by the consumption effect.[23] In accordance with the type and degree of over-all bias, the developing country's offer curve will then shift, and a new international trade equilibrium will tend to result. The type of over-all bias will determine the direction of movement of the offer curve, while the extent of the shift in the offer curve will depend on the degree of the over-all bias and on the rate of growth in total production.[24] Once the offer curve shifts, we can then note the change in the volume of trade and the terms of trade.

The over-all bias in the development of country E is neutral if the biases on both the production and consumption sides are neutral.[25] In this case, the country's demand for importables and its supply of exports increase proportionately to the expansion in total output. But since imports are equivalent to the excess of consumption over the domestic production of importables, the domestic supply of importables is necessarily a smaller fraction of total output than the consumption of importables as a fraction

[23] In the case of complete specialization in production, however, the over-all bias depends only on the consumption effect as national output expands, since the country itself produces none of the commodity which it imports.

[24] A rigorous geometric proof of the position of the new offer curve, under various cases of growth, is presented by Frederic L. Pryor, "Economic Growth and the Terms of Trade," *Oxford Economic Papers*, March, 1966, pp. 49–52, 57.

[25] It may be noted, however, that the over-all bias will not be neutral even though production is export-biased and consumption is import-biased, and the biases are of the same degree. This is because the consumption of imports initially represents an excess demand over the domestic supply of importables, so that to have neutrality on balance the import-bias in consumption must be offset by a sufficiently greater opposite bias in production. If the degree of bias in the production change is not sufficiently greater than the degree of bias on the side of consumption, the consumption bias will dominate on balance.

of total consumption. Initially, the demand for importables is greater than the domestic supply of importables, so that under conditions of neutral total bias, the difference between the demand for and the home supply of importables at constant prices must become larger. Country E's offer curve is then displaced from OE to, say, OE_N in Fig. 3, indicating that at each level of the terms of trade the demand for imports by E and the supply of exports from E are greater than before E's production frontier shifted outwards. Assuming, for simplicity, no development in country G, and hence no change in G's offer curve, the new position of trade equilibrium is at C'. In this case, the volume of trade has expanded, and the commodity terms of trade have deteriorated for country E.

If both the production effect and the consumption effect are export-biased, the total effect is also export-biased. Or if the production effect is neutral, but the consumption effect is export-biased, the total effect will be export-biased. The total effect will also be export-biased if the production effect is export-biased and the consumption effect is neutral. The demand for imports and supply of exports then increase more than proportionately to the growth of total output. E's offer curve shifts from OE to, say, OE_X in Fig. 3, and the new equilibrium is at C''. The volume of trade expands, and the terms of trade worsen for country E. Given the same rate of growth in total production, the increase in the volume of trade and the deterioration in the terms of trade are greater in this case than when the total bias was neutral.

If the consumption effect is import-biased, and the production effect is neutral or import-biased, the total effect is import-biased or possibly ultra-import-biased, depending on the degrees of bias in production and consumption. Or if there is import-bias in production, and a neutral consumption effect, the total effect will again be import-biased or possibly ultra-import-biased.

When production is not sufficiently import-biased to more than offset the greater absolute demand for imports, the total effect will be simply import-biased. The demand for imports and the supply of exports then increase less than proportionately to total output. The offer curve shifts to the right of OE, but not as far as OE_N to, say, OE_M. Given the unchanged offer curve for G, the absolutely greater demand for imports tends to worsen E's terms of trade, although for the same rate of growth in total output the deterioration will now be less than in the neutral case of an increased demand for imports proportional to output.

If the import bias in production is sufficient to meet not only the increased absolute demand for importables that results from the output expansion but also some of the original demand for imports, the total effect will be ultra-import-biased. The absolute demand for imports and the supply of exports will be diminished; the offer curve will then shift to the left of OE to, say, OE_{UM}. At the new equilibrium position C''', the volume of trade is less than before development occurred, and the terms of trade are improved for country E.

If there is an ultra-import-bias on the production side, the total effect must also be ultra-import-biased; for the ultra-import-bias in production means that the domestic output of importables will increase more than total output, so that the demand for imports and the supply of exports fall absolutely.

If, however, there is an ultra-export-bias in production, there cannot be an over-all ultra-import-bias because the domestic output of importables falls absolutely. Depending on the consumption effect, the total effect may be ultra-export-biased, export-biased, or import-biased. If it is ultra-export-biased, the absolute demand for imports increases by more than the entire increase in national income, and the supply of exports increases more than in even the case of export-bias. Given the same rate of

growth in total output, the offer curve would thus shift from
OE to the right beyond OE_X. The volume of trade would then
be larger, and the deterioration in country E's terms of trade
would be greater than in the case of an over-all export-bias.

The variety of over-all biases that may result from different
combinations of production and consumption effects can be summarized as follows, where the different total effects are indicated
within the table:[26]

Type of Consumption Effect	Type of Production Effect				
	N	X	M	UM	UX
N	N	X	M or UM	UM	X or UX
X	X	X	Not UX	UM	X or UX
M	M or UM	Not UX	M or UM	UM	Not UM

N = neutral M = import-bias UX = ultra-export-bias
X = export-bias UM = ultra-import-bias

11. Although the foregoing model could be embellished at many
points, especially by incorporating additional countries, commodities, or factors, we are concerned here only with the central
logic of how the structure of comparative costs may change in
the course of development. What is important to recognize is
that comparative advantage is not given to a country, whether
rich or poor, once-for-all; it evolves as a consequence of changes
in factor supply and technical progress. In a developing world,
it is essential to realize that the demand and supply of exportables and importables are ever changing. Even though we have
not ventured beyond the method of comparative statics, our analysis in this chapter certainly indicates that changes in compara-

[26] Cf. Black and Streeten, *op. cit.*, p. 308.

tive costs can be readily incorporated into traditional trade theory.

More than that, the analysis provides a framework for interpreting a range of international development problems. The analysis may be used to explain historical relationships between the spread of development in the international economy and changes in the volume and pattern of trade.[27] And it may offer insights into whether the future spread of industrialization will lead to an increase or decline in world trade. As already undertaken by other writers, some elements of the analysis may also be related to the adjustments required for the maintenance of international equilibrium between manufacturing and primary-producing countries,[28] or the analysis may be applied to the problem of the effects of a population increase on a country's foreign trade,[29] or to the question of whether technical change is likely

[27] Using this type of analysis, one would find it illuminating to reinterpret such earlier studies as D. H. Robertson, "The Future of International Trade," *Economic Journal*, March, 1938, pp. 1–14; Folke Hilgerdt, *Industrialization and Foreign Trade*, League of Nations, 1945. In this connection, some stimulating questions are provided by J. R. Hicks, *International Trade: The Long View*, Central Bank of Egypt Lectures, 1963.

The analysis of this chapter might also be related to more recent studies: H. B. Chenery, "Patterns of Industrial Growth," *American Economic Review*, September, 1960, pp. 624–654; Karl Deutsch and Alexander Eckstein, "National Industrialization and the Decline of the International Economic Sector, 1890–1957," *World Politics*, January, 1961, pp. 267–299; P. Lamartine Yates, *Forty Years of Foreign Trade*, Allen & Unwin, 1959; Alfred Maizels, *Industrial Growth and World Trade*, Cambridge Univ. Press, 1963; Bela Balassa, *Trade Prospects for Developing Countries*, Richard D. Irwin, 1964; Richard N. Cooper, "Growth and Trade: Some Hypotheses About Long-Term Trends," *Journal of Economic History*, December, 1964, pp. 609–628.

[28] Johnson, *International Trade and Economic Growth, op. cit.*, chap. III.

[29] W. M. Corden, "The Economic Limits to Population Increase," *Economic Record*, November, 1955, pp. 242–260.

to promote or inhibit international trade.[30] Instead of pursuing these specific applications, we shall in subsequent chapters use this analysis in a more general fashion to help sort out the forces governing secular movements in the terms of trade, the developmental effects of an inflow of foreign capital, and the impact of commercial policy on a country's development.

[30] Johnson, "Effects of Changes in Comparative Costs as Influenced by Technical Change," *op. cit.*, pp. 107–112.

3

Terms of Trade

1. Despite all the ambiguities obscuring their use, the terms of trade still receive considerable attention in discussions of economic development. This is so not only because the terms of trade have sizeable quantitative significance for most poor countries, but also because they are a convenient indication of the net result of many diverse forces, and may have important welfare implications. We shall therefore analyze in this chapter the determinants of secular changes in the terms of trade and attempt to assess the influence of these changes on the development of a poor country.[1]

2. Several different concepts of the terms of trade may be distinguished: the gross barter, net barter or commodity, income,

[1] The short-run problem of cyclical fluctuations in the terms of trade and export earnings is analyzed in Chapter 9.

single-factoral, double-factoral, real cost, and utility terms of trade.[2] These several concepts fall into three groups: (1) those that relate to the ratio of exchange between commodities—the gross barter, net barter, and income terms of trade; (2) those that relate to the interchange between productive resources—the single-factoral and double-factoral terms of trade; and (3) those that interpret the gains from trade in terms of utility analysis—the real cost and utility terms of trade.

In considering the barter terms of trade, Taussig introduced the distinction between "net" and "gross" barter terms.[3] The commodity or net barter terms of trade (N) are expressed as $N = P_x/P_m$, where P_x and P_m are price index numbers of exports and imports, respectively. A rise in N indicates that a larger volume of imports could be received, on the basis of price relations only, in exchange for a given volume of exports. According to Taussig, however, the net barter terms are relevant only when nothing enters into the trade between countries except sales and purchases of merchandise.

If the balance of payments includes unilateral payments, so that there is an excess in money value of either exports or imports, then the relevant concept is the gross barter terms (G). This measures the rate of exchange between the whole of a country's physical imports as compared with the whole of its exports, and is expressed as $G = Q_m/Q_x$, where Q_m and Q_x are vol-

    [2] Jacob Viner, *Studies in the Theory of International Trade*, Harper & Row, 1937, pp. 558–564; W. W. Rostow, "The Terms of Trade in Theory and Practice," *Economic History Review*, Second Series, Vol. III, No. 1, 1950, pp. 1–20; R. G. D. Allen and J. E. Ely, eds., *International Trade Statistics*, John Wiley, 1953, pp. 207–209; Gottfried Haberler, *A Survey of International Trade Theory*, International Finance Section, Princeton University, rev. ed., 1961, pp. 24–29.
    [3] F. W. Taussig, *International Trade*, Macmillan Co., 1927, pp. 113, 117, 248–249.

ume index numbers for imports and exports, respectively. A rise in G represents a "favorable" change in the sense that more imports are received for a given volume of exports than in the base year. Since $G = N$ only if the value of imports and value of exports are equal,[4] G and N diverge when there are unilateral transactions. But one must distinguish among the different types of unilateral transactions that cause changes in G. It is then more meaningful to consider the significance of various unilateral transactions directly, instead of incorporating them in the terms of trade index.[5]

Since it is especially important for a poor country to take changes in its volume of exports into account, we may want to correct the movements in N for changes in export volume. The income terms of trade (I) do this, and are expressed as $I = N \cdot Q_x$, where Q_x is the export volume index.[6] A rise in I indicates that the country can obtain a larger volume of imports from the sale of its exports; its "capacity to import"—based on exports—has increased. The export-based capacity to import should be distinguished, of course, from the total capacity to import, which depends not only on exports but also capital inflow and other invisible exchange receipts. Nor should a change in

[4] If V_m and V_x are index numbers of values of imports and exports, respectively, $\dfrac{G}{N} = \dfrac{Q_m}{Q_x} \cdot \dfrac{P_m}{P_x} = \dfrac{V_m}{V_x}$.

[5] Cf. Gottfried Haberler, *The Theory of International Trade*, William Hodge & Co., 1936, pp. 164–165; Viner, *op. cit.*, p. 563; Erick Schiff, "Direct Investments, Terms of Trade, and Balance of Payments," *Quarterly Journal of Economics*, February, 1942, pp. 310–316.

[6] G. S. Dorrance, "The Income Terms of Trade," *Review of Economic Studies*, 1948–49, pp. 50–56. The income terms of trade have also been referred to as "the export gain from trade"; A. H. Imlah, "The Terms of Trade of the United Kingdom, 1798–1913," *Journal of Economic History*, November, 1950, p. 176.

the income terms of trade be interpreted as a measure of the gain from trade or an indicator of welfare; it should be used simply as a measure of the quantity of imports bought by exports.

It is significant that, according to the direction and magnitude of the changes in P_x and Q_x, the changes in I and N may be in opposite directions. If, for example, with unchanged import prices, export prices have fallen, but export quantities (Q_x) have increased by a greater percentage than the decrease in P_x, the income terms of trade will have improved despite a deterioration in the commodity terms of trade.

Changes in productivity are obviously also of prime significance in considering development, and one may therefore want to refer to the factoral terms of trade. The single-factoral terms (S) correct the commodity terms for changes in productivity in producing exports, and may be expressed as $S = N . Z_x$, where Z_x is an export productivity index. A rise in S is a favorable movement in the sense that a greater quantity of imports can be obtained per unit of factor-input used in the production of exportables.

If N is corrected for changes in productivity in producing imports as well as exports, the result is the double-factoral terms of trade (D), expressed as $D = N \cdot Z_x/Z_m$, where Z_m is an import productivity index. A rise in D shows that one unit of home factors embodied in exports now exchanges for more units of the foreign factors embodied in imports. D will diverge from S when there is a change in the factor cost of producing imports, but this has no welfare significance for the importing country, even though it indicates a change in productivity in the other country from which commodities are imported. What matters to the importing country is whether it receives more goods per unit of its "exported factor-input" (an improvement in S)—not whether these imports contain more or less foreign inputs than before.

It may also be noted that N will equal D when constant returns to scale prevail, and there are no historical changes in costs and no transport costs. But if costs are variable with respect to output or time, or there are transport costs, N and D will diverge. Although this divergence is analytically significant, it is difficult to measure as long as a productivity index remains an elusive concept. In the offer curve analysis of the preceding chapter, the terms of trade as determined at the positions of equilibrium in Fig. 3 are the commodity terms. If, however, we had followed Marshall, and considered on each axis "representative bundles" or "bales" of commodities that contained a constant quantity of "productive resources," the terms of trade would have been the double-factoral terms.

Proceeding more directly to the level of welfare analysis, we may define in utility terms the total amount of gain from trade as the excess of the total utility accruing from imports over the total sacrifice of utility involved in the surrender of exports.[7] To consider the amount of disutility involved in the production of exports, we may correct the single-factoral terms of trade index by multiplying S by the reciprocal of an index of the amount of disutility per unit of productive resources used in producing exports.[8] The resultant index would be a real cost terms of trade index (R). If R rises as a result of a change in the methods of producing exports, or a change in the factor proportions used in exports, this would indicate that the amount of imports obtained per unit of real cost was greater.

On the side of demand, we may want to allow for changes in the relative desirability of the imports and the domestic commodities whose home consumption is foregone because of the use of resources in export production. It is then necessary to in-

[7] Viner, *op. cit.*, p. 557.
[8] *Ibid.*, p. 559.

corporate into R an index of the relative average utility per unit of imports and of foregone domestic commodities. The resultant index is the utility terms of trade (U), equal to R multiplied by an index of the relative utility of imports and foregone commodities.[9]

The difficulty with the use of R and U is, of course, that of calculating the disutility involved in export production, or the relative average utility of various commodities. The welfare significance of changes in the terms of trade must therefore be considered only indirectly, along the lines suggested below in section 5, and not directly through any measurement of R or U.

Having minimized the significance of changes in G, D, R, and U, we are thus left with N, S, and I as the most relevant concepts of the terms of trade for poor countries. Movements in N, S, and I may diverge, however, and these divergences are not merely technical but are due to fundamentally different circumstances. Accordingly, they have different consequences for the country's development. To assess the significance for a poor country of an alteration in its commodity terms of trade—the most frequently cited change—we must therefore analyze the determinants of this change and also the attendant movements in the income and single-factoral terms of trade.

3. Over the short period, the terms of trade may vary as a consequence of changes in commercial policy, exchange rate variations, unilateral transfer payments, or cyclical fluctuations. Over the long period, however, the determinants of changes in the terms of trade are associated with more fundamental structural variations in production and consumption that may be examined in the light of the offer curve analysis of the preceding chapter.

[9] *Ibid.*, pp. 560–561.

As already noted, the shifts in the offer curves will cause movements in the terms of trade, and the various possible shifts in the offer curves can be attributed, in turn, to different types of development.[10]

Assuming that development occurs only in country E, so that G's offer curve remains fixed while E's offer curve shifts, we can summarize the various changes in E's commodity terms of trade, according to the different total biases in development, as follows:

Type of Total Bias in Development	Direction of Change in Commodity Terms of Trade
N	$(-)$
X	$(-)$
M	$(-)$
UM	$(+)$
UX	$(-)$

N = neutral	UX = ultra-export-bias
X = export-bias	$(-)$ = deterioration
M = import-bias	$(+)$ = improvement
UM = ultra-import-bias	

When development occurs only in E, and G's offer curve is not infinitely elastic, the terms of trade for E deteriorate for each

[10] For other analyses of the effects on international trade of shifts in reciprocal demand schedules of different elasticities, see Murray C. Kemp, "The Relation between Changes in International Demand and the Terms of Trade," *Econometrica*, January, 1956, pp. 41–46; W. R. Allen, "The Effects on Trade of Shifting Reciprocal Demand Schedules," *American Economic Review*, March, 1952, pp. 135–140; J. Bhagwati and H. G. Johnson, "Notes on Some Controversies in the Theory of International Trade," *Economic Journal*, March, 1960, pp. 84–93; Frederic L. Pryor, "Economic Growth and the Terms of Trade," *Oxford Economic Papers*, March, 1966, pp. 45–57.

type of total bias except an ultra-import-bias. As indicated previously (Fig. 3), the deterioration for a given increase in total output is least, however, when there is an import-bias, and the demand for imports increases less than proportionately to the expansion in total output. The deterioration is greatest when there is an ultra-export-bias, and the absolute demand for imports increases more than total output. In general, the rate of deterioration in E's commodity terms of trade will be greater under the following conditions: the larger is the degree of export-bias on balance in E; the higher is the rate of increase in E's total output; the lower is E's elasticity of demand for G's goods; and the lower is G's elasticity of demand for imports from E.

4. When development occurs in both E and G, the movement of the terms of trade depends on the rate of increase in each country's demand for imports from the other country—in other words, on the relative shifts of the offer curves as determined by the type of total bias and the rate of development in each country.

If the total bias in the development of each country is neutral, each country's offer curve shifts outwards, with the extent of the shift depending on the rate of development. The terms of trade will therefore deteriorate for the country that has the higher rate of development.

If in each country development is ultra-export-biased, or export-biased, or import-biased, each country's offer curve again shifts outwards. The terms of trade would then remain constant only if the types and degrees of bias and rates of development had the same total effect on the growth of demand for imports in each country. In the general case, the terms of trade deteriorate for that country which has the greater rate of growth of demand for imports as determined by its degree of bias, as well as rate of development.

If the over-all effects are export-biased in E, but import-biased in G, then, assuming the rate of development is the same in each country, the terms of trade will deteriorate for E. If, however, the rate of development in E is sufficiently lower than in G, the terms of trade will improve for E, even though its development is export-biased.

The relative rates of development in the two countries may, in many cases, be significant in offsetting the different degrees or types of bias. If, however, the development is ultra-import-biased in only one of the countries, the terms of trade will improve for that country regardless of the type of bias in the other country and the relative rates of development.

From these diverse cases it is apparent that there is no invariant relationship between a country's development and movements in its commodity terms of trade. Depending on the type and degree of bias and the rate of development in each country, the terms of trade may either improve or deteriorate.

5. The connection between changes in the terms of trade and economic welfare is an especially difficult problem: In what sense may a movement in a country's terms of trade be accepted as an index of the trend in economic welfare? Considerable care must be exercised to avoid the fallacy of equating a change in any of the various terms of trade with a variation in the amount or even direction of change in the gains from trade. Such an equation cannot be adduced until we determine the underlying forces associated with the change in the terms of trade, and until we connect the terms of trade, relating to a unit of trade, with the volume of trade.

The welfare implications of a change in the commodity

terms of trade are most directly seen in the effect on real national income. When a country's commodity terms of trade improve, its real income rises faster than output, since the purchasing power of a unit of its exports rises. This increase in real
income will supplement the benefit that the country derives from
its own development.[11] If, however, a country experiences a deterioration in its terms of trade as it develops, part of the benefit
from an expansion in its own output is thereby cancelled.

Insofar as a slower rate of development might allow a country's commodity terms of trade to improve, whereas a higher
rate would cause a deterioration, it is possible that the gain from
the improvement in the terms of trade might be more than sufficient to compensate for the output foregone by the slower expansion in home output. In the case of an ultra-import-bias,
however, a lower rate of development would not tend to aug-
ment the improvement in the commodity terms of trade. On the
contrary, unlike the other cases, a higher rate of development in
this situation will not only increase domestic output further, but
will also cause a greater improvement in the commodity terms of
trade.

As an extreme case, it is possible that the type and rate of
development may cause so severe a deterioration in the terms of
trade that the gain from the growth in output is more than offset
by the loss from adverse terms of trade, so that the country ends
up with a lower real income after growth. This theoretical possibility has been demonstrated by Professor Bhagwati, who de-

[11] An improvement in the commodity terms of trade might facilitate
an expansion in domestic output by permitting the release of resources
from export production to domestic production. If the improvement is
due to a rise in export prices, this may contribute to an increase in public
saving through export taxes, income taxes, or a rise in the profits of governmental marketing boards.

scribes it as a case of "immiserizing growth."[12] For example, an increase in factor supply or technical progress would raise real income by the amount of the change in output at constant prices, but if the factor accumulation or "factor-saving" is so export-biased that the terms of trade worsen, the negative income effect of the actual deterioration in the terms of trade may then be greater than the positive effect of the expansion in output.

Although analytically interesting, the practical bearing of this possibility is very limited. The conditions necessary for immiserization to result are highly restrictive. In the case of incomplete specialization, the possibility can arise only if the increased quantity of the factor is allocated to export industries, and either the foreign demand for the growing country's exports is inelastic or the country's expansion actually reduces the domestic production of importables.[13] But if external demand is so unfavorable, then additional resources will not flow into the export sector when the situation is such that the very growth of factor supplies may actually have to be induced by the existence of profitable

[12] Jagdish Bhagwati, "Immiserizing Growth: A Geometrical Note," *Review of Economic Studies*, June, 1958, pp. 201–205; "International Trade and Economic Expansion," *American Economic Review*, December, 1958, pp. 941–953; "Growth, Terms of Trade and Comparative Advantage," *Economia Internazionale*, August, 1959, pp. 395–398.

Some classical and neoclassical economists also recognized this possibility when they considered the impact of technological change upon the terms of trade. See J. S. Mill, *Principles of Political Economy*, Longmans, Green, 1848, Book III, chap. XVIII, sec. 5; C. F. Bastable, *The Theory of International Trade*, Macmillan Co., 1903, appendix C, pp. 185–187; F. Y. Edgeworth, "The Theory of International Values, I," *Economic Journal*, March, 1894, pp. 40–42.

[13] Bhagwati, "International Trade and Economic Expansion," *op. cit.*, pp. 949–952. In the case of complete specialization, it is necessary that both the foreign demand for exports and the domestic demand for imports be inelastic. This proposition is demonstrated by Bhagwati and Johnson, *op. cit.*, pp. 80–81.

openings for the employment of these additional factors. Moreover, even if there is an autonomous increase in factors, there is
still no basis for "immiserizing growth," inasmuch as increments
in factor supplies are as a rule mobile and the economy has some
capacity for transforming its structure of output. Factor increments, therefore, need not flow into the export sector in accordance with a predetermined pattern of production.[14] To be valid,
the "immiserizing growth" argument depends on highly restrictive conditions with respect to elasticities of demand and supply
—conditions which are unlikely to apply when an economy has
some flexibility in its structure of output and some capacity for
adapting to changed circumstances. It should also be realized
that, even if the necessary conditions do exist, the country can
still institute offsetting policies and impose taxes on its trade sufficient to gain some of the benefits of the expanded production.[15]

If we examine the welfare implications of a change in the
terms of trade more broadly, we can readily identify circumstances under which a country need not be worse off, even
though its commodity terms deteriorate. When the deterioration
results from a shift only in the foreign offer curve, with the
country's own offer curve unchanged, the resultant deterioration
in the country's terms of trade is clearly unfavorable. If, however, the domestic offer curve also shifts, then it is necessary to
consider the causes of this shift and also the possible changes in
the factoral and income terms of trade.

[14] Ragnar Nurkse, *Patterns of Trade and Development*, Wicksell Lectures, Almqvist & Wiksell, 1959, pp. 56, 58–59 (reprinted in *Equilibrium
and Growth in the World Economy. Economic Essays by Ragnar Nurkse*,
Harvard Univ. Press, 1961, pp. 332–334).

[15] R. A. Mundell, "The Pure Theory of International Trade," *American Economic Review*, March, 1960, p. 85; Bo Södersten, *A Study of Economic Growth and International Trade*, Almqvist & Wiksell, 1964, pp.
53–54.

For instance, development may occur in both countries E and G, but the rate of growth of demand for imports may be greater in E than in G, so that E's commodity terms of trade deteriorate. Nonetheless, E may still be better off than before if the deterioration in its commodity terms is due to export-biased increases in productivity. In this case the single-factoral terms of trade improve, and the deterioration in the commodity terms is only a reflection of the increased productivity in E's export industries. As long as productivity in E's export sector is rising faster than the prices of its exports are falling, its real income rises despite the deterioration in its commodity terms of trade. If the prices of exports in terms of imports fall by a smaller percentage than the percentage increase in productivity, the country clearly benefits from its ability to obtain a greater quantity of imports per unit of factors embodied in its exports.

Classical and neoclassical economists recognized this possibility and attempted to go behind the quantities of exports and imports to consider what, as Pigou remarked, "underlie the exports, namely a given quantity of labor and service of capital." It may then be that although the commodity terms of trade deteriorate when the production costs of exports fall, the country may receive more imports than previously for what "underlies its exports." A divergence between the commodity terms and the factoral terms was meant to be avoided by J. S. Mill's conception of "cost," Bastable's "unit of productive power," and Marshall's "representative bales of commodities," each of which contains a constant quantity of "productive resources." But as already noted, if we allow for more than two commodities, transportation costs, or variable costs of production, the commodity terms and the factoral terms of trade may diverge.

It is also relevant that even if productivity is not rising in the export sector, and the commodity terms of trade are deteriorating, it is still possible for the real income of the factors to rise. This may occur under conditions of a "dual economy" in which factors are initially employed in the backward domestic sector with lower productivity than exists in the advanced export sector. If export production should then expand and attract these factors into the export sector, the factors will gain to the extent that their marginal productivity in the export sector remains above their marginal productivity in the sector from which they withdraw. At the same time, the real prices of export products may be falling, and the commodity terms of trade may be worsening.[16]

A high degree of export-bias on the side of consumption may also cause a deterioration in E's commodity terms of trade. But if this export-bias is due to a change in tastes or a redistribution of income, it is difficult to reach any welfare conclusion. For the intervening change in the preference system makes it impossible to conclude that the later result is inferior to the previous situation merely because the commodity terms have deteriorated. If the terms worsen because demand increases for imports, it may not be true that from the criterion of "utility" a loss is incurred. What must be considered is not the utility of the import alone, but also its utility relative to that of the domestic commodities whose domestic consumption is precluded by allocation of resources to production for export. Were it measurable, the utility terms of trade index would be appropriate for this type of change.

We should also realize that it is possible for the country's income terms of trade to improve despite, or sometimes even because of, a deterioration in the country's commodity terms of

---

[16] Theodore Morgan, "The Long-Run Terms of Trade Between Agriculture and Manufacturing," *Economic Development and Cultural Change,* October, 1959, pp. 17–18.

trade. If the foreign offer curve is elastic,[17] or if the foreign offer curve shifts out sufficiently, the volume of exports may increase enough to improve the income terms of trade despite the deterioration in the commodity terms. The country's capacity to import is then greater, and this can be of decided significance for a developing country. Such an improvement in the capacity to import is especially important for a poor country which has a high average propensity to import. It would, of course, be even better for the country if its greater volume of exports could be traded at unchanged prices. But this involves a comparison with a hypothetical situation, whereas the relevant consideration is the effect of the actual change between the previous and present situations.

In contrast, a country's development program may be handicapped, despite an improvement in its commodity terms, if its capacity to import is reduced because of a fall in the volume of exports that is not offset sufficiently by the improved commodity terms. If, for example, a country's development is ultra-import-biased so that its commodity terms improve, but the foreign offer curve is not inelastic, or it shifts inwards relatively more than does the domestic offer curve, the country's income terms will deteriorate. Regardless of its more favorable commodity terms, the country's capacity to import is then reduced, and this may hamper the country's developmental efforts if the growth in output has not been sufficiently import-saving.

These examples illustrate that the mere knowledge of a change in the commodity terms of trade does not in itself allow a firm conclusion as to the effect on the country's economic welfare. It is essential to proceed beyond this superficial level and consider whether the change has been caused by a shift only in

---

[17] When the offer curve is of the normal "elastic" sort, more imports are demanded and more exports are supplied as the price of imports falls.

the foreign offer curve or by a shift in the domestic offer curve. If by the latter, then the cause of the shift becomes relevant and may deserve more emphasis than the fact of the change itself. Attention to the underlying cause is especially needed for recognizing movements in the single-factoral terms as well as commodity terms of trade, and for determining possible changes in the pattern of demand. Finally, changes in the volume of trade must always be considered along with price variations.

6. With the foregoing general considerations in mind, we may now examine the validity of the often-repeated contention that the poor countries have suffered a secular deterioration in their commodity terms of trade.[18] On the basis of inferences from the United Kingdom's commodity terms of trade, proponents of this view claim that "from the latter part of the nineteenth century to the eve of the second world war . . . there was a secular downward trend in the prices of primary goods relative to the prices of manufactured goods. On an average, a given quantity of primary exports would pay, at the end of this period, for only 60 percent of the quantity of manufactured goods which it could buy at the beginning of the period."[19]

---

[18] This allegation appears in several reports of the United Nations and in various writings by Raúl Prebisch, Hans Singer, W. A. Lewis, and Gunnar Myrdal, among others. It is noteworthy that this view is completely at variance with that commonly held by classical economists who believed that the operation of diminishing returns in primary production would cause the prices of primary products to rise relatively to prices of manufactures. Keynes restated the classical view in his "Reply to Sir William Beveridge," *Economic Journal*, December, 1923, pp. 476–488; also, D. H. Robertson, *A Study of Industrial Fluctuation*, P. S. King & Son, 1915, p. 169.

[19] United Nations, Department of Economic Affairs, *Relative Prices of Exports and Imports of Underdeveloped Countries*, 1949, p. 72. The

The causes of this deterioration are supposedly associated with differences in the distribution of the gains from increased productivity, diverse cyclical movements of primary product and industrial prices, and disparities in the rates of increase in demand for imports between the industrial and primary producing countries. Since technical progress has been greater in industry than in the primary production of poor countries, it is suggested that if prices had been reduced in proportion to increasing productivity, the reduction should then have been less for primary products than for manufactures, so that as the disparity between productivities increased, the price relationship between the two should have improved in favor of the poor countries. It is alleged, however, that the opposite occurred: In respect to manufactured commodities produced in more developed countries, it is contended that the gains from increased productivity have been distributed in the form of higher wages and profits rather than lower prices, whereas in the case of food and raw material production in the underdeveloped countries the gains in productivity, although smaller, have been distributed in the form of price reductions.[20]

---

indices used are based on Werner Schlote, *Entwicklung und Strukturwandlungen des englischen Aussenhandels von 1700 bis zur Gegenwart*, Probleme der Weltwirtschaft, No. 62, Jena, 1938. Other indices constructed by Professors Imlah and Kindleberger do not show as marked an improvement for Britain as do Schlote's; A. H. Imlah, *Economic Elements in the Pax Britannica*, Harvard Univ. Press, 1958, chap. IV, Table 8; C. P. Kindleberger, *The Terms of Trade, A European Case Study*, John Wiley, 1956, pp. 53 ff.

W. A. Lewis' consideration of the prices of primary products and manufactures also relies heavily on Schlote's data; Lewis, "World Production, Prices and Trade, 1870–1960," *Manchester School of Economic and Social Studies*, May, 1952, Table II.

[20] United Nations, Department of Economic Affairs, *The Economic Development of Latin America and Its Principal Problems*, 1950, pp. 8–14;

This contrasting behavior of prices in industrial and primary producing countries is also attributed to the different movements of primary product prices and industrial prices over successive business cycles and to the greater number of monopoly elements in industrial markets.[21] According to this reasoning, the prices of primary products have risen sharply in prosperous periods, but have subsequently lost their gain in the downswing of the trade cycle. In contrast, it is asserted that although manufacturing prices have risen less in the upswing, they have not fallen as far in depression as they have risen in prosperity, because of the rigidity of industrial wages and price inflexibility in the more monopolistic industrial markets. It is therefore concluded that over successive cycles the gap between the prices of the two groups of commodities has widened, and the primary producing areas have suffered an unfavorable movement in their terms of trade.

Proponents of the secular deterioration hypothesis also argue that the differential price movements between poor and rich countries have been accentuated by a relative decrease in the demand for primary products and a relative increase in the demand for industrial products. This is attributed to the operation of Engel's law, and also, in the case of raw materials, to technical progress in manufacturing, which reduces the amount of raw ma-

---

Relative Prices of Exports and Imports of Underdeveloped Countries, op. cit., pp. 13–24, 126; H. W. Singer, "The Distribution of Gains Between Investing and Borrowing Countries," *American Economic Review, Papers and Proceedings*, May, 1950, pp. 477–479; W. A. Lewis, "Economic Development with Unlimited Supplies of Labour," *Manchester School of Economic and Social Studies*, May, 1954, pp. 183–184; F. Mehta, "The Effects of Adverse Income Terms of Trade on the Secular Growth of Underdeveloped Countries," *Indian Economic Journal*, July, 1956, pp. 9–21.

[21] *The Economic Development of Latin America and Its Principal Problems, op. cit.*, pp. 12–14.

terials used per unit of output.[22] The low income elasticity of demand and the structural changes result in a secular decline in the demand for primary products. In other words, the consumption effect of development in the poor country is export-biased (pro-trade-biased), whereas in the rich country it is import-biased (anti-trade-biased).

If the alleged secular deterioration in the terms of trade of poor countries were true it would mean that there has been an international transfer of income away from the poor countries, and this decrease in purchasing power would be significant in reducing their capacity for development. The thesis is, however, highly impressionistic and conjectural. When its content is examined more rigorously, the argument appears weak—both statistically and analytically.[23]

Although the relevant long-run data for individual poor countries are not readily available, the substitution of the "inverse" of the United Kingdom's terms of trade is merely an expedient and does not provide a sufficiently strong statistical foundation for any adequate generalization about the terms of

---

[22] Singer, *op. cit.*, p. 479; Raúl Prebisch, "Commercial Policy in Underdeveloped Countries," *American Economic Review, Papers and Proceedings*, May, 1959, pp. 261–264. For a quantitative approach to some of the factors considered by Singer and Prebisch, see M. K. Atallah, *The Terms of Trade Between Agricultural and Industrial Products*, Netherlands Economic Institute, 1958.

[23] The most systematic and thorough-going critiques of the argument have been presented by Gottfried Haberler, "Terms of Trade and Economic Development," Howard S. Ellis, ed., *Economic Development for Latin America*, St. Martin's Press, 1961, pp. 275–297; M. June Flanders, "Prebisch on Protectionism: An Evaluation," *Economic Journal*, June, 1964, pp. 309–316. On the basis of several objections, largely similar to those we discuss below, both of these papers conclude that the reasons which have been advanced for the alleged trend are either fallacious or are entirely inadequate in their explanation.

trade of poor countries.[24] The import-price index is a mixed bag, concealing the heterogeneous price movements within and among the broad categories of foodstuffs, raw materials, and minerals. An aggregation of primary products cannot be representative of the wide variety of primary products exported by poor countries. Nor, of course, is it legitimate to identify all exporters of primary products as poor countries. Some primary producing countries are also importers of primary products. Moreover, the composition of exports from other industrial countries differs markedly from the United Kingdom's, making it unlikely that the United Kingdom's terms of trade can be truly representative for other industrial countries. It has been shown that the terms of trade for other industrial countries have behaved quite differently from those of the United Kingdom.[25]

Even if we were willing to use the British terms of trade as indirect evidence for the terms of trade between industrial and nonindustrial countries, we should still have to be extremely skeptical about the reliability of the British data. Apart from all

[24] Morgan, *op. cit.*, pp. 6–20. From a consideration of six countries other than the United Kingdom, Professor Morgan concludes that the highly diverse demand and supply experience for particular commodities of the different countries emphasizes the importance of refraining from generalizing about the experience of other countries by using the experience of the United Kingdom. Particular supply influences, and particular demand changes, for different commodities, countries, and times, have dominated the historical picture (p. 20).

Also see Morgan, "Trends in Terms of Trade and Their Repercussions on Primary Producers," R. F. Harrod and D. C. Hague, eds., *International Trade Theory in a Developing World*, Macmillan Co., 1963, pp. 57–59; Robert E. Lipsey, *Price and Quantity Trends in the Foreign Trade of the United States*, Princeton Univ. Press, 1963, pp. 8–24, 76; Harry G. Johnson, *Economic Policies toward Less Developed Countries*, Brookings Institution, 1967, appendix A.

[25] Kindleberger, *op. cit.*, pp. 53 ff., 233.

the statistical pitfalls connected with the construction of import and export price indices, there are strong biases in the United Kingdom series that make the terms of trade appear less favorable to poor countries than they actually were.[26] No allowance is made for changes in the quality of exports and imports; nor is there adequate coverage for the introduction of new commodities. Insofar as the improvements in quality and the introduction of new commodities have undoubtedly been more pronounced for industrial products than for primary products, a simple inversion of the United Kingdom's terms of trade would thus overstate any unfavorable movement for countries exporting primary products to the United Kingdom and importing industrial products from it.

Furthermore, there is no allowance for the fact that transportation costs were falling, making it invalid to infer from the British data what the terms of trade were for the primary producing countries trading with Britain. If the recorded terms of trade were corrected for the decline in transportation costs that occurred, the improvement in the United Kingdom's terms would appear substantially less. This is because British exports are valued at the port of exit, while the value of imports includes shipping costs. A large part of the decline in British import prices, however, was caused by the fall in ocean freights, and if Britain's export price index were corrected for transportation costs it would show a greater decline than does the recorded British export price index.[27] A proper consideration of transportation costs

[26] Morgan, "The Long-Run Terms of Trade Between Agriculture and Manufacturing," *op. cit.*, pp. 4–6; R. E. Baldwin, "Secular Movements in the Terms of Trade," *American Economic Review, Papers and Proceedings*, May, 1955, pp. 267–268.

[27] Statistical confirmation is given by L. Isserlis, "Tramp Shipping Cargoes and Freights," *Journal of Royal Statistical Society*, 1938, p. 122;

makes the terms of trade of primary producers appear less unfavorable.

These statistical imperfections do not allow much support
for the hypothesis of a secular deterioration in the terms of trade
for poor countries. It might even be maintained that their terms
of trade improved because of quality improvements in their imports, access to a wider range of imports, and the great relative
decline in transportation costs as compared with the prices of the
commodities transported.

If the empirical evidence does not bear close scrutiny, still
less does the analytical explanation. The validity of the appeal to
monopolistic elements in the industrial countries depends on the
existence of monopoly in not only factor markets but also product markets,[28] so that the increasing productivity could be distributed in the form of rising money wages and profits, with
stable or rising prices. It is an open question whether trade unions
and firms actually possessed and exercised sufficient monopoly
powers. But even if they did, the existence of such monopoly elements would at most explain movements in the absolute domestic
price level and not changes in relative world prices of manufactures and primary products. World price levels depend on
world conditions of supply and demand, and a country with a
relatively high domestic price level may simply find itself priced
out of international markets unless it makes some adjustment in
its domestic prices or exchange rate.

Further, allowing for the neglected influence of transport

Kindleberger, *op. cit.*, pp. 20–21, 336–339; C. M. Wright, "Convertibility
and Triangular Trade as Safeguards against Economic Depression," *Economic Journal*, September, 1955, pp. 424–426; P. T. Ellsworth, "The
Terms of Trade Between Primary Producing and Industrial Countries,"
Inter-American Economic Affairs, Summer, 1956, pp. 47–65.

[28] Kindleberger, *op. cit.*, pp. 246–247, 304.

costs over the cycle, we may also note many instances in which during a recession the prices of primary products declined in the United Kingdom, while actually rising at the ports of shipment in the primary producing countries.[29] Nor is the pre-1914 evidence on the purchasing power of primary products consistent with the cyclical explanation: Britain's terms of trade actually deteriorated during most depressions before 1914; Britain's food import prices fluctuated less in most trade cycles before 1914 than did British export prices; and a substantial number of primary products—especially foodstuffs—actually gained in purchasing power during many pre-1914 depressions.[30]

As for the appeal to disparities in the rates of increase in the demand for imports, it is true that, *ceteris paribus*, different Engel curves could cause a deterioration in the terms of trade. It is, however, essential to consider also the rates of development and changes in supply conditions, as has been stressed in the analysis of shifts in the offer curves. For even though the percentage of expenditure on a given import might be a decreasing function of income, the absolute demand for the import may still be greater as development proceeds. In addition, shifts of the long-term supply elasticities within industrial countries may be such as to prevent the domestic output of importables from keeping up with demand, so that the import requirements may rise relatively to income growth in the industrial countries. It should also be remembered that Engel's law applies only to foodstuffs—not to industrial raw materials or minerals. And even if an income

[29] Wright, *op. cit.*, pp. 425–426.

[30] K. Martin and F. G. Thackeray, "The Terms of Trade of Selected Countries, 1870–1938," *Bulletin of the Oxford University Institute of Statistics*, November, 1948, pp. 380–382; W. W. Rostow, "The Historical Analysis of the Terms of Trade," *Economic History Review*, Second Series, Vol. IV, No. 1, 1951, pp. 69–71.

elasticity of demand of less than unity is accepted as reasonable for primary products, what is significant for a specific primary producing country is not this over-all elasticity but the expansion in demand for its own exports.

Finally, aside from its statistical and analytical weaknesses, the entire argument has been unduly restricted to only the commodity terms of trade. Also significant are changes in the income terms of trade and especially the single-factoral terms. It is clearly possible, as already noted, that a country's income terms and single-factoral terms might improve at the same time as its commodity terms deteriorate. Since the exports from poor countries have grown so considerably, and productivity in export production has increased, the income terms and single-factoral terms have undoubtedly improved for poor countries. This is actually implicit in the secular deterioration argument, insofar as it relies on productivity increasing in both primary producing and industrial countries, but at a higher rate in the latter. Although their double-factoral terms of trade may have deteriorated, this did not affect the welfare of poor countries; they were better off when their own single-factoral terms improved and they received more imports per unit of their "exported factors," regardless of whether the single-factoral terms also improved for other countries exporting to them. Their capacity to import and their imports per unit of productive resources exported have increased—regardless of any changes in the relative prices for their products.

The most favorable situation, of course, would be an improvement in the commodity terms of trade as well as in the single-factoral and income terms. But the ruling conditions may frequently be incompatible with such a simultaneous improvement. Nonetheless, to look only at changes in the commodity terms is to neglect the favorable effects of the greater capacity to import through improvement in the income terms and the benefits from the improvement in the single-factoral terms. When it is assessed within this wider analysis, a change in the commodity terms of trade may prove to be of small moment for a developing economy in comparison with the more fundamental changes that have occurred at the same time.

4

External Balance

1. So far, in examining how the "real" forces of development manifest themselves internationally through changes in comparative advantages and variations in the terms of trade, we have assumed the existence of balance of payments equilibrium. We must now remove this assumption and consider one of the major problems confronting a poor country—the likelihood that an increase in its rate of development will place a severe strain on its balance of payments. The persistent tendency towards external disequilibrium has indeed become of foremost concern to countries engaged in development programming.[1]

The problem of external imbalance in relation to a development program has been clearly posed as follows:

[1] This was the major area of discussion at the first session of UNCTAD, Geneva, 1964. The Trade and Development Board, established since the Conference, has continued to focus attention on this problem.

"[I]nternational trade and the problems of international payments that are involved in it may affect the process of development in two diametrically opposite ways. On the one hand, by permitting specialization and the introduction of new techniques in those activities in which productivity of economic resources is highest and by thus facilitating accumulation, international trade may speed up the rate of development. On the other hand, in an economy in which, as it grows, the propensity to import tends to run ahead of the power to export there may be constant danger of developing crises of the balance of payments. It may be forced into patterns of development which tend to diminish rather than to increase productivity. It will almost certainly suffer from more or less severe constraints both on the pattern and on the priorities and phasing of its development. Its development is likely to be much more severely affected by minor as well as by major errors and failures in particular sectors of the economy. It may be forced to protect its currency reserves by a high interest rate which, while it may serve to diminish and control the volume of imports, will do so by putting the brake on development. An uneasy equilibrium may be secured through underloading of the economy and a slow rate of development."[2]

Of the various sources of balance of payments pressure, those associated with capital accumulation are of particular significance to a country undertaking a development program. Although cyclical instability or specific sectoral imbalances may imperil a poor country's external balance,[3] a more prevalent cause of ex-

[2] Austin Robinson, "Foreign Trade in a Developing Economy," K. Berrill, ed., *Economic Development with Special Reference to East Asia*, Macmillan Co., 1964, pp. 212–213.

[3] The view that balance of payments difficulties are due to specific input-output imbalances and disproportionalities which arise in the course of growth is argued by A. O. Hirschman, *The Strategy of Economic Development*, Yale Univ. Press, 1958, pp. 166–173.

ternal imbalance is likely to be the internal disequilibrium connected with the inability of the country to mobilize sufficient domestic savings to fulfill the capital requirements of its development program. In most development programs, a policy of accelerated capital formation entails a fundamental and chronic need for foreign exchange, and the country's rate of development becomes highly dependent on the ability to finance a large imbalance on current account. If to support its development program, a country has to run its international reserves down to a minimum, it will then be in a vulnerable position of not having adequate cover for shorter-run swings in its balance of payments. As its international reserves become deficient, the country finds itself under pressure to correct its external deficit. Out of consideration for the balance of payments, the development targets may then have to be compromised. The necessity of avoiding a conflict between the objectives of accelerating capital formation and maintaining balance of payments equilibrium is therefore a primary restraint on the country's rate of development.

For an attempt to attribute chronic disequilibrium in the balance of payments to a structural disequilibrium inherent in the process of development, see Celso Furtado, "The External Disequilibrium in the Underdeveloped Economies," *Indian Journal of Economics*, April, 1958, pp. 403–410. An extensive literature now exists on the structural balance of payments problem, particularly as related to Latin American economies. See, for example, Dudley Seers, "A Theory of Inflation and Growth in Underdeveloped Economies Based on the Experience of Latin America," *Oxford Economic Papers*, June, 1962, pp. 173–195; Seers, "Normal Growth and Distortions: Some Techniques of Structural Analysis," *Oxford Economic Papers*, March, 1964, pp. 78–104.

More recently, in clarifying the structural problem, it has been argued that a developing country may be subject to a "foreign exchange constraint" even if there is no internal disequilibrium in the sense of a shortage of domestic savings. We shall examine, in section 7, the validity of this distinction between a "savings constraint" and a "foreign exchange constraint" on development.

Several definitions of "balance of payments equilibrium" are possible, differing by the extent to which they incorporate normative elements. For present purposes we shall consider the balance of payments to be in equilibrium if over the relevant time period a country can meet its international payments out of its international receipts from current transactions and autonomous ("ordinary" or "acceptable") capital inflows, without being compelled to endure excessive unemployment or to restrict imports merely to avoid a deficit in the balance of payments. When a passive balance on current account is not covered by an autonomous capital inflow, there is a need for induced ("accommodating" or "distress") capital transactions or a gold outflow. The country then suffers from an external disequilibrium which requires remedial action.

2. As a basis for examining how the forces of development may disturb the balance of payments, we should first recall some fundamental relationships between national income and the balance of payments. Although national output, national income, and national expenditure are necessarily equal in a closed economy, they may diverge in an open economy.

National output (O) is expressed as

$$O = C + I + X - M$$

where consumption (C) and home investment (I) include imported consumption and investment goods, X represents value of all exports, and M the value of all imports of goods and services in the balance of trade. If allowance is made for other items in the balance on current account, the national income (Y) may differ from the national output according to

$$Y = O \pm R$$

where $+ R$ represents the net payments received from abroad on account of interest and dividends from foreign investments, private unilateral transfers, and government aid ($- R$ would represent net payments made abroad on these items). The total domestic expenditure (E), or the "total absorption" of consumption and investment goods, is

$$E = C + I = O - (X - M).$$

It follows that

$$X - M = O - E, \text{ and } (X - M) \pm R = Y - E.$$

From the last equation, it is clear that an external deficit consists in an excess of aggregate expenditure over real national income (output). If a country's level of national expenditure—or total absorption of resources—is larger than its home output plus the resources that it can import with an ordinary capital inflow, the consequence is a balance of payments deficit which must be financed by an accommodating capital inflow or gold outflow. In this situation the external imbalance is a direct manifestation of internal disequilibrium, and we may as readily speak of excess spending as of a balance of payments deficit, or as easily of "overabsorption" as of "overimporting."[4]

This essential relationship between internal imbalance and

[4] This principle is fully elaborated by Ragnar Nurkse, "The Relation Between Home Investment and External Balance in the Light of British Experience, 1945–1955," *Review of Economics and Statistics*, May, 1956, pp. 137–147. The "absorption approach" to balance of payments policy was introduced by S. S. Alexander, "The Effects of a Devaluation on a Trade Balance," *International Monetary Fund Staff Papers*, April, 1952, pp. 263–278. For a generalization of the "absorption approach" to balance of payments theory, see H. G. Johnson, *International Trade and Economic Growth*, Allen & Unwin, chap. VI. A concise survey of balance of payments theory is presented by W. M. Corden, *Recent Developments in the Theory of International Trade*, Princeton University, March, 1965, chap. I.

external imbalance is also apparent when the Harrod-Domar theory of equilibrium growth is applied to the balance of payments. Harrod writes his fundamental equation in the form $GC = s - b$, where: G, representing growth, is the increment of total production in any unit period expressed as a fraction of total production; C, capital, represents the investment of the period divided by the increment of production in the same period; s is the fraction of income saved; and b is the balance of trade expressed as a fraction of income.[5] The equation can therefore be rewritten as

$$\frac{\triangle Y}{Y} \cdot \frac{I}{\triangle Y} = \frac{S}{Y} - \frac{(X - M)}{Y} \text{ or } I + X = S + M[6]$$

Although this equation always holds true in the "realized" or *ex post* sense for an actual rate of growth, the values of $I + X$ and $S + M$ need not be equal in the "intended" or *ex ante* sense. If they are not, the level of national income changes. At an equilibrium level of national income, $I + X$ equals $S + M$ in both the intended and realized senses. But the equilibrium condition of national income is no guarantee of external balance. There may be a passive balance on current account equal to the excess of home investment over home saving. This passive balance will be financed by a net capital inflow or gold outflow; in effect, the foreigner is providing the deficiency in home savings. Or there may be an active balance on current account equal to the excess of home saving over home investment; foreign investment is

[5] R. F. Harrod, *Towards a Dynamic Economics*, Macmillan Co., 1948, p. 105. If allowance is made for other items in the current account, credits may be added to exports, and debits to imports, so that b is then the balance on current account expressed as a fraction of income.

[6] This does not allow for government expenditures and taxes, or else assumes that these are equal. More generally, the equation may be written $I + X + G = S + M + T$, where G represents government expenditures and T taxes.

then covering the excess saving, and the active balance is being matched by a net flow of investment abroad or gold inflow.

This fundamental relationship can also be expressed diagrammatically, as in Fig. 6. The export function X, which includes all credit items on current account, is represented as autonomous with respect to the country's national income, since it is assumed that changes in the country's imports are too small to have a substantial influence upon the income of foreign countries to which the country exports. The other functions, however, are represented as dependent on the level of national income: imports M, which include all debits on current account, home investment I, and saving S are all shown to be greater the higher the level of national income.[7] Added horizontally, the functions give $I + X$ and $S + M$.

The intersection of $I + X$ with $S + M$ denotes the equilibrium level of income OY_o, to which actual income tends if a departure is made from P.

Even if this equilibrium condition of national income holds, however, it does not follow that the balance of payments will necessarily also be in equilibrium at that level of income. The balance of payments will be in equilibrium only if X equals M, unless the deficit on current account is being offset by an equivalent amount of acceptable borrowing which gives a surplus on long-term capital account. But at the income level of OY_o, in Fig. 6, M exceeds X by the amount AB. Indeed, as long as the level of

---

[7] For simplicity, we assume that the marginal and average propensities to consume are equal and remain constant through the time under consideration; similarly, for the marginal and average propensities to import. The savings schedule and the import schedule then begin at the origin, rather than at some point on the ordinate above the origin. The steepness of the investment function is due to the small amount of induced investment in a poor country.

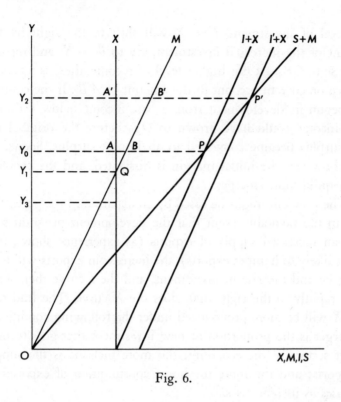

Fig. 6.

income is greater than OY_1, there will be a passive balance on current account which will require a gold outflow or a short-term capital inflow, if it is not counterbalanced by a long-term capital inflow.

3. We may now explore the more common sources of external imbalance for a developing country. Assume that the country's level of income is initially OY_1 in Fig. 6 (the initial $I + X$ line would then be to the left of that drawn in Fig. 6). At this level of income, exports equal imports. If the country then embarks upon a development program which provides for an increase in the level of investment, $I + X$ will shift to the right by the amount of the increased investment, say to $I' + X$, and income will rise to OY_2. At this higher level of income, there is a passive balance on current account in the amount of $A'B'$. If the country had begun its development from a base income below OY_1, say OY_3, income could have grown to OY_1 before the original export surplus became converted to an import surplus. Sooner or later, however, the initial margin is dissipated, and the problem of disequilibrium emerges.

The problem might be eased by an expansion in exports. But even in the favorable event that the development program supports an increased supply of exports (as experience shows, it is just as likely to hamper exports), the increase in exports will tend to lag behind the rise in investment, and the I curve then shifts more rapidly to the right than does the X curve. The lead of I over X will be more pronounced under the following conditions: the larger is the proportion of new investment that goes to non-export sectors of the economy; the more inelastic is the supply of exports; and the more the home consumption of exportables increases as income rises.

Nor will the difficulty be easily removed even if after a certain time lag the exports do increase more readily. For as exports increase, the level of income will also rise, and so will imports. It is therefore a problem of not only increasing exports by an amount sufficient to remove the initial gap $A'B'$, which has resulted from the increase in investment, but also by an additional amount which will offset the induced rise in imports. The increase in imports may be expressed as $\triangle M = m(\triangle Y)$, where m is the marginal propensity to import. We know that income will rise until the increase in $M + S$ equals the increase in $X + I$, or until $(m + s - i)\triangle Y = \triangle X$, where s and i are the marginal propensities to save and invest, respectively. Thus,

$$\Delta Y = \frac{1}{m + s - i} (\Delta X),$$

and the induced imports are equal to

$$m(\Delta Y) = \frac{m}{m + s - i} (\Delta X).$$

To remove the deficit on current account which appears after investment increases, exports must therefore expand not only by the amount of the original gap $A'B'$, but by

$$A'B' + \frac{m}{m + s - i} (A'B').$$

The analysis has so far assumed constant propensities. But it is extreme—especially in the case of a developing country—to suppose that the import, saving, and investment coefficients remain constant over any long period. Insofar as the propensity to import is likely to rise, particularly during the early phases of the country's development, the balance of payments problem may become even more severe, unless there is a sufficient increase in the propensity to save. Although it will differ according to the character of the particular investment plan, the proportion of investment expenditure that must be directed to imports of capital goods is likely to be high. Since the import component of aggregate investment is generally higher than the import component of consumption, there will be a rise in imports as the share of investment in the national product increases in relation to that of consumption. Moreover, as personal incomes rise, the demand for imported consumer goods also tends to be high. Even if the additional investment is designed to produce substitutes for these imported consumer goods, there will still be a high income elasticity of demand for these imports during the gestation period of the investment. Alternatively, if prior to the investment the government had already imposed controls on these imports in order to promote a home market for the larger output of import substitutes, the import content of the investment would then exceed the import coefficient of consumption *a fortiori*.

There is also a tendency for a developing country's marginal propensity to import to become greater as the level of income rises.[8] In part, this is because there is not a once-for-all introduction of the advanced countries' exports, but rather a more gradual process of preliminary "want development" for such commodities;[9] and these commodities, especially consumer goods, are of such a nature that they enter into the poor country's standard of consumption only after the country's income has risen above a certain minimum level. Over the long period the distribution of income in the poor country might also shift in favor of profits and rents, since, as the level of activity rises, numerous intermediary traders emerge and benefit from the secular inflationary pressures, the demand for land increases, and money wages do not rise commensurately because of the abundance of unskilled labor without bargaining power. Traders and landlords may be expected to have a higher marginal propensity to import than other classes, so that again the marginal propensity to import for the community will tend to increase as the level of income rises. With the shift of population away from a rural to an urban environment, the demand for imported goods will also increase as the pattern of consumer expenditures changes, and a higher proportion of income is used for the purchase of imported goods.

Thus, there remains the basic problem that, in the course of development, the rate of growth of imports tends to be more rapid

[8] The import function would then, of course, no longer be represented by a straight line in Fig. 6.

[9] Elizabeth E. Hoyt, "Want Development in Underdeveloped Areas," *Journal of Political Economy*, June, 1951, pp. 194–202.

than the rate of growth of national output, and the demand for imports tends to exceed the export-based capacity to import.[10] Unless there is a sufficiently large capital inflow, the poor country then confronts a conflict between accelerating its internal development and maintaining external balance.

4. Another method for determining whether the pace of development has to be restrained for the sake of external balance is to specify the critical level of investment above which external imbalance will result. This can be done in terms of the Harrod-Domar theory, as follows.[11]

Let σ, $\left(\dfrac{\triangle O_t}{\triangle K_{t-1}}\right)$, be the reciprocal of the marginal capital-output ratio, assumed constant. The expansion of productive capacity in period t will then equal the investment of the previous period $t - 1$ (the length of the gestation period of the investment), multiplied by σ, or $\triangle O_t = I_{t-1} \cdot \dfrac{\triangle O_t}{\triangle K_{t-1}}$. Since the marginal pro-

---

[10] This problem is now commonly termed that of the "widening trade gap." See Raúl Prebisch, *Towards a New Trade Policy for Development*, Report by the Secretary-General of UNCTAD, United Nations, 1964, pp. 3–5, 107–108.

We shall frequently refer to this problem as we review the policies actually adopted by developing countries. It will be seen that import-substitution policies, subsidization of manufacturing, inflation, and over-valued exchange rates have created in many of the poor countries a distorted price structure that in effect taxes their exports and imparts an anti-trade bias to their development programs. Although the analysis in this section has been in terms of income analysis, the underlying price structure should not be ignored.

[11] J. C. Ingram, "Growth in Capacity and Canada's Balance of Payments," *American Economic Review*, March, 1957, pp. 95–97; K. K. Kurihara, "Economic Development and the Balance of Payments," *Metroeconomica*, March, 1958, pp. 16–27.

pensity to consume domestic goods (c) is equal to ($1 - s - m$), the portion of the increased output that is available for an increase in domestic investment and for exports is

$$\triangle I_t + \triangle X_t = \triangle O_t - (1 - s - m) \triangle O_t.$$

Or, $$\triangle I_t + \triangle X_t = (s + m) I_{t-1} \cdot \sigma.$$

While the rise in exports is $\triangle X_t = (s + m) I_{t-1} \cdot \sigma - \triangle I_t$, the increase in imports is $\triangle M_t = m \cdot I_{t-1} \cdot \sigma$, assuming that money income rises by the same proportion as output rises. If we now impose the condition that the economy expands without any deterioration in the balance on current account ($\triangle X = \triangle M$), it follows that

$$(s + m) I_{t-1} \cdot \sigma - \triangle I_t = m \cdot I_{t-1} \cdot \sigma.$$

Or,

$$\frac{\triangle I_t}{I_{t-1}} = s \cdot \sigma.$$

That is, the maximum rate of growth in investment that can be sustained without encountering balance of payments difficulties is equal to $s \cdot \sigma$. If investment grows at a higher rate, the growth in imports will outstrip the rise in exports, and the developing country will have to lose international reserves, or else receive an inflow of capital. If it is stipulated that only domestic saving, and not a balance of payments deficit, is available for financing the investment, then the maximum sustainable rate of growth in investment is clearly below what it would be if a balance of payments deficit were allowed.

5. In demonstrating that there will be no change in the balance on current account as long as any increase in desired investment is matched by a concurrent increase in desired saving, the preceding analysis reiterates the fundamental principle that external imbalance can be avoided if the investment is financed by non-inflationary methods.[12] The output created by the investment removes pressure on the balance of payments. When the output is either export-creating or import-saving, it will directly improve the balance of payments. But the remaining alternative—an expansion in output for the domestic market—will also be import-saving, even though the substitution of domestic goods for imports is made only indirectly. Since the investment is non-inflationary, national expenditure does not exceed national output; therefore, to buy the additional output from the new investment on the home market, there must be a reduction in imports. Such a switch of expenditure from imports will offset any increase in imports caused by the investment in the home industry.[13]

---

[12] But even if *ex ante* savings and investment are equal, there is the possibility that structural problems in an underdeveloped country that lacks a diversified economic structure may, in turn, lead to payments difficulties. The balance of payments difficulties of a developing country would then not necessarily be a reflection of inadequate savings or inflationary fiscal and monetary policies. Cf. I. G. Patel, "Trade and Payments Policy for a Developing Economy," R. F. Harrod and D. C. Hague, eds., *International Trade Theory in a Developing World*, Macmillan Co., 1963, p. 310. This possibility is discussed more fully in section 7.

[13] A. E. Kahn, "Investment Criteria in Development Programs," *Quarterly Journal of Economics*, February, 1951, pp. 42–47; Ragnar Nurkse, "International Trade Theory and Development Policy," H. S. Ellis, ed., *Economic Development for Latin America*, St. Martin's Press, 1961, pp. 259–260.

In Nurkse's words: "If the new industry sells its products on the domestic market, the rest of the economy will have to divert its expenditure away from imported products, provided that expenditure is not increased by inflationary means, through a reduction in saving, through dishoarding, or through credit expansion. If inflation can be avoided, then the products sold by the new industry—given the constraint of limited in-

It must be emphasized that since inflation is an over-all problem in the economy, its adverse effects on the balance of payments do not depend on any particular distribution of investment. What matters for the avoidance of balance of payments problems is not the composition of the investment, but whether the investment is financed by noninflationary means and whether it provides the highest possible social marginal product. It is erroneous to believe that balance of payments problems can only be avoided if the investment is directed toward export or import-competing industries. For, as long as investment is making the greatest possible contribution to an expansion in national output, and is not giving rise to inflation, it will also be aiding the balance of payments. To allocate investment arbitrarily to import-competing or export industries, instead of in accordance with the principle of acquiring the maximum marginal productivity from investment, is to be misled by a narrow "commodity approach" to balance of payments policy; it fails to recognize the over-all contribution of investment to national output and thereby indirectly to the balance of payments.[14]

---

come in the rest of the economy—will necessarily act as import substitutes indirectly, even if they look totally different from anything imported previously. If there is a balance of payments deficit it is a result of inflation, not of output expansion for the home market. In the absence of inflation the rest of the economy will have to reduce its imports in order to buy the products of the new industry, and this will tend to offset the increase in imports caused by the new industry."

For a critical review of this issue, see Hang-Sheng Cheng, "A Theory of Balance-of-Payments Adjustments Following upon Output Expansions in the Foreign-Trade and Domestic-Trade Industries," *Southern Economic Journal,* October, 1966, pp. 197–211.

[14] Ragnar Nurkse, *Problems of Capital Formation in Underdeveloped Countries,* Basil Blackwell, 1953, pp. 137–138; "International Trade Theory and Development Policy," *op. cit.,* pp. 262–263.

In view of the distorted domestic price structure that commonly pre-

When, however, national expenditure increases by inflationary methods—through private or public deficit spending, or through dissaving—the expenditure will exceed the increase in output, and an external imbalance will result. For, in this case, to buy the new products on the home market, expenditure does not have to be diverted away from imports. An excess of spending over income at home will be taken out in an external deficit; the imbalance between imports and exports is simply the reflection of an imbalance between domestic investment and saving or between government expenditure and taxation. If domestic output remains unchanged, then an increase in savings (or taxation), with unchanged domestic investment (or government expenditure), must improve the balance of payments by an equal amount. This is the essence of the absorption approach to balance of payments problems as outlined in the foregoing sections.

While this is necessarily true, *ex post*, in terms of the accounting identity, the important question remains whether there is a causal connection such that an increase in savings will always reduce the balance of payments deficit. Given a fixed exchange rate, if domestic output declines when domestic demand falls, there need not be a reduction in imports and increase in exports equivalent to the reduction in domestic demand.[15] Or if the elasticity of foreign demand for a country's exports is so low that exports cannot be increased, or can only be sold at the

---

vails in a poor country, it should be stressed that the maximum rate of return on new investment must be computed at the correct set of internal prices. To make an economic payoff calculation as distinguished from a commercial one, the calculation should be at "honest unsubsidized prices"; Wolfgang Stolper, "Comprehensive Development Planning," *East African Economic Review*, Vol. I, New Series, 1964, pp. 11–12.

[15] I. M. D. Little and J. M. Clifford, *International Aid*, Allen & Unwin, 1965, pp. 141–142.

expense of a deterioration in the country's terms of trade, and imports are required for investment, then the balance of payments acts as a real restraint on the level of investment, even though the additional saving would make more resources available for the supply of exports. If exports cannot expand sufficiently to cover the imports required by the investment program, a balance of payments problem will remain even though additional investments are covered by savings. Thus, if a country cannot invest more without additional foreign exchange, and if domestic saving cannot be transferred into foreign exchange, the basic development bottleneck may then more appropriately be considered as that of foreign exchange rather than savings. In section 7 we shall return to a discussion of this distinction.

6. According to the absorption approach, it now appears that if a poor country has an external deficit caused by inflationary pressures, and it cannot borrow more from abroad, its national expenditure must then be reduced to the level of its national output. Until there is internal stabilization the external disequilibrium will persist, since the total absorption of goods and services by households, firms, and government will continue to exceed the country's aggregate production plus any autonomous capital inflow. In this inflationary situation neither import restrictions nor devaluation alone will prove effective in removing the external imbalance; these measures must be supplemented by policies that will also lower the rate of absorption.

Only under highly restrictive conditions would import regulations or devaluation automatically have effects of the right character on absorption. Import regulations will not create their own "disabsorption" if the income formerly spent on imports is now simply diverted to domestic consumption. Barring a reduction in investment, if the income previously spent on imports does not now remain unspent, then domestic consumption increases, prices rise, and the volume of exports falls. Under these conditions, the strain on the balance of payments would be lessened only if there were an inelastic demand for exports, so that export revenue increased as export prices rose, and this increase in export revenue were saved. It is more likely, in the generality of cases, that the balance of payments repercussions of inflationary pressures will take the form of a weakening of the competitive position of exports, an increase in imports, a deterrence to the inflow of foreign capital, and an encouragement to capital flight.

Moreover, since import controls in themselves will not help to remove the cause of the disequilibrium, they can only continue to suppress the disequilibrium when they are retained on a long-run basis. The disadvantages of maintaining import regulations over long periods are, however, especially severe in a developing economy, for the continual reliance on import restrictions to protect international reserves will react adversely on production.[16] Bottlenecks in production will tend to occur when stocks of imported materials have been worked down to low levels. Behind the protection of the import regulations, monopoly elements and oligopolistic market structures may be strengthened, and distortions in production may give rise to unusual opportunities for private profits. Without an increase in saving and taxation, import controls are especially likely to create profitable opportunities in luxury consumption industries, and a large proportion of imported "essential" capital goods may simply be diverted to

[16] For an elaboration of the following points, see Eric Lundberg, "International Stability and the National Economy," Douglas Hague, ed., *Stability and Progress in the World Economy*, St. Martin's Press, 1958, pp. 216–218; H. G. Johnson, "Fiscal Policy and the Balance of Payments in a Growing Economy," *Malayan Economic Review*, April, 1964, pp. 1–13.

these industries. In the absence of external competition, new projects appear profitable, but the result is low productivity as the economy strains in too many directions. Further, the protection given by import control will tend not only to increase costs and thereby weaken the competitive position of the export industries, but also to divert resources to import-competing industries at the expense of export development. In conformity with the comparative cost analysis of Chapter 2, this diversion of resources from the exporting to the import-substituting sector is wasteful because the resources are shifted from indirect production of importable goods to domestic production at a higher real cost. To the extent that import restrictions constitute in essence a tax on real incomes in the export sector, they actually aggravate the balance of payments problem by indirectly impeding rather than fostering an expansion of exports.[17] All these adverse effects attest to the basic difficulty that, when import controls are superimposed on an inflationary economy, the allocation of resources becomes even more distorted, and the resultant misallocation of resources can be extremely expensive—and self-perpetuating.

A common cause of import restrictions is the overvaluation of the developing country's exchange rate. With the excessive rise in aggregate demand and the inflation of domestic wages and prices, the demand for imports increases, and an excess demand for foreign exchange results. If devaluation is ruled out, there is then a need for import restriction or distress borrowing.[18] Under

---

[17] Johnson, "Fiscal Policy and the Balance of Payments in a Growing Economy," *op. cit.*, pp. 3–4.

[18] Instead of pursuing a policy of outright devaluation, many developing countries have attempted to meet this situation by first imposing higher duties and exchange controls on imports, and then trying to promote exports through devices such as direct export subsidies, favorable exchange rates for export proceeds, and tax remissions. The result is the equivalent of a *de facto* devaluation, in the sense of a rise in the local cur-

inflationary conditions, however, an adjustment of the country's exchange rate may prove ineffective. If the elasticity of foreign demand for exports is extremely low, and imports are already being restricted, it is quite possible that devaluation may actually worsen the balance of payments, at least in the short run, by decreasing the foreign exchange earnings of exports, while the foreign exchange cost of imports would not fall. But even if the elasticities are sufficiently high to rule out this perverse case of devaluation, it is still essential, under conditions of full employment, that the devaluation should be accompanied by a fall in aggregate real expenditure so as to allow an improvement in the trade balance through an increase in export volume and a fall in the import volume. When devaluation changes relative prices, resulting in an increase in the local currency prices of exports and imports relative to home prices, there must be a shift in demand away from export and import goods to domestic goods and a shift in home production in favor of exportables and import substitutes. These shifts have inflationary effects which will cancel the devaluation, unless they are counteracted by deflationary

---

rency prices of both exports and imports relative to domestic prices. But instead of having a general devaluation across the board for all exports and imports, the covert devaluation brought about by a combination of import duties and export subsidies is only a partial devaluation and has a differential impact upon different categories of imports and exports. See Johnson, "Fiscal Policy and the Balance of Payments in a Growing Economy," *op. cit.*, pp. 3–4.

These piecemeal measures, involving distortions of the price structure, also inevitably introduce significant distortions in the allocation of resources. It may be argued that a developing country ideally should adopt a floating exchange rate, so that the inflationary effects and balance of payments pressures that accompany development planning might be offset automatically, without interfering with the allocation of resources according to comparative advantage as modified by development planning; *ibid.*, pp. 4–6.

measures. If when a country devalues it does not also adopt measures to hold aggregate domestic expenditure constant, any increase in exports or decrease in imports resulting from devaluation will simply lead to an inflation of expenditure and renewed pressures on the balance of payments. It is therefore essential that monetary expansion not be allowed to offset the equilibrating effects of devaluation.

In order to stress the principle that domestic expenditure is a basic and deliberate policy variable for the maintenance of external balance, we have focused on an aggregate spending approach to balance of payments adjustment. But this approach should not be overemphasized to the neglect of the complementary role played by changes in relative prices (the elasticities approach). It should be recognized that if the money supply is kept constant, real absorption will be automatically reduced by the rise in the price level and the reduction in the real value of total cash balances as a result of the devaluation. Besides the effects on absorption of the rise in the level of prices, the relative price changes associated with a change in the terms of trade will also affect absorption, through both the income effects and substitution effects of the change in the terms of trade. In general, relative price changes and income-expenditure adjustments combine to determine the effects of a devaluation.[19]

When a policy of import control or devaluation is supple-

[19] For a well-balanced exposition, see S. C. Tsiang, "The Role of Money in Trade-Balance Stability: Synthesis of the Elasticity and Absorption Approaches," *American Economic Review*, December, 1961, pp. 912–936. Also, S. S. Alexander, "Effects of a Devaluation: A Simplified Synthesis of Elasticities and Absorption Approaches," *American Economic Review*, March, 1959, pp. 22–42; Johnson, *International Trade and Economic Growth, op. cit.*, chap. VI; F. Machlup, "Relative Prices and Aggregate Spending in the Analysis of Devaluation," *American Economic Review*, June, 1955, pp. 255–278.

mented by adequate monetary and fiscal policies of "disabsorption," it may then be possible to remove the external imbalance without sacrificing internal balance. Such a combined policy of deflation accompanied by either import restriction or devaluation will allow a given improvement in the balance of payments to be attained at a higher level of employment than if deflation is used alone.[20] But since it will conflict with the development program if the required "disabsorption" of resources is sought through a restriction of investment and government expenditures, the brunt of the "disabsorption" must fall on consumption. It is, however, difficult to mobilize additional saving out of current consumption. Reliance must then be placed on additional saving out of current increases in output. Although there is unlikely to be a voluntary increase in saving, even out of additions to income, the saving might be forced through taxation. If the import content of investment is higher than the import content of marginal consumption expenditures, the balance of payments situation will not be improved immediately, but it will be eased eventually as the investment results in additional domestic production and as resources are released from the domestic consumption sector for the export and import-competing sectors.

[20] For an illuminating, albeit highly formal, analysis of the optimum combination of import restrictions, devaluation, and deflation, see M. F. W. Hemming and W. M. Corden, "Import Restriction as an Instrument of Balance of Payments Policy," *Economic Journal*, September, 1958, pp. 483–510. Also, see S. S. Alexander, "Devaluation versus Import Restrictions as an Instrument for Improving Foreign Trade Balance," *International Monetary Fund Staff Papers*, April, 1951, pp. 379–396; H. G. Johnson, *Money, Trade and Economic Growth*, Allen & Unwin, 1962, chap. 1.

For a comparison of the use of direct controls and of price adjustments in the light of their effects on the balance of payments and the level of real income in the different countries, see J. E. Meade, *Balance of Payments*, Oxford Univ. Press, 1951, chaps. XXI, XXIII, XXIV.

7. The foregoing analysis has emphasized the traditional view of international trade theory that a chronic balance of payments deficit is due to a chronic state of excess demand. If there is over-absorption, an increase in savings and taxation or decrease in investment and government expenditure is then necessary to remove the deficit. The "savings constraint" thus sets a limit to the rate of development that can be sustained without incurring external imbalance.

In contradistinction to this view, however, it has been increasingly argued that from the perspective of development planning, the lack of foreign exchange can be a bottleneck limiting the rate of development even if saving is not a constraint.[21] The strands in the argument are as follows. Foreign exchange is essential for an increase in investment because for technological reasons the level of investment depends on the availability of im-

[21] The distinction between the "savings gap" and "foreign exchange gap" has been stressed particularly for the case of India: I. M. D. Little, "The Strategy of Indian Development," *National Institute Economic Review*, May, 1960, pp. 23–25; Little and Clifford, *International Aid, op. cit.*, pp. 141–145; G. D. A. MacDougall, "India's Balance of Payments," *Bulletin of Oxford Institute of Statistics*, May, 1961, pp. 153–155; J. Bhagwati, "Indian Balance of Payments Policy and Exchange Auctions," *Oxford Economic Papers*, February, 1962, pp. 56–58; J. P. Lewis, *Quiet Crisis in India*, Brookings Institution, 1962, pp. 40–47; W. B. Reddaway, *The Development of the Indian Economy*, Richard D. Irwin, 1962, pp. 215–216. More generally, the foreign exchange constraint has been emphasized by H. B. Chenery and M. Bruno, "Development Alternatives in an Open Economy: The Case of Israel," *Economic Journal*, March, 1962, pp. 79–103; H. B. Chenery and A. M. Strout, "Foreign Assistance and Economic Development," *American Economic Review*, September, 1966, pp. 679–731; R. I. McKinnon, "Foreign Exchange Constraints in Economic Development and Efficient Aid Allocation," *Economic Journal*, June, 1964, pp. 388–409; Jaroslav Vanek, *Estimating Foreign Resource Needs for Economic Development*, McGraw-Hill, 1967, chaps. 1, 6; Staffan Burenstam Linder, *Trade and Trade Policy for Development*, Praeger, 1967, chap. II.

ported complementary goods. An increase in savings will, however, make more foreign exchange available for the purchase of these necessary import-inputs for investment only if it results in an increase in export earnings or a decrease in other expenditures. But export earnings may not expand with an increase in savings: On the one hand, the home demand for exportables may be negligible, so that a rise in domestic savings will not release from home consumption goods that can be exported; on the other hand, even if the export supply does increase, it is maintained that foreign demand may be so inelastic that a greater supply of exports will only yield lower export revenue. And imports will not be reduced by additional savings because consumption-goods imports are already being limited to a minimum requirement, and it is not technically feasible to produce domestically the remaining goods in the import bill. Hence, it is concluded that an increase in savings cannot be translated into the necessary foreign exchange to sustain a higher level of investment. The rate of development thus encounters a balance of payments barrier—notwithstanding the increase in savings. If, however, there were no foreign exchange constraint and necessary imports could rise, then production could increase by several times the value of the increase in imports; by raising income, this would in turn raise savings and investment and thereby the rate of development. In short, when the poor country's export capability is limited and its import requirements are fixed and large, the foreign exchange bottleneck can limit the country's rate of development, independently of the savings constraint.

To recognize the possibility of such a situation, the analysis in section 4 can now be modified. Instead of assuming, as was done in section 4, that the developing country has no difficulty in raising its export receipts, we now postulate that it is not domestic savings but the limited quantity of exports and thereby limited import-goods for investment that constitute the real restraint on the country's growth. An increase in investment $(\triangle I_t)$ is then limited by the foreign exchange increment $(\triangle X_t - m\triangle O_t)$, where $\triangle X_t$ is given by world markets, and m represents the marginal propensity to import consumer goods. Insofar as foreign exchange, and not saving, now limits investment, an increase in $\triangle X_t$ or a decrease in m would permit a rise in the rate of increase in investment. Thus, the foreign exchange constraint operates when it is impossible to increase exports and decrease consumption imports sufficiently to fulfill the requirement of additional imports for a higher rate of investment. The exports of the developing country are then insufficient to pay for the imports of capital goods and intermediate inputs that are needed to sustain the rate of growth that would be achieved by its rate of domestic saving and over-all capital-output ratio ($s\sigma$). Instead, the country can grow only at a lower rate ($< s\sigma$), determined by the ratio of export capabilities to national income and the ratio of imported capital goods and foreign-materials inputs required to produce an additional unit of domestic output. The "foreign exchange constraint" will then be encountered before the "savings constraint," and a part of domestic savings which could have supported a higher rate of growth will not be fully utilized because of the inability to obtain the additional imports necessary for a higher level of investment.[22]

This distinction between a foreign exchange gap and a savings gap is analytically useful, especially from the standpoint of a development plan. But the essential question is how valid are

---

[22] McKinnon, *op. cit.*, pp. 389–395. Where the *ex ante* gap between total imports and exports is greater than the *ex ante* difference between investment and savings, the realized level of savings will be less than originally projected. In the *ex post* sense, the actual difference between investment and savings will, of course, equal the actual difference between imports and exports.

the assumptions on which the conceptual distinction rests. To maintain a "dual gap" analysis, it is necessary to rule out devaluation as a feasible policy instrument and to assume very significant rigidity and lack of substitution possibilities in the developing economy between: (1) production for export or import substitution and nontraded goods, and (2) a high degree of complementarity in the use of domestically produced capital goods and imported capital goods as well as other intermediate inputs in the aggregate production function.[23] The crucial question therefore is whether or not the "structural" assumptions of extremely limited substitution possibilities in both the output-mix and factor-inputs are empirically relevant.

Regarding the assumption that the imported capital goods and other inputs are required in rigidly fixed proportions with domestic inputs, one may argue that at the most this is plausible only for the import-substituting industries in the modern sector of the economy, based on imported technology and requiring inputs that cannot be easily supplied from domestic production. But this assumption does not hold for wider import-substituting possibilities that may be realized through the expansion of domestic agriculture, and in some countries through the expansion of smaller scale industries using local materials and techniques. Nor is the existence of industries operating at less than their full technical capacity necessarily indicative of a shortage of imported materials and a foreign exchange constraint: It may well be that even if the imported inputs could be obtained, the industries would still operate below capacity because their costs are too high or the domestic market is too narrow.[24] Moreover, instead

---

[23] McKinnon, *op. cit.*, pp. 403–406; McKinnon, "Foreign Exchange Constraints in Economic Development and Efficient Aid Allocation: Rejoinder," *Economic Journal*, March, 1966, p. 170.

[24] Hla Myint, "The 'Widening Trade Gap' of the Underdeveloped Countries: A Critical View" (unpublished paper).

of being due to an irreducible technically determined relationship between imported inputs and domestic output, the high import "requirements" in a developing economy may be simply a
reflection of domestic policies that result in a misallocation of
domestic resources.

As for the assumption that the country's export capability is
low relative to its import requirements, there is some merit in
the argument that the trade restrictions of advanced countries
limit the exports from developing countries. But inhibiting factors are also again to be found in the domestic policies of the
developing countries—especially those policies that stem from a
belief in growth through import-substitution rather than growth
through trade.[25] Inflationary policies with resultant import controls have unfavorable effects in impeding the growth of export
supply; to this extent, the previous analysis of the savings constraint becomes of direct relevance. Other policies, such as direct
taxation of exports, discriminatory exchange rates, taxation
through marketing boards, and the general "squeeze on agriculture" may also have deleterious effects on exports. Thus, even
though it may well be true for some countries that an increase
in domestic savings would not lead directly to a higher level of
export earnings by directly releasing home consumption goods
that can be exported, it is nonetheless possible that a rise in savings would do so indirectly, particularly when home inflation is
restraining a rise in exports. For many countries, a ceiling on exports is being imposed through the supply side by the use of domestic policies that overemphasize import-substitution, maintain
an overvalued exchange rate, and result in a distorted price structure. These policies are commonly rationalized by appealing to
the alleged inelasticity of export demand and low elasticity of

[25] See further, Chapters 7 and 8.

domestic demand for imports; but once they are adopted, the policies do react on exports and become self-justifying. Finally, unlike India which has a low ratio of exports to national income but a potentially large domestic market, there are many other poor countries with high ratios of exports to national income— export ratios that are in fact considerably higher than their ratios of saving to national income. For these countries, it is especially difficult to believe that a balance of payments bottleneck as distinct from the savings limitation is at present the operative constraint.[26]

In view of the highly restrictive assumptions upon which the structural interpretation of a foreign exchange constraint depends, we may conclude that it is unlikely to be generally true that the problem of developing economies is primarily one of a foreign exchange constraint.[27] The foreign exchange approach is

[26] Myint, *op. cit.*

[27] Little and Clifford, *op. cit.*, pp. 142–143; but cf. Patel, *op. cit.*, p. 311. India and a few Latin American countries may be examples of countries where the foreign exchange constraint bites before the savings constraint. In most of the African countries, however, exports would be enough to pay for materials and the essential import component of such investment as can be absorbed, provided savings were enough.

Much of the literature on the foreign exchange constraint was originally related to India: see n. 21, above. But even for India, the assumption of rigid import "coefficients" may be considered extreme: see J. Bhagwati, "The Development of Trade Theory in the Context of Underdeveloped Countries," A. K. Das Gupta, ed., *Trade Theory and Commercial Policy*, Asia Pub. House, 1965, pp. 25–26. It has also been suggested that India could expand exports of commodities for which India is a marginal exporter: see M. Singh, *India's Export Trends and the Prospects for Self-Sustaining Growth*, Clarendon Press, 1964, pp. 150–153. The view that government policy rather than world demand has been the dominating factor in limiting the growth of India's exports is also presented by Anne Krueger, "Export Prospects and Economic Growth: India: A Comment," *Economic Journal*, June, 1961, pp. 436–442.

useful in reminding us that to secure a balance of payments "margin" for greater maneuverability in its development plan, a developing country should engage in efforts to increase its export earnings and diminish the import-intensity of its import-substitution industries. At the same time, it is still true that in many cases a large part of the pressure for imports is due to excess demand, and the absorption approach—with its emphasis on the savings constraint—remains of general and fundamental importance for a majority of the less developed countries that face the problem of keeping attempted absorption within the bounds of current income.

If efforts to increase domestic saving fail, the overabsorption must be covered by foreign borrowing of an autonomous or acceptable character. As long as a development program emphasizes investment, and there is a deficiency of home savings, an increased supply of long-term capital from foreign countries is needed. Historically, the investment expenditure which touched off the development process in many poor countries was financed by an inflow of foreign capital acceptable to both lender and borrower. At present, however, new problems are being encountered through international aid measures and foreign investment policies designed to both encourage and regulate private foreign capital. The next two chapters consider these problems.

5

International Aid

1. The traditional theory of international capital movements has been concerned mainly with the mechanism of adjustment in the balance of payments. But in the context of development, the effects of a foreign capital inflow raise a number of questions that extend beyond the adjustment mechanism. While the literature on development emphasizes the importance of foreign capital, the discussion is still at too remote a level of generality and is insufficiently related to fundamental problems of development. There is still, as Nurkse observed, a need for "a theory of capital movements that is concerned with capital as a factor of production" and a theory that "would direct attention to the unequal proportions in which capital cooperates with labor and land in the different parts of the world; to the technical forms which capital should assume in response to different relative factor endowments; to the relations between capital movements, population growth and migration; and to other such fundamental matters. Only fragments of this type of capital-movement theory exist today, but the great awakening is forcing the attention of economists all over the world to these basic questions—with some benefit, one may hope, not only to the theory of capital formation and development, but to international economics generally."[1]

Responding to some of these questions, this chapter and the next analyze the role of foreign capital in the development process. In considering international aid, we shall concentrate in the present chapter on the flow of long-term financial resources (not commodity aid as under Public Law 480, or technical assistance); and we shall be primarily concerned with the effects of international aid on the economies of the recipient countries (not the donor countries). Special attention will be given to the objectives of foreign aid, criteria for its allocation, measures to increase its effectiveness, and the increasingly acute problem of debt servicing.

2. Properly defined, external financial "aid" refers to only that part of the capital inflow which is not based on normal market incentives but is instead made on concessionary terms. Thus, grants of freely convertible currency constitute aid in the full sense; loans contain only an element of aid (the aid-component being greater, the longer the grace and maturity periods, and the lower the interest rate); and private foreign investment and short-term capital movements are excluded.[2]

---

[1] Ragnar Nurkse, *Problems of Capital Formation in Underdeveloped Countries*, Basil Blackwell, 1953, p. 131.

[2] On problems of measuring the flow of international aid, see Goran Ohlin, *Reappraisals of Foreign Aid Policies*, OECD Development Center, 1966, chap. V; United Nations, Report of the Secretary-General, *Measurement of the Flow of Long-Term Capital and Official Donations to Developing Countries: Concepts and Methodology*, A/5732, February 1, 1965.

At the outset, we should recognize that the transfer ʊɪ ᴄˣternal resources must now be considered in conjunction with development planning. Even though the argument for accelerated capital accumulation as the central objective of a development program is often based too naively on aggregative capital-output ratios and saving ratios, nevertheless most of the less developed countries do view their need for foreign capital in terms of their national development programs. Through a variety of policy measures, the recipient countries attempt to influence the magnitude, composition, and use of the capital transfer. Aid-giving countries also encourage the practice of development planning as a prerequisite for the receipt of external financial aid. Thus, unlike the classical context of international capital movements, or historical interpretations of earlier periods of foreign investment, the present role of foreign capital in poor countries cannot be examined apart from development planning.

In the context of a development program, foreign capital has a dual role in enabling the recipient country to raise its level of investment and increase its imports. Although within a general development program it is not possible to identify any one source of funds with a specific type of use, a net capital inflow can offset or "finance" all three of the following differences as aggregates: (1) value of products used *minus* value of products produced domestically; (2) net investment *minus* net domestic savings; (3) value of imported goods and services, including factor payments *minus* value of exported goods and services, including factor receipts.[3] The foreign capital requirements of a

---

[3] Simon Kuznets, "International Differences in Capital Formation and Financing," National Bureau of Economic Research, *Capital Formation and Economic Growth*, Princeton Univ. Press, 1955, pp. 34–35.

The volume of net capital imports is arrived at by deducting interest and amortization on loan capital, dividends and amortization on direct investments, and flight of capital.

development plan can therefore be expressed either as the need to fill the "savings gap" or to cover the "foreign exchange gap."

3. If the development program entails greater investment than can be sustained by the level of domestic savings, and it is desired to undertake the additional expenditure without inflation, then the excess of domestic expenditure over current output must be covered by external financing. When the claims of the development plan exceed the available domestic resources, the shortfall in real resources must be removed by using foreign resources. An import surplus then permits domestic investment to exceed domestic savings, and the external aid can be viewed as having the effect of supplementing domestic savings. In this sense, the transfer of capital to a developing country is very much the international counterpart of the domestic problem of mobilizing savings for a higher rate of domestic capital formation.

An estimate of the amount of external capital "required" to remove the savings constraint is derived by calculating the difference between the recipient country's absorptive capacity (ability to derive an acceptable rate of return from additional capital) and its saving capacity. A target rate of growth of income is first designated, based on some judgment of the country's absorptive capacity. Assuming a capital-output ratio, it is next decided what would be the required ratio of net investment to national income in order to fulfill the target growth rate in income. Given the initial domestic saving rate, and postulating a marginal saving rate, it is then possible to estimate the capital requirements and expected domestic savings over the plan period. The difference is the amount of foreign capital required. To the extent that private foreign investment or foreign exchange reserves do not fill the gap, public funds from abroad are needed.

A number of studies have estimated the need for external

financial aid based on the savings gap.[4] All these estimates, however, are obviously subject to large margins of uncertainty insofar as they depend on estimates of absorptive capacity, the capital-output ratio, and an expected marginal saving ratio. In formulating a development plan, it is only too simple to consider foreign capital as merely the residual means of financing the plan. The full implications of external financing cannot, however, be appreciated without undertaking a more comprehensive analysis of the role of the foreign capital. In the broadest sense, the analysis should consider how the capital inflow relates to a greater national effort to increase the rate of development. More specifically, it should examine the differential impact of various forms of foreign capital receipts, their costs and benefits, and the transfer problem.

At the outset of a development plan, the demand for foreign capital should be restrained to a level that is economically warranted. If current consumption were to be bolstered through external financing, the scope for the use of foreign capital would be practically without bounds. When we exclude this use, the economically warranted demand for foreign capital is limited by the recipient country's absorptive capacity. At least in the short-run, even if not in the longer run, there may be a limit to how much foreign investment can be effectively used when the investment must not only cover its costs but also yield a reasonable increase in income.

The country's technical absorptive capacity will initially be determined by the extent to which certain conditions necessary for the productive utilization of capital already exist in the econ-

[4] See, for example, P. N. Rosenstein-Rodan, "International Aid for Underdeveloped Countries," *Review of Economics and Statistics*, May, 1961, pp. 107–117. A convenient summary of several studies is presented by Ohlin, *op. cit.*, chap. V.

omy. In general, the capacity to absorb external resources for productive investment purposes will be low when there are inadequate public overhead facilities,[5] administrative and organizational bottlenecks, deficient qualities of entrepreneurship, shortages of complementary natural resources, scarcities of trained manpower, low geographic and occupational mobility of labor, and narrow localized markets.[6] These handicaps may prevent some of the projects in the development plan from ever being implemented in the first instance. In other cases, the project may be completed but not utilized fully or efficiently. And in still other situations, the limited supply of complementary factors and facilities may result in a sharp decline in the marginal productivity of capital as capital accumulates. The marginal productivity of capital in a poor country may be high at the outset of an investment program, but if diminishing returns to capital are to be forestalled, it is necessary to eliminate the bottlenecks, increase the supply of factors cooperating with capital, and achieve more rapid technological progress. Once the pace of development gains momentum, the absorptive capacity will be higher. With greater productivity and a better mechanism for resource allocation, the rate of effective utilization of foreign capital would continually increase.

4. Instead of focusing on the savings gap, it may be more appropriate for some countries to calculate the requirements of foreign

---

[5] The very object of public foreign investment may, of course, be the creation of these facilities. In the absence of public overheads, however, the capacity to absorb private direct investment will be limited.

[6] Noneconomic aspects of the social systems in the poor countries are also important in accounting for the low capacity to absorb capital productively. See, for instance, Marion J. Levy, Jr., "Some 'Social Obstacles' to 'Capital Formation' in 'Underdeveloped Areas,'" National Bureau of Economic Research, *Capital Formation and Economic Growth, op. cit.*, pp. 450–497.

capital on the basis of the country's foreign exchange gap. As we have already noted,[7] the foreign exchange constraint can conceivably operate before the savings constraint as a bottleneck limiting the rate of development. Foreign assistance is then needed to allow the projected investment of the development plan to take the desired form—that is, investment may require necessary imports that cannot be alternatively supplied from substitute domestic sources.[8] If domestic saving does not result in an adequate increase in exports or reduction in imports of consumer goods so as to provide sufficient foreign exchange for the imports needed to support the higher rate of capital formation, foreign assistance will then be required for balance of payments reasons quite distinct from the need for aid as an adjunct to savings. When this is the case, the primary objective of external aid is to fill the gap in foreign exchange resources, and foreign aid requirements must then be based on the expected gap between foreign exchange earnings and import requirements during the plan period. Although by definition the contribution made by foreign resources to available savings and foreign exchange availability will necessarily be identical *ex post*, the savings gap may differ from the foreign exchange gap *ex ante*, as we have seen. If the *ex ante* foreign exchange gap is larger than the savings gap, and the inflow of external financial aid is designed to overcome only the savings gap, the developing country will not be able to fulfill its import requirements. External balance will then have to be attained by a variety of adjustment measures that sacrifice the planned rate of development. The question of capital provision is therefore not merely a matter of saving: It is a balance of pay-

---

[7] Chapter 4, section 7.

[8] Even if all investment projects were labor-intensive, but the country had to import foodstuffs, the amount of additional labor that could be employed would then be effectively limited by the amount of foreign exchange available to buy food (the real wages of the workers).

ments question.[9] Since the investment program depends on greater imports, the plan has to be financed by an inflow of capital to the extent that foreign exchange receipts on current account fall short of foreign exchange requirements, unless the country is able and willing to fill the gap with international reserves.

When the primary limit to development is the foreign exchange bottleneck, the productivity of aid is likely to be high: A relatively small increase in the availability of foreign exchange may yield a considerable increase in national income. By breaking a production bottleneck and allowing the utilization of previously underutilized capacity, the importation of strategic capital goods or foreign materials provided by external aid can permit a sizeable expansion of output from complementary domestic resources that would otherwise remain unused. If the function of external aid were merely to supplement domestic savings and finance additional investment, the productivity of aid would be equal to only the marginal productivity of additional capital; but when foreign aid removes a balance of payments bottleneck, its productivity is higher and has a proportionately greater effect on the rate of development.[10]

Since they depend on projections of foreign exchange earnings and expenditures during the plan period, estimates of the foreign

[9] An illuminating discussion of the practical consequences to be drawn from this argument is given by John R. Hicks, *Essays in World Economics*, Oxford Univ. Press, 1959, pp. 204–207; I. M. D. Little, "The Third Five Year Plan and the Strategy of Indian Development," *The Economic Weekly*, June, 1960, pp. 887–888.

[10] H. B. Chenery and A. M. Strout, "Foreign Assistance and Economic Development," *American Economic Review*, September, 1966, pp. 701–703; R. I. McKinnon, "Foreign Exchange Constraints in Economic Development and Efficient Aid Allocation," *Economic Journal*, June, 1964, p. 392.

capital requirements based on the foreign exchange gap are also necessarily inexact. The total foreign exchange resources available for imports are estimated from the sum of export earnings, net invisible receipts (excluding official donations), and net capital transactions (excluding fresh receipts of official loans and private foreign investment). From this total, a deduction may be made for essential imports that might be termed "maintenance imports"—that is, inescapable imports such as raw materials, intermediate products, foodstuffs, and capital goods for replacement. The balance then constitutes the foreign exchange resources available for "development imports"—that is, for the direct import requirements of the plan's investment targets in the public and private sectors. To the extent that foreign exchange requirements for "development imports" exceed the availability of foreign exchange, the plan will have to be financed by foreign savings in the form of a capital inflow (neglecting any possible use of existing foreign exchange reserves).[11]

When estimates of the need for foreign capital are made at the beginning of the plan period, they are likely to turn out to be quite wide of the mark during the course of the plan period, and the plan must then be revised. Most programs have been in error in underestimating foreign capital requirements. In some cases this has been due to overoptimistic projections of export earnings; more frequently, it has resulted from underestimating import requirements for both "maintenance imports" and "development imports."

A more fundamental difficulty in estimating foreign capital requirements by this method is to determine whether the foreign exchange gap is truly due to structural causes (and hence is to be

[11] For an instructive exercise, cf. Jaroslav Vanek, *Estimating Foreign Resource Needs for Economic Development*, McGraw-Hill, 1967.

relieved only by foreign aid) or, in contrast, is due to the repercussions of domestic policies (which could be altered to reduce
the foreign exchange gap). As we shall see in Chapter 7, a plausible case can be made that inflationary measures, an overvalued
exchange rate, and uneconomic import-substitution policies have
accentuated the foreign exchange gap in many developing countries. If the shortage of foreign exchange is not due to an irreducible technically determined relationship between imported
inputs and domestic output, but is instead related to domestic
policies, then a change in these policies is required. Indeed, under
these conditions, foreign assistance might simply have the effect
of making it easier to maintain the uneconomic domestic policies
that lead to the foreign exchange gap.

5. A detailed empirical study is needed to determine whether a
shortage of foreign exchange or deficiency of savings is currently
the controlling limitation in any individual country's development program. But regardless of whether the savings gap or foreign exchange gap is used in calculating the need for external
aid, most students of the problem conclude that the present
amount of aid falls substantially below the calculated requirements. And regardless of errors in estimating the extent to which
fulfillment of a development plan must rely on foreign capital,
the fundamental principle remains: The dependence on external
capital limits the size of the plan.

Using various combinations of assumptions with respect to
target growth rates, marginal saving rates, export growth, and
import substitution, Chenery and Strout submit that the net capital inflow requirements in 1970 will be in the range of $10–$17
billion, corresponding to a rate of growth of external capital of
3 percent to 10 percent from its value in 1962.[12] This range com-

---

[12] Chenery and Strout, *op. cit.*, pp. 721–722.

pares with the UNCTAD Secretariat's estimate for 1970 of $20 billion to raise the average growth rate in gross domestic product of the underdeveloped world to 5 percent per annum, and Balassa's estimated range of $9 to $12 billion.[13] Little and Clifford have suggested that less developed countries might usefully absorb another $1 to $1.5 billion per annum,[14] and studies by the World Bank indicate that between now and 1970 aid recipients could productively use $3 to $4 billion a year more external capital than has been provided in the recent past.[15]

Even though the estimates of aid requirements emphasize the inadequacy of the present level of foreign assistance, the net official flow of long-term capital to the less developed countries has actually leveled off since 1961. And with a rise in national income in the donor countries, the amount of net official aid has actually constituted a declining proportion of the donors' national income. Compared with the commonly stated target that the developed countries should aim at transferring a minimum of 1 percent of their "national incomes" by way of "capital flows" to the developing countries,[16] the annual net contribution of official assistance from the major donor countries has been only about .6 of 1 percent of their national income.[17] Especially distressing is the fact that just at a time when the volume of aid has

[13] See Chapter 8, p. 253.

[14] I. M. D. Little and J. M. Clifford, *International Aid*, Allen & Unwin, 1965, p. 235.

[15] International Bank for Reconstruction and Development, *Annual Report, 1964–1965*, Washington, D.C., p. 62.

[16] This target may have some political value, but it is economically ambiguous because the several donors provide aid in various forms and on different conditions, so that the real value of aid may differ markedly from the nominal value. See n. 18.

[17] United Nations, *International Flow of Long-Term Capital and Official Donations, 1961–1965*, New York, 1966, p. 15. This refers to nominal aid; in real terms, the percentage is less.

levelled off, the capacity of the developing countries to use external resources productively has increased markedly. If in the early postwar period of foreign assistance, many of the recipient countries experienced nonfinancial difficulties in making productive use of aid, this is no longer true for most of the developing countries. Nonetheless, while the ability to absorb more aid has been expanding during recent years, the net flow of assistance has not.

The need to increase the amount of external financial aid is but one of the conclusions to be drawn from the several studies of aid requirements. It is also important to recognize that the real value (net transfer of resources) of present aid programs is considerably less than the nominal value (the flow of financial resources).[18] Given the same nominal amount of capital inflow, the real resource transfer can be increased by softening the conditions and terms on which this capital is received. The less aid is tied to purchases from the donor country, so that recipients may import from the lowest-cost source, the greater will be the purchasing power of aid. Also, the higher the percentage of grants in the total inflow of capital, or the lower the interest rate, and the longer the grace and amortization periods on loans, the greater will be the real value. If the adverse effects of aid-tying can be reduced, and more lenient financial terms introduced, so

[18] For various estimates of the difference between the real value and nominal amount of aid, see John Pincus, *Economic Aid and International Cost-Sharing*, Johns Hopkins Press, 1965, chap. 5; Pincus, *Trade, Aid and Development*, McGraw-Hill, 1967, pp. 315–317; Little and Clifford, *op. cit.*, chap. II.

It should also be noted that the real cost of aid to the donor and the real benefit to the recipient are not necessarily symmetrical. Cf. Pincus, *Trade, Aid and Development, op. cit.*, pp. 309–315; Wilson Schmidt, "The Economics of Charity: Loans versus Grants," *Journal of Political Economy*, August, 1964, pp. 387–395.

as to increase the value of the subsidy implicit in the total flow of resources, the real value of external resources can more closely approach the nominal value.

It is also frequently asserted that increased trade can substitute for more aid. But this is true only under special conditions. Whereas foreign aid can close a prospective balance of payments gap without additional domestic saving on the part of the developing country, this gap can be closed by trade only if there is also an increase in domestic saving equal to the rise in export proceeds.[19] Over the longer run, to the extent that more trade raises national income, and this results in increased savings, trade will reduce the need for more aid; but the rise in savings is a necessary condition.

The view that trade can substitute for aid is also limited because it recognizes only the balance of payments constraint and considers only the foreign exchange side of aid—not the transfer of additional real resources for investment that aid also provides. If the developing country is only able to export more at prevailing prices, there is no provision of additional real resources as under aid; only if the less developed countries were enabled, because of international commodity agreements or preferential trading arrangements,[20] to charge higher prices for their exports than would otherwise prevail, would there be an explicit transfer of resources through trade.

6. When aid is limited, and trade is not a perfect substitute, it becomes all the more important to achieve the most effective use

[19] H. G. Johnson, *The World Economy at the Crossroads*, Oxford Univ. Press, 1965, pp. 88–89; Johnson, *Economic Policies toward Less Developed Countries*, Brookings Institution, 1967, pp. 53–54; Little and Clifford, *op. cit.*, pp. 150–155.
[20] See Chapter 9.

of the amount of aid that is forthcoming. By attaining high standards of performance the recipient countries may also help strengthen the case for generating larger amounts of aid.

Both capital-supplying and receiving countries can contribute to increasing the effectiveness of aid. To this end, donor countries should adopt the goal of accelerated development in the recipient country as the primary objective of aid-giving, and should not impose conditions on aid according to their own needs or national advantage. The economic effectiveness of aid can only be assessed in terms of the goal of development, not in terms of commercial, political, or military advantage to the donor country. Two important implications follow from the emphasis on the development goal: Aid should be untied, and a country's over-all development program (instead of individual projects) should be the basis for allocating and controlling aid.

The tying of aid funds to expenditure in the capital-supplying country is convenient in gaining political support for the appropriation of aid and in giving the appearance of promoting the balance of payments position of the aid-giving country. But the tying of aid to purchases in the donor country is implicitly a form of protection, and it can only too readily degenerate into a means of trade promotion by the capital-supplying country instead of being a means of accelerating the development of the recipient country. There are then adverse effects for the recipient country. The real value of aid is reduced to the extent that import prices from the donor country are above competitive world market prices. This may be of less concern when the recipient country receives aid in the form of a grant; but in the case of a loan, the extra cost of tying (represented by the difference between the purchasing power of untied aid and tied aid) may have a substantial effect in reducing the element of subsidy or the "grant component" in the loan.

Beyond diminishing the real value of aid, the practice of aid-tying is also undesirable because it distorts the recipient's allocation of investment resources. When procurement is limited to the aid-giving country, the recipient's development program tends to become biased towards those projects that have a high component of the special import content allowed for under the conditions of tied aid. Aid tied to purchases in the donor country can also limit the choice of technology used in investment projects and may thereby cause the recipient country to adopt by necessity a technology that is less appropriate for its factor endowment than would be true if it could import freely.

If, of course, the choice is between having to accept tied aid or having the capital-supplying country reduce its aid because of strains on its balance of payments, the tied aid is preferable to no aid, and recipient countries must live in a "second-best" world. Obviously, however, protection of the balance of payments does not justify tying by a surplus country; to the extent that the aid of a surplus country is tied, it serves the commercial interest of promoting the aid-giving country's export industries. Development of the aid-receiving economy is then not the primary objective of the aid, and recipient countries and other donor countries in balance of payments deficit can legitimately argue that surplus countries should untie their aid and increase the volume of their economic assistance.

It has been common to tie aid not only by restricting procurement to the aid-giving country, but also by limiting the aid to specific projects. Again, it has been the interests of the donor countries that have dictated reliance on project aid, rather than general purpose or program aid. For project aid has a number of advantages from the donor's viewpoint in gaining political and popular approval; giving the appearance of being devoted to something "concrete" and "permanent," with a minimum risk of failure; supposedly facilitating the capacity to service the foreign debt; being readily linked to procurement-tying; and providing a direct mechanism of control by the donor.

If, however, accelerated development of the recipient country is adopted as the purpose of aid, there are serious objections to project aid. The granting of aid for particular projects may be in large part illusory, insofar as the project actually financed by aid may be quite different from the one to which the aid is ostensibly tied.[21] If the project to which aid is tied would have been undertaken in any event by the recipient country, then the aid really enables the recipient to finance an additional project instead of the project to which aid is tied. In this case, the aid may just as correctly be interpreted as financing the marginal project, although the aid was granted on the basis of the donor's evaluation of the first project, and the technical and economic soundness of the additional project has never come under the donor's purview.

If, however, aid is given only for the import content of specific projects, and these projects would not otherwise have been undertaken, then the project-tying of aid will distort the recipient's investment priorities and twist its import pattern in favor of the import components of the tied projects. To absorb this type of aid, the country may have to forego other investments that it would otherwise have undertaken. This is because imports will also indirectly result from domestic expenditure on the project; the recipient may then not be able to meet the "local cost" of the projects for which the imported goods under tying are intended and still undertake, without inflation, the other investments for which no aid is forthcoming.

----

[21] H. W. Singer, "External Aid: For Plans or Projects?", *Economic Journal*, September, 1965, p. 539. But see A. Carlin, "Project Versus Programme Aid: From the Donor's Viewpoint," *Ibid.*, March, 1967, pp. 48–58.

The excessive tying of aid to particular goods (usually capital goods) from the donor country is especially deleterious when it results in the underutilization of domestic resources in the recipient country—either of labor, because the recipient country does not have the capacity to import the additional consumer goods that would result from greater employment; or of local industrial capacity, because the country cannot import the necessary components, raw materials, spare parts, etc. "Double-tying" —by donor procurement and project restriction—can too readily make the recipient country encounter a "local cost" or balance of payments problem which alters the relative priority of different projects and biases investment toward import-intensive projects.[22] Project-tying can only be of more benefit to the recipient country than program aid if the tied project would not otherwise have been included in the development program and is superior to other investments that are now foregone.

The underlying weakness of project aid is its failure to recognize that a development program or plan is more than a list of discrete projects. Resources may be substituted among projects, and resources may be diverted from some alternative use to the tied project, so that it is impossible to limit the effects of aid only to the project to which aid is ostensibly tied. The efficiency of any one project is very much a function of the country's entire investment program, and the impact of aid cannot be assessed without a general analysis of resource allocation in the recipient country. When the donor country acts as if it were simply a banker or private foreign investor, concerned only with projects, then a given amount of financial assistance will not contribute as much to the objective of accelerating development as would program aid.

[22] Little and Clifford, *op. cit.*, pp. 161–164, 285–286, 334–335; OECD, *Development Assistance Efforts and Policies, 1966 Review*, Paris, 1966, pp. 70–72.

Program aid has distinct advantages. To qualify for aid, recipients are not compelled to put forward projects with a high foreign exchange content, or to emphasize investment in specific projects over other expenditures that might be classified as current or as consumption but which may be in reality much more developmental than expenditures classified as "projects" or capital expenditure.[23] In practice, project-aid has tended to be concentrated in large infrastructure projects, but program aid may allow more assistance in fields that now merit special emphasis—agriculture, education, smaller-scale industry, administrative services. Program assistance might also improve the allocation of aid among recipient countries by allowing aid to be granted according to the over-all performance of the recipient, as determined by the recipient's entire set of development policies, instead of merely on the basis of the recipient's project preparation which is only one aspect of the country's capacity to make effective use of aid.[24]

The arguments for untying aid and shifting to nonproject aid are also arguments for supporting multilateral aid instead of bilateral aid. When foreign assistance is provided through a multilateral agency it is less likely to be oriented to the donors' interests in the way that some bilateral programs are. The undesirable effects of procurement-tying and project-tying are more easily avoided, and economic criteria rather than the political interests of the donors are more likely to determine the allocation of aid. Multilateral aid also has merit in avoiding the piecemeal and fragmented character of bilateral aid programs, and in removing the disparity of criteria and terms of aid from various sources that work independently of one another, and sometimes even at cross-purposes. Multilateralism also increases the active participation of

---

[23] Singer, *op. cit.*, p. 544.
[24] Chenery and Strout, *op. cit.*, pp. 723–728. See also, pp. 115–116.

recipient countries in the aid process, and this can have considerable educative effects, as well as being politically beneficial. For these reasons, it is understandable why UNCTAD adopted the recommendation that "[international financial cooperation] should encourage the channeling of external resources, wherever possible and appropriate, through multilateral institutions—including regional development institutions."[25]

The distinction between bilateral and multilateral aid can, however, be overdrawn. The difference is, after all, only one of degree; but in denigrating bilateral aid, there is the danger that the result will be a reduction in the total amount of aid forthcoming. Although a bilateral program may be motivated by historical associations with recipients and by political reasons, it nonetheless increases the volume of aid. If all aid were to be only multilateral, the amount of aid might be reduced; and it is questionable whether a smaller amount of multilateral aid is preferable to a larger amount of bilateral aid. Instead of contraposing bilateral and multilateral assistance, we should emphasize the best elements in each type of aid and seek to incorporate these elements in the total aid program. Thus, instead of overemphasizing multilateral aid to the neglect of bilateral aid, it would be more appropriate to reform bilateral programs and coordinate the programs of several donors through consultative groups and consortia. The World Bank can be an especially appropriate agency for exercising a leadership role in coordinating bilateral programs, bringing about a harmonization and improvement of the financial terms on which aid is provided, and strengthening the movement toward regional cooperation among the developing countries so that aid might have a more substantial regional impact.

While, in terms of donor policies, the effectiveness of aid

[25] United Nations, *Proceedings of* UNCTAD, Vol. I, 1964, p. 42.

would be increased by untying aid and granting program assistance, the recipient countries must also share a greater responsibility for improving their utilization of aid. Specific recommendations for the better utilization of aid depend on the particular arrangements and circumstances of the individual country, but some general principles have wide relevance for making aid a more effective component of development planning.

If there are economic advantages to program assistance, then it is obviously necessary at the outset that the recipient country be able to produce a well-formulated development plan and have the capacity to implement the plan. Otherwise, the donor has no choice but to tie its aid to projects, or impose its own strategy for development, or else be indifferent to whether its aid is for development or any other purpose.[26] Given that the requisite conditions exist for distributing aid on a program basis, the effective use of aid will depend on the extent to which it is successfully integrated into the recipient's development plan. The essence of external financial aid is the provision of additional economic resources, but external assistance must add to—not substitute for—the developing country's own efforts. If financial assistance from abroad is to result in a higher rate of domestic investment, it must be prevented from simply replacing domestic sources of financing investment, and it cannot be dissipated in supporting higher consumption or an increase in nondevelopmental current expenditure by the government. Regardless of the amount of aid received, all policy considerations must heed the dictum that "capital is made at home."[27]

Since the effective utilization of foreign capital is highly dependent on the borrowing country's ability and willingness to adopt complementary domestic policies, there can be no simple

[26] Little and Clifford, *op. cit.*, pp. 188–191.
[27] Nurkse, *op. cit.*, p. 141.

equivalence between the amount of the country's foreign borrowing and its rate of development. The entire rationale of program aid will be lost, and external aid may be incapable of yielding significant results, unless the recipient undertakes complementary domestic measures ranging from improvements in the organization and management of specific activities to more general policies—such as fiscal policy and balance of payments policy—that affect total resource use. Broadly stated, the objectives of self-help measures should be to increase the aid-receiving country's ability, in terms of institutions and skilled manpower, to plan and implement development programs; extend the scale of its development program; raise the income yielded by its development expenditure; increase its own financing of development; and promote exports and economize on imports.[28]

In order to encourage self-help measures and exert positive leverage in having the recipient countries meet specified standards, it has been suggested that aid should be allocated on the basis of the recipient's development performance.[29] If aid were varied in accordance with performance, this would provide an incentive system for recipients to improve their performance by undertaking policies to raise the rate of domestic saving and reduce the balance of payments deficit. Program-aid, self-help measures, and aid-allocation on the basis of performance are thus to be considered as interdependent elements in the aid mechanism, and each element should be reinforced by the others. The total effect should be to accelerate the rate of development and

[28] Clarence S. Gulick and Joan M. Nelson, *Promoting Effective Development Policies: AID Experience in the Developing Countries*, AID Discussion Paper No. 9, September, 1965, p. 2; AID, *Principles of Foreign Economic Assistance*, 1963, pp. 29–32.

[29] Chenery and Strout, *op. cit.*, pp. 728–729. But see the distinction drawn between the capacity to use more capital and the need for more aid, p. 130.

hasten the time when aid might be replaced by the recipient's own capacity for self-sustaining growth.

Although some consideration of performance is needed to improve the allocation of aid, the performance criterion should not be applied mechanically. Beyond consideration of quantitative targets, it is also necessary to give due weight to qualitative factors in any assessment of a country's performance. In some cases, what is termed "poor performance" may just as readily be attributed to unreasonable expectations by donors. Nor should poor performance in the past necessarily foreclose future aid if the causes of the inadequate performance are expected to be eliminated in the future. In other cases, "need" rather than performance may still be a compelling argument for aid. Although the principle of allocating aid according to its "productivity" is appealing to the economist, the recipient countries are actually a heterogeneous lot, and the purposes of aid are varied, so that the inter-country allocation of aid on a strict basis of the same criteria of performance is likely to be overly formal and artificial. Instead of being used for deciding the allocation of aid among countries, the emphasis on performance requirements may be more relevant for considering changes in the amount of aid to an individual country over time. Finally, if performance is interpreted *ex ante* instead of simply as an *ex post* reward, aid will frequently be a prerequisite for the improvement of performance and will itself lead to more effective use of aid in the future.

7. The question of the termination of aid may now be examined more systematically.[30] Given the same initial conditions, the pe-

[30] For a comprehensive quantitative analysis, see John C. H. Fei and Douglas S. Paauw, "Foreign Assistance and Self-Help: A Reappraisal of Development Finance," *Review of Economics and Statistics*, August, 1965,

riod of reliance on foreign assistance will be shorter, the greater is the long-run productivity of the assistance. Beyond the initial increment in GNP that results from the additional resources provided through aid, it is essential that the subsequent use made of this initial increment be as productive as possible. Studies undertaken by the Agency for International Development emphasize that the increments in GNP can be used to reduce any or all of the major types of restrictions to further growth: labor training, additional savings and taxes, and import-substitution or additional exports. By considering the uses made of the stream of additional production, these studies attempt to measure the long-run productivity of assistance.[31] The higher the marginal productivity of assistance—as measured by the ratio of the cumulative increment in GNP over a given period to the corresponding increment in capital inflow—the earlier will the recipient country be able to finance its development out of its own resources. The crucial importance of the indirect effects of aid can be shown by varying the recipient's marginal saving rate and marginal capital-output ratio: the higher the marginal saving rate and the lower the marginal capital-output ratio, the greater will be the marginal productivity of external assistance, and the sooner may such assistance be terminated.[32]

---

pp. 251–260. This study provides numerical answers to such questions as the duration of aid, the time-path of its flow, the peak-year volume, and the accumulated value over time.

[31] See Irma Adelman and H. B. Chenery, "Foreign Aid and Economic Development: The Case of Greece," *Review of Economics and Statistics*, February, 1966, pp. 1–14; J. G. Williamson, "Projected Aid Requirements for Turkey: 1960–1975," A. I. D. Discussion Paper, 1964; J. Vanek, "A Case Study in Development Analysis: Future Foreign Resource Requirements of Columbia," A. I. D. Discussion Paper, 1964.

[32] Chenery and Strout, *op. cit.*, pp. 701–705, 724–726; McKinnon, *op. cit.*, pp. 396–403. But cf., Little and Clifford, *op. cit.*, pp. 103–106.

While the dependence on external financing may have to be large during the early years of the development program, most plans aim for a progressive reduction in foreign aid and an eventual approach to a self-financing plan. To achieve this, the plan relies on a high marginal rate of saving; it is expected that the proportion that can be saved out of an increase in output will be much higher than average savings at the start of the plan period. The proportion of national income invested and financed by domestic savings would then increase, and the ratio of net foreign capital imports to additional investment would fall. Since profits provide a major source of savings, there are grounds for expecting an increase in home savings relative to income when an expansion of the capitalist sector is facilitated and government enterprises begin to yield operating surpluses.[33] A higher saving rate may also result if the composition of output changes in favor of more industrial activities with high marginal rates of saving. It will still be difficult, however, to realize a substantially higher marginal saving rate without forcing public saving through additional taxation and increasing tax revenues as a proportion of national income.

From the standpoint of the balance of payments, the reliance on foreign capital will also diminish if, as development proceeds, the composition of investment alters toward projects with a lower import content. Provided there is no inflationary financing, import-saving will also be indirectly fostered by the growth in total domestic output and a diversion of purchasing power to the products of the expanding industries. In countries that import

---

[33] W. A. Lewis, *The Theory of Economic Growth*, Allen & Unwin, 1955, pp. 236–239. The expected increase in profits applies not only to private capitalists; as Lewis states, it is just as relevant to State capitalism, or to any form of economic organization where capital is used to employ people, and where, after payment of wages and salaries, a substantial surplus remains, of which a large part is reinvested productively.

foodstuffs, the success of agricultural development in expanding the home production of foodstuffs will be especially instrumental in replacing imports. Finally, export promotion policies may increase export revenue, not merely from efforts to raise productivity in traditional export activities, but even more so by adding to the value of exports by selling them at a more highly processed stage and by extending the range of export items.

There are undoubtedly wide errors involved in the quantitative projections of aid requirements and possible termination dates. Nonetheless, we can certainly appreciate the basic importance of stressing (as these projections do) a rise in the savings rate, an improvement in the efficiency with which capital and human resources are used, and the overcoming of balance of payments pressures. Without these achievements, the rate of development cannot become self-sustaining, and aid for the purpose of development can never end.[34]

8. Although access to foreign capital will ease the undertaking of a development program, we should be aware that it may also give rise to problems of balance of payments adjustment. If the transfer mechanism does not operate rapidly and smoothly, disequilibrium will persist in the balance of payments of donor and recipient countries. We have seen that a developing country is

[34] In making "self-sustained growth" the condition for the termination of aid, the analysis in this section has implicitly rejected the notion that aid should go on forever as part of the process of redistributing the world's wealth. The question of equity is acutely faced if one country reaches self-sustaining growth and receives no further aid, but still has a lower per capita real income than a second country which has not yet reached self-sustaining growth and receives aid even though its per capita real income is higher than the first country. To some, the argument that aid should cease when a country becomes capable of self-sustained growth has, of course, no more ethical justification than the argument that aid should continue forever; see Little and Clifford, *op. cit.*, pp. 92–102, 235.

especially susceptible to a large potential deficit on current account. The problem of effecting the real transfer is therefore not so much that of generating in the first instance an import surplus on current account equal to the surplus on long term capital account as it is to prevent the potentially larger deficit on current account from becoming actually realized—in other words, restraining the demand for foreign exchange within the limits given by the supply of foreign exchange. Subsequently, the amount of foreign exchange required to service the accumulated foreign debt might become larger than the amount of foreign exchange being supplied by new foreign loans and grants; the transfer mechanism will then have to generate sufficient foreign exchange receipts to cover the payment of interest and amortization on the foreign borrowings.

When the aid-receiving country is still a young debtor receiving a net capital inflow, the very forces of development will facilitate balance of payments adjustment. During this period, the net capital imports will be filling the savings gap, and also covering interest and amortization payments on previous developmental loans. Although the external debt is rising (and at an accelerated rate), the donor countries are financing interest and amortization so that no burden of debt servicing is being placed on the recipient's domestic savings. Nor is there a problem in effecting a real transfer of resources into the recipient country. When attention is given to the forces of development, a full explanation of the transfer mechanism extends beyond the classical analysis of sectional price changes among domestic, export, and import-competing commodities. Especially relevant for the aid-receiving country is the fact that the capital borrowings stimulate employment and output and thereby induce imports through the increase in real income. In a developing country, all foreign exchange receipts tend to be spent rather than saved in the form of additions to foreign exchange reserves; a passive balance on current account therefore readily offsets the active balance on capital account.

To the extent that financial assistance is directly expended in the donor country, there is no transfer problem. If, however, foreign aid is not tied to exports of goods and services from the donor country, only a portion of the capital inflow may induce imports directly from the donor country. The donor may then have difficulty in generating a transfer of real resources which corresponds to its foreign assistance program. In order to minimize the adverse balance-of-payments impact of foreign assistance, the donor may then reduce the volume of its aid program or else impose a number of conditions on the receipt of aid in order to ensure that the financial assistance generates an export surplus on current account sufficient to cover the capital outflow.[35]

Although the expansionary forces in the recipient country facilitate the initial transfer of capital, they may at the same time create so high a demand for imports that the country has to avoid a "transfer problem in reverse." This type of "negative" transfer problem emerges when the complementary demands of the aid recipient are so strong that they give rise to an increased demand for foreign exchange that exceeds the increase in foreign exchange available from the capital inflow. This problem can be expressed more precisely in terms of an "expansion ratio," defined as the actual ratio of the rate of investment in the borrowing country over the initial rate of capital inflow.[36] Given the rate of capital inflow, marginal propensity to consume, and marginal

[35] For a fuller discussion, particularly in terms of the United States balance-of-payments problems, see Richard N. Cooper, "External Assistance and the Balance of Payments of Donor Countries," United Nations, *Proceedings of* UNCTAD, *op. cit.*, Vol. V, pp. 360–373.

[36] J. J. Polak, "Balance of Payments Problems of Countries Reconstructing with the Help of Foreign Loans," *Quarterly Journal of Economics*, February, 1943, p. 214.

propensity to import, there will be a certain maximum expansion ratio which designates the limit to which domestic investment, financed by foreign loans and by domestic credit expansion, can be increased without endangering the balance of payments.[37]

9. The costs of balance of payments adjustment are likely to be most pronounced when the aid-receiving country encounters the problem of debt service. No debt servicing problem would arise, of course, if the capital inflow were always sufficient to allow the developing country to meet its debt servicing obligations and also maintain its imports at a desired level. In reality, however, sooner or later—depending on the growth in new foreign borrowing, rate of interest, and amortization rate—the debt servicing charges may require a net capital outflow from the developing country. When the return flow of interest and amortization payments exceeds the inflow of new loans and grants, the country becomes a "mature debtor" and confronts a transfer problem in servicing the debt. The debt service payments are a charge on domestic real income and savings, and the debtor country will have to generate an export surplus equivalent to the net outward transfer of amortization on capital account and of income payments on current account. In this stage of the debt cycle, domestic savings

---

[37] If the marginal propensity to save is $\frac{1}{4}$, and the marginal propensity to import is $\frac{1}{4}$, the maximum expansion ratio would be 2—that is, a level of investment of two times the level of capital inflow could be maintained without encountering an import surplus greater than the capital inflow. In this simple model, the multiplier (k) is 2, and the import demand ($\triangle M$) is $\frac{1}{2}$ of the amount of investment ($\triangle I$), $[\triangle M = m\ (k \triangle I)]$, so that one dollar of domestic investment for each dollar of foreign-financed investment would use up the foreign aid in induced imports. If, in addition to the indirect demand for imports via the multiplier, we also allowed for imports caused directly by the investment, the maximum expansion ratio would be correspondingly lower.

in the developing country will have to be sufficient to finance all domestic investment, and in addition the interest cost of accumulated debt and the repayment of the principal of its loans. In order to convert the surplus of savings into the foreign currencies that it needs for debt servicing, the developing country will have to generate an export surplus by reallocating resources so as to expand exports or replace imports. And to accomplish this, the country may have to impose internal and external controls or experience exchange depreciation. The adverse effects of these measures of balance of payments adjustment must then be considered as indirect costs of foreign aid, to be added to the direct costs of the foreign payments.

The direct costs of foreign debt service, however, should not in themselves be a cause for concern. True, part of the increased production from the use of foreign capital has to be repaid abroad —and this is a deduction which would not be necessary if the savings were provided at home. But this is merely to say that the developing country cannot expect to get an income from savings if it does not make the savings.[38] The significant result is that the country does have additional investment, and the benefits from this may exceed the direct costs of the foreign savings that made possible the accumulation of additional capital.

Of prime concern are the indirect costs of the foreign capital —that is, the need to institute measures of balance of payments adjustment in order to acquire sufficient foreign exchange for the remittance of the debt service obligations. To minimize these indirect costs, a development program must give attention to the "debt servicing capacity" of the country. The long-term productivity of foreign aid must be sufficiently high to yield an increase in real income greater than the interest and amortization charges.

[38] Hicks, *op. cit.*, p. 191.

Not only must the rate of return on individual projects be in excess of the international rate of interest; in addition, to maintain a desired rate of development, the savings out of the income stream generated by the investment must eventually be sufficient to enable the developing country to finance its domestic investment requirements and meet the service payments. If the social rate of return on investment is lower than the interest cost, and if a sufficiently high marginal saving rate is not achieved, the debt burden will become unmanageable: the country will not be able to meet the interest payments on accumulated debt, let alone begin net repayment.

In order to provide a sufficient surplus of foreign exchange to avoid a transfer problem, the capital should also be utilized in such a way as to generate a surplus in the other items of the balance of payments equal to the transfer payments abroad. The total supply of foreign exchange, including gross capital inflow and net use of foreign exchange reserves, must exceed the value of imports of goods and services by the amount of service payments on the foreign debt.

In the light of these requirements, it is apparent that the limits of a country's capacity to service foreign capital cannot be determined without taking into account the country's development program as a whole. Reference to the entire program is necessary for an appraisal of the conditions under which the competing claims on total resources, on saving, and on foreign exchange can be adjusted so as to release the amount required for debt service.[39]

Moreover, the effects of a specific investment project on the balance of payments cannot be considered only from the stand-

[39] For a conceptual framework within which debt-servicing capacity can be appraised, and for some attempts at quantitative projections, see "Economic Growth and External Debt—An Analytical Framework," in United Nations, *Proceedings of* UNCTAD, *op. cit.*, Vol. V, pp. 72–107.

point of the particular sector to which the investment is directed: The development of one sector may influence the development of other sectors, and the balance of payments effects of any given investment will then depend on the spatial and temporal interdependence of other investments. The effects will also depend on the mobility of the factors of production and the economy's capacity to reallocate resources into export and import-competing sectors. The greater is this transforming capacity, the more indirect, but no less important, will be the balance of payments effects of a specific investment project.

Once we appreciate the relationship between total resource availabilities and uses, the interdependence of investments, and the transforming capacity of the economy, we can perceive that the transfer problem can still be solved without stipulating that the investment of foreign capital should create its own means of payment by directly expanding exports or replacing imports. If it is realized that the ability to create a sufficiently large export surplus depends on the operation of all industries together, not simply on the use made of foreign investment alone, it is then apparent that a project financed by foreign borrowing need not itself make a direct contribution to the balance of payments.[40] Instead of such a narrow balance of payments criterion, the basic test for the allocation of foreign capital is that it should be in-

---

[40] A similar view was taken in Chapter 4, section 5. Nurkse's statement of this point is worth quoting: "When additional capital becomes available to a country, the country will want or should be urged to invest it in the form that yields the highest possible return, taking into account any external economies created by the project as well as the direct commercial yield. On the other hand, the particular goods through which the interest is transferred abroad are determined by the scale of comparative costs in international trade (though this scale need not be regarded as fixed and may well change as a result of the investment itself). No particular relation is required between the marginal-productivity-of-capital schedule and the comparative-cost schedule." Nurkse, *op. cit.*, pp. 136–137.

vested in the form that yields the highest social marginal product. The essential point is that the allocation of capital according to its most productive use will also be the most favorable for debt servicing, since it maximizes the increase in income from a given amount of capital and thereby contributes to the growth of foreign exchange availabilities. In a fundamental sense, the continuing growth in per capita production and the underlying process of rapid accumulation of productive capital will make the process of debt servicing less burdensome.

The transfer problem will also be eased, of course, if the policies of the lending country facilitate the creation of an export surplus from the borrowing country. Although we are concentrating on the borrower's position, it is obvious that the servicing of the foreign debt will be easier when the lender follows a more expansionary domestic policy and a more liberal commercial policy.

To the extent that these policies help maintain imports from the developing country, the country's cyclical problem of "overborrowing" and relying unduly on supplier credits and other forms of short-term borrowing will also be mitigated. If short-run fluctuations result in a fall in export receipts for the poor country, the burden of debt servicing becomes heavier as the ratio of aggregate service payments to total foreign exchange receipts rises. This investment service ratio can be held down, however, if importing countries maintain their demand for the developing country's exports and if the donor countries provide assistance at lower interest, for longer terms, and with more stability.

10. In light of the foregoing, it should be clear that if a less developed country's debt burden is allowed to go on rising without a sufficient growth in domestic savings and foreign exchange

earnings, more foreign aid on soft terms and in sufficient amount will eventually be needed simply to service some part of the past debt; or else the country will have to curtail imports and restrict its rate of development as more resources are devoted to meeting the debt service. Several countries have already encountered difficulties in servicing their debt, and the rapidly rising debt-service liabilities threaten to become a burdensome problem for many more countries in the near future.

The total volume of outstanding public and publicly-guaranteed foreign debt of the less developed countries increased from approximately $10 billion in 1955 to more than $35 billion in 1965.[41] Annual servicing costs on this debt grew from less than $1 billion in 1955 to nearly $4 billion in 1965; from less than 4 percent of the developing countries' total export earnings in the mid-1950s, the debt servicing rose to about 10 percent in the mid-1960s. In most of the aid-receiving countries, the growth of international debt and debt-service obligations has been considerably higher than the rate of growth in GNP, exports, or savings. In large part, the heavy servicing charges—almost three-quarters of which consist of repayment of principal—reflect the concentration of foreign indebtedness in early maturities: as of the end of 1962, the proportion of outstanding external public debt that was due for repayment within the period 1963–1967 was as high as 55 percent in Latin America, 52 percent in East Asia, and 50 percent in Africa.[42] As a result of the continuing rise in debt-service liabilities, a large part of new gross lending is offset by interest and amortization charges on past debt—some 30 percent

[41] The debt situation for a number of the principal developing countries is analyzed in United States Agency for International Development, *Loan Terms, Debt Burden and Development*, Washington, D.C., 1965.

[42] United Nations, *Proceedings of* UNCTAD, *op. cit.*, Vol. V, pp. 108–117.

of external assistance in 1965, compared with only 8 percent a decade earlier.

These unfavorable trends have several implications for the future effectiveness of development assistance. In view of the present size, structure, and terms of the external debt of the developing countries, it is clear that the gross amount of long-term, low-interest loans will have to be increased in the future, merely in order to maintain a given net capital transfer. If the gross capital transfer should level off at a constant amount, the net loan receipts will become smaller, and foreign assistance will rapidly diminish in effectiveness. To avoid having the foreign debt become a net burden on the recipients' balance of payments, the level of gross aid must be raised.

An especially burdensome feature of the debt structure in many developing countries is the heavy borrowing on short-term. While long-term loans have been difficult to obtain, short-term money has been overabundant, particularly in the form of suppliers' credits to finance imports of industrial equipment.[43] The resulting concentration of repayment obligations within a few years creates undue pressure on the balance of payments; lenders will then have to relend if the debtor is not to default, or else (as recommended by UNCTAD) there will have to be an agreement "on the rescheduling or consolidation of debt, with appropriate periods of grace and amortization and reasonable rates of interest."[44] To avoid making short-term borrowing either necessary or so attractive for the developing countries, it may be proposed that some scheme of compensatory or supplementary financing should be instituted to provide an alternative to the need for short-term

---

[43] See W. A. Lewis, *Development Planning*, Allen & Unwin, 1966, pp. 140–142; Little and Clifford, *op. cit.*, pp. 209–210, 250–252.

[44] United Nations, *Proceedings of* UNCTAD, *op. cit.*, Vol. I, Annex A.IV.5.

credits when export receipts decline;[45] advanced countries should not support through government guarantees short-term private export credits as a means of promoting their exports to developing countries; and a greater flow of grants-in-aid and longer-term loans with softer terms should be available.

If the foreign capital inflow is to be within the limit of the recipient's capacity to repay, the terms of development loans must also be improved for many of the developing countries. As has been emphasized, until the recipient's growth is more than self-sustaining the interest on loans must itself be paid from loans or grants; if the country is to be able to finance its own investment and be in a position both to pay interest on the past inflow of capital and to make repayments, the savings accruing from the investment of foreign capital must become larger than the total annual debt charges.[46] Any hardening of aid terms will intensify the magnitude of the debt burden and prolong the time before self-sustaining growth is achieved. It will, therefore, be more advantageous to the developing countries if new loan commitments are available at lower interest rates and with longer grace and amortization periods. To the extent that there is increased emphasis on program aid instead of project aid, this too may allow more attention to the servicing of loans from the standpoint of total resource use, domestic saving performance, and foreign trade performance of the aid-recipient.

It should also be noted that the combination of grants and loans, and degree of softness or hardness in terms, should vary among the aid-receiving countries in order to adapt the debt burden to the individual circumstances of each country. Greater

[45] See Chapter 9, section 7.

[46] For calculations showing that the long-term burden of debt is governed by the level of interest rates, see Little and Clifford, *op. cit.*, pp. 204–212.

harmonization in terms, along with softer terms, would also be desirable. At present, the same recipient may be receiving aid from a number of different donors, and all on different terms. The result is that those who are lending on more lenient terms are in effect servicing the debt to those who impose harder terms. This makes it more difficult for those donors who have been lending at relatively soft terms to maintain their easier terms. The presence of loans at harder terms may also increase the risks of default for all lenders.

Finally, a distinction should be drawn between those countries that can use more capital and those that require more aid proper. Not all recipient countries need the same degree of concessionary terms. Indeed, those countries with a better promise of attaining self-sustaining growth may merit more capital, but with a smaller component of aid. In contrast, other countries that are farther from self-sustaining growth need a larger component of aid, even though they have the capacity to use effectively only a smaller amount of capital.

6
Private Foreign Investment

1. Although the international financing of development has been dominated by foreign aid, there is now reawakened interest in the potential role of private foreign investment. Unlike earlier historical episodes of international investment, however, the widespread practice of national economic planning in developing countries is moving the problems of foreign investment into a new context. To appreciate more fully the issues that are emerging, we need an analytical framework for appraising how a less developed country might attain the double policy objective of encouraging a greater inflow of private foreign capital while, at the same time, obtaining from this capital a more substantial contribution to the country's development program. This chapter attempts to provide such a framework.

Our concern throughout is with "direct" private investment and with the national regulation of such investment by the capital-recipient countries.[1] The experience of the past two decades has made it increasingly evident that policies of the capital-receiving countries are more decisive in determining the quantity and quality of the private capital inflow than are the measures taken by the capital-exporting countries to encourage and protect foreign investment.[2] For the host country has controlling power as the ultimate policy-maker and can neutralize action taken initially by the investing country.[3] Controls exercised by

[1] The justification for considering only investments in which the foreign investor exercises managerial control is that portfolio investment is now of negligible quantitative importance for newly developing countries and can be expected to remain so.

An illuminating discussion of the differences between present-day and nineteenth-century international investment is provided by Ragnar Nurkse, "The Problem of International Investment Today in the Light of Nineteenth-Century Experience," *Economic Journal*, December, 1954, pp. 744–758.

[2] In an attempt to promote a larger flow of private capital to less developed countries, several capital-exporting countries have adopted a range of measures that include tax incentives, state guarantees, and financial assistance to private investors. For a sampling of the extensive literature on these measures, see generally, E. R. Barlow and I. T. Wender, *Foreign Investment and Taxation*, Harvard Law School, 1955; J. N. Behrman, "U.S. Government Encouragement of Private Direct Investment Abroad," R. F. Mikesell, ed., *U.S. Private and Government Investment Abroad*, Univ. of Oregon Books, 1962, chap. VIII; Marina von Neuman Whitman, *Government Risk-Sharing in Foreign Investment*, Princeton Univ. Press, 1965.

[3] American businessmen have consistently believed that the over-all role of the United States government in impeding or promoting profitable private foreign investment is minor compared with the role of foreign governments and with market and economic forces outside the control of the investor's government: National Industrial Conference Board, *Obstacles and Incentives to Private Foreign Investment 1962–1964*, Report No. 115, 1965, pp. 39–42; United States Department of Commerce, *Factors Limiting United States Investment Abroad, Part 2*, U.S. Government Printing Office, 1964.

the host country over the conditions of entry of foreign capital, the operation of foreign enterprises, and the remittance of profits and repatriation of capital are of crucial importance in determining the flow and contribution of external private capital.

By shifting the emphasis to the policies connected with development planning in the recipient countries, our discussion might focus more directly on the primary determinants of the flow and contribution of foreign private capital. We shall, therefore, begin by sorting out the various benefits and costs of private foreign investment from the viewpoint of a national development program. Against this conceptual background, we may then appraise the effects of policy measures being taken by developing countries to encourage an inflow of private capital and to regulate the operation of the foreign enterprise in conformity with developmental objectives.

2. Even though only a small amount of private capital, relative to government loans and grants,[4] has gone to poor countries, the belief persists that capital from official sources is only a transitional arrangement, and that foreign economic aid should be gradually replaced by a flow of private financial resources. To this end, considerable interest is being shown in measures that might promote foreign investment and allow it to contribute more effectively to the development of the recipient countries.[5]

[4] For summary statistical data on the flow of official and private long-term capital to less developed countries, see OECD, *Development Assistance Efforts and Policies, 1966 Review*, Paris, September, 1966, Tables 3–8; IMF, *Balance of Payments Yearbook*, annual editions; Samuel Pizer and Frederick Cutler, "Foreign Investments 1965–1966," *Survey of Current Business*, September, 1966, pp. 30–40.

[5] United States Agency for International Development, *Foreign Aid through Private Initiative*, Report of the Advisory Committee on Private Enterprise in Foreign Aid, July, 1965; see also the recommendations of

When one examines the policies taken by the developing countries, however, they reveal a mixed picture of restrictions and incentives. On the one side, the foreign investor's freedom of action may be constrained by a variety of governmental regulations that exclude private foreign capital from certain sectors of the economy, impose limitations on the extent of foreign participation in ownership or management, specify conditions for the employment of domestic and foreign labor, limit the amount of profits, and impose exchange controls on the remission of profits and the repatriation of capital. And yet, during recent years, a progressive liberalization of policy toward private foreign investment has occurred, and a number of investment incentive measures have been recently adopted or are under consideration. These incentive devices include establishment of overhead facilities such as in industrial estates, protective tariffs on imports that compete with local commodities produced by foreign enterprise, exemptions from import duties on necessary equipment and materials, the granting of exchange guarantees or privileges, tax concession schemes for the encouragement of desired new investments, and special legislation for the protection of foreign capital.

The current trend toward greater encouragement of private foreign investment reflects, in part, a retrenchment from the earlier postwar reliance on a "heavy" comprehensive type of detailed economic planning to a "lighter" framework type, in which there is greater scope for the private sector, and, in part, a growing awareness that a community of interest might be established between the foreign enterprise and host country.

More directly, many countries have come to realize that an

----

earlier special Presidential commissions: The Gray Report (1950); Rockefeller Report (1951); Paley Commission Report (1952); and the Randall Commission Report (1954).

inflow of private capital can offer some unique qualitative advantages over public capital. For no problem of productive use arises with foreign direct investment: by its very nature, a foreign investment necessarily entails the identification of an economic opportunity, the formulation of a productive project, and its efficient implementation. Especially significant is the merit that foreign direct investment has in carrying with it an integral ingredient of technical assistance—the managerial and technical knowledge which are usually in even shorter supply than capital. As an instrument for transmitting technical and organizational change, integrating technical and financial assistance, and helping to overcome the skill and management limitations in development, the private foreign investment has a distinct advantage over foreign public capital.

If recipient countries have assumed a more positive attitude toward foreign enterprise, so too have foreign investors come to appreciate that the practice of development planning need not in itself be inimical to the promotion of a larger inflow of private capital. Development planning now involves much more than a public investment program, and the practice of planning is not to be confused with the issue of public ownership and control. The essence of development planning is the formulation and coordination of a set of policies to achieve explicit objectives. In doing this, a plan may stress the complementary relationship between the public and private sectors and may include policies designed to induce and assist action in the private sector. Although a development plan reserves some areas of investment for the public sector, there is at least, on the other side, a clear statement of policy regarding areas in which private investment is desired. A development plan can be of service to the foreign investor when it expressly defines the particular role assigned to the private sector, indicates clearly the existence of investment opportunities, facilitates advance calculation, and reduces the foreign investor's uncertainties regarding his position vis-à-vis the domestic private and public industrial sectors.

An American government report, for example, lists several advantages that private enterprise may gain from the emphasis on national planning by developing countries:

a. Competent development planning, by emphasizing statistical information and a quantitative framework for future targets and goals, creates a more dependable environment for evaluating business opportunities and risks than now exists in many less developed countries.

b. Planning may define more exactly and more reliably the fields of activity in which government and private business, respectively, are expected to provide the main leadership and activity.

c. Careful planning facilitates the timely provision of publicly financed installations, such as roads, irrigation facilities or power plants, which are important to the growth of private investment. To the extent that development planning improves the use of resources for development, the basic facilities to support a vigorous private sector are provided more rapidly and effectively.

d. The planning process forces the planners to recognize the size of the requirements for sustained economic growth, and the consequent necessity of enlisting the forces of private enterprise in helping to meet these requirements.[6]

Although development planning does not necessarily limit the scope for private activity and may actually promote more attractive business opportunities, it does mean that private investors must share with the government a common interest in accelerating development. The tasks of development require both more

[6] U.S. President's Task Force on Foreign Economic Assistance, *Act for International Development, Summary Presentation*, Department of State Publication 7224, July, 1961, pp. 102–103.

effective governmental activity and more international investment. But the private investor must be aware of the developmental objectives and priorities of the host country in order to determine how his investment will fit into the country's development strategy. As long as the host country remains serious about accelerating its development, the continued beneficial economic performance of foreign investment (in terms of our analysis, a high benefit-cost ratio) will be the decisive determinant of the investment's security.

No longer is it simply a matter of private investors dismissing investment prospects with the complaint that a "favorable climate" does not exist; the meaning of a "favorable climate" calls for reinterpretation in terms of development planning. Nor need host countries contend that an inflow of private capital entails nothing but "foreign domination"; in the context of development planning, the effects of foreign investment need no longer be feared as being a repetition of the undesirable features in the history of colonialism. Development planning now allows the government to influence the performance of private foreign investment, but in doing this, the government should appreciate fully the potential contribution of this investment, and should devise policies that will encourage a greater inflow of private capital and gain the maximum contribution toward the achievement of the country's development. This calls for more intensive analysis of the consequences of foreign investment and for more thought and ingenuity in devising new approaches that favor the mobilization of private foreign capital while ensuring its most effective "planned performance" in terms of the country's development program.

3. To provide an analytical basis for understanding the rationale and effects of foreign investment policies in the host countries, we should weigh the benefits of foreign investment against its

costs.[7] After assessing what difference the presence of foreign-owned capital might make to the real income of the recipient country, we may then appraise existing policies.

Just as we have already noted for public foreign capital, an inflow of private capital contributes to the recipient country's development program in two general ways—by helping to reduce the shortage of domestic savings and by increasing the supply of foreign exchange. To this extent, the receipt of private foreign investment permits a more rapid expansion in real income, eases the shortage of foreign exchange, and removes the necessity of resorting to a drive toward self-sufficiency and the deliberate stimulation of import-substitution industries out of deference to foreign exchange considerations.

Beyond this initial contribution, the essence of the case for encouraging foreign investment is that in time, as the investment operates, the increase in real income resulting from the act of investment is greater than the resultant increase in the income of the foreign investor. There is a national economic benefit if the value added to output by the foreign capital is greater than the amount appropriated by the investor: social returns exceed private returns. As long as foreign investment raises productivity, and this increase is not wholly appropriated by the investor, it follows that the greater product must be shared with others, and there must be some direct benefits to other income groups. These benefits can accrue to (1) domestic labor in the form of higher real wages, (2) consumers by way of lower prices, and (3) the government through expanded revenue. In addition, and of most

[7] Much of the following analysis has been suggested by G. D. A. MacDougall, "The Benefits and Costs of Private Investment from Abroad: A Theoretical Approach," *Economic Record*, March, 1960, pp. 13–35; also see Paul Streeten, *Economic Integration*, 2d ed., A. W. Sythoff, 1964, chap. 5.

importance in many cases, there are likely to be (4) indirect
gains through the realization of external economies.

An inflow of foreign capital may be a major influence in
raising labor's marginal productivity and increasing total real
wages. Assuming two factors of production—capital and labor—
the line *EG* in Fig. 7 relates the marginal physical product of
capital to the physical capital stock, given the amount of labor.

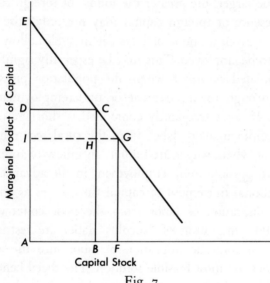

Fig. 7.

If initially the capital stock is *AB*, total output is *ECBA*. Assuming that profits per unit of capital equal the marginal product of
capital, and that the total capital stock *AB* is domestically owned,
total profits on domestic capital are *ABCD*, and total real wages
are *CDE*.

If there is now an inflow of foreign capital in the amount
BF, total output increases by the amount *BFGC*. The foreign

capital now earns *BFGH* of this amount. Since the marginal product of capital, and hence the profit rate, have fallen, total profits on domestic capital are reduced to *ABHI*, but the total real wages of labor are now *GIE*. Although the increase in real wages amounts to *DCGI*, most of labor's gain—the amount *DCHI*—is merely a redistribution from domestic capitalists. Given the marginal product curve, both the redistribution effect and the net gain to domestic factors, represented by the triangle *CGH*, will be larger, the greater the inflow of foreign capital.

The presence of foreign capital may not only raise the productivity of a given amount of labor; it may also allow a larger labor force to be employed. This may be especially significant for heavily populated countries where the population pressures are taken out through unemployment or underemployment in the rural sector. If, as is frequently contended, a shortage of capital limits the employment of labor from the rural sector in the industrial sector where wages are higher, an inflow of foreign capital can make possible more employment in the advanced sector. The international movement of capital thus serves as an alternative to the migration of labor from the poor country: When outlets for the emigration of "surplus" labor are restricted, the substitution of domestic migration of labor into the advanced sector becomes the most feasible solution. The social benefit from the foreign investment in the advanced sector is then greater than the profits on this investment, for the wages received by the newly employed exceed their marginal productivity in the rural sector; and this excess should be added as a national gain.[8]

---

[8] MacDougall, *op. cit.*, pp. 21, 35; T. Balogh and P. P. Streeten, "Domestic versus Foreign Investment," *Bulletin of the Oxford University Institute of Statistics,* August, 1960, p. 220. But it should be noted that even if rural labor is in disguised unemployment, the social cost of transferring labor to the advanced sector is not zero. See Chapter 7, section 8.

Some benefits from foreign investment may also accrue to consumers. When the investment is cost-reducing in a particular industry, there may be a gain not only to the suppliers of factors in this industry through higher factor prices but also to consumers of the product through lower product prices. If the investment is product-improving or product-innovating, consumers may then enjoy better quality products or new products.

In order that labor and consumers might gain part of the benefit from the higher productivity in foreign enterprises, the overseas withdrawal by the investors must be less than the increase in output. But even if the entire increase in productivity accrues as foreign profits, there will still be a national benefit when the government taxes these profits or receives royalties from concession agreements.[9]

From the standpoint of contributing to the development process, the major benefits from foreign investment are likely to arise in the form of external economies. Besides bringing to the recipient country physical and financial capital, direct foreign investment also includes nonmonetary transfers of other resources —technological knowledge, market information, managerial and supervisory personnel, organizational experience, and innovations in products and production techniques—all of which are in short supply. By being a carrier of technological and organizational change, the foreign investment may be highly significant in providing "private technical assistance" and "demonstration effects" that are of benefit elsewhere in the economy. New techniques accompany the inflow of private capital, and by the example they

[9] If the borrowing country is party to a double-taxation agreement with the investing country, with full credit allowed on foreign taxes, it may enjoy this fiscal benefit by taxing the earnings of imported capital up to the rate of taxation in the investing country without impeding the inflow of capital.

set, foreign firms promote the diffusion of technological advance in the economy.[10] Technical assistance may also be provided to suppliers and customers of the foreign enterprise. In addition, foreign investment frequently leads to the training of labor in new skills, and the knowledge gained by these workers can be transmitted to other members of the labor force, or the newly trained workers might be later employed by local firms.

Private foreign investment can also stimulate additional domestic investment in the recipient country. If the foreign capital is used to develop the country's infrastructure, it may directly facilitate more investment. Even if the foreign investment is in one industry, it may still encourage domestic investment by reducing costs in other industries; profits may then rise and lead to expansion in the other industries. Since there are so many specific scarcities in a poor country, it is common for investment to be of a cost-saving character by breaking bottlenecks in production. This stimulates expansion by raising profits in all underutilized productive capacity and by allowing the exploitation of economies of scale that had previously been restricted.

There is also considerable scope for the initial foreign investment to create external investment incentives by raising the demand for the output of other industries. The foreign investment in the first industry can give rise to profits in industries that supply inputs to the first industry, or that produce complementary products, or that produce goods bought by the factor-owners who now have higher real incomes as a result of the inflow of foreign capital. A foreign investment that is product-improving or product-innovating may also have similar effects. A whole series of domestic investments may thus be linked to the foreign investment.

[10] For a broader discussion of the process by which new techniques are transferred from one country to another, see A. K. Cairncross, *Factors in Economic Development*, Allen & Unwin, 1962, chap. 11.

These external effects raise production outside the foreign enterprise, but the foreign investor cannot appropriate this additional output. The spill-over goes unpriced and constitutes an uncompensated service. To the extent that the foreign investment yields an external economy, the marginal social net product of the foreign capital is greater than its marginal private net product. According to the criterion of national economic benefit, the case for governmental encouragement of private foreign investment is then strong.

4. Against these benefits, however, there are a number of costs to foreign investment that may be detrimental to the host country's development plan. These costs may arise from (1) special incentives and concessions offered by the host country, (2) adverse effects on domestic saving, (3) deterioration in the terms of trade, and (4) pressure on the country's balance of payments.[11]

To attract foreign capital, the government of the host country may have to provide special facilities, undertake additional public services, extend financial assistance, or subsidize inputs to the foreign enterprise. These have a cost in absorbing governmental resources that could be used elsewhere. Tax concessions may also have to be offered, and these may have to be extended to domestic investors, since the government may not be able to discriminate, for administrative and political reasons, in favor of only the foreign investor. In encouraging foreign investment, there is thus a fiscal cost through increased government expenditure or foregone revenue.

Once foreign investment has been attracted, it should lead to a higher level of real income and hence to an increase in do-

---

[11] While the discussion here is theoretical, Chapter 8 considers the broader contention that foreign investment has historically limited the development of the borrowing country; see pp. 228–239.

mestic saving. This effect may be offset, however, by a redistribution of income away from domestic capital if the foreign investment competes with home investment and reduces profits in domestic industries. The consequent reduction in home savings would then be another indirect cost of foreign investment.

The possible effects of foreign investment on the terms of trade are usually related to the transfer problem—the terms of trade normally tend to improve with an inflow of capital, then tend to worsen when there is, subsequently, a return flow of capital from the borrowing country. We shall consider these effects as part of the broader problem of balance of payments adjustment.

Aside from these transfer effects, foreign investment may also affect the terms of trade through structural changes associated with the pattern of development that results from the capital inflow. If foreign investment leads to an increase in the host country's rate of development without any change in the terms of trade, then the country's growth of real income will be the same as its growth of output. Only under exceptional conditions, however, is this likely. Instead, it is to be expected that the terms of trade will alter—improving or worsening, depending on various possible changes at home and abroad in the supply and demand for exports, import-substitutes, and domestic commodities. We have already considered in Chapters 2 and 3 under what conditions the commodity terms of trade will turn against a country when it accumulates capital. The same analysis can be applied to an inflow of foreign capital when it results in a higher rate of capital formation.

If the pattern of development associated with foreign investment involves a deterioration in the country's commodity terms of trade, then the net gain from foreign capital will be diminished. It is improbable, however, that foreign investment would cause any substantial deterioration. For if an unfavorable shift resulted from an export bias on the side of consumption, it would probably be controlled through import restrictions. And if it resulted from private direct investment in the export sector, this inflow of foreign capital would diminish as export prices fell, thereby limiting the deterioration in the terms of trade. Moreover, if the deterioration comes through an export bias in production, it is possible that the factoral and the income terms of trade might still improve even though the commodity terms worsen.

The most significant costs of foreign investment tend to be associated with balance of payments adjustment. We have already considered in the preceding chapter the burden of debt servicing. A similar problem arises when the return outflow of interest, profits, and dividends on the accumulated investments, and repatriation of capital put pressure on the developing country's balance of payments.[12] Again, when the country is not currently earning sufficient foreign exchange to cover the external servicing of the foreign investment, the adverse effects of measures designed to reequilibrate the balance of payments will entail indirect costs of foreign investment, to be added to the direct costs of the foreign payments.

5. We have now classified the major consequences of foreign investment into those benefits or positive gains that contribute to the developing country's objective of increasing real income and

[12] It might be thought that, if foreign private investment is in export industries, direct investment payments would be correlated with fluctuations in export receipts, and hence not be so burdensome. The correlation is absent, however, if the investment is in import-substitute industries: export earnings may decline, but profit remittance on direct investments may rise.

those costs or negative effects that involve some sacrifice of the objective. The rational approach to the economic regulation of foreign investment would be to ensure that each foreign investment project meets the criterion of yielding a benefit-cost ratio greater than unity.[13]

With the foregoing conceptual framework in mind, we may now evaluate the investment laws and regulatory measures of developing countries. No attempt will be made to present in detail the variety of policies that are being used to affect the import of private investment capital. But the foregoing analysis might help us concentrate on the essential features of these measures and gauge their effectiveness in fulfilling the benefit-cost criterion.

The host country's regulatory measures over foreign investment are embodied for the most part in investment statutes, tax laws, controls over foreign trade, and foreign exchange regulations. Although these measures have generally arisen in an unsystematic and ad hoc fashion, rather than as a closely coordinated set of policies, we can conveniently analyze the consequences of these policies in terms of an "allocation effect," a "distribution effect," and a "balance of payments effect." By considering alternative investment policies in terms of these effects, we shall be able to evaluate the effectiveness of these policies in increasing benefits or decreasing costs.

---

[13] It would be a misconception to express the criterion as "maximum benefit with minimum cost"; there is no policy that will meet the criterion of simultaneously maximizing gains while minimizing costs. See Roland McKean, *Efficiency in Government through Systems Analysis*, John Wiley, 1958, pp. 34–49.

For a more refined analysis, we should consider the time-stream of benefits and the time-stream of costs, and then discount these two streams down to the present value excess of benefits over costs. The rate of discount to be used depends on when it is most desired that the benefits should accrue, i.e., "social time preference."

The "allocational effect" of investment policies has two aspects: the inducement of foreign investment to one country rather than to another country and, within the recipient country, the allocation of the investment to one activity rather than to another. Most of the developing countries have now consolidated legislation regarding foreign investment in an investment statute which sets forth both the privileges and obligations of foreign investors and specifies the administrative procedures, rules and regulations governing the entry and operation of foreign investment.[14] The statute attempts to encourage an inflow of foreign capital through the use of tax exemptions, tariff concessions, relaxation of exchange controls, some guarantee of nonexpropriation and nondiscrimination, and assurances for the repatriation of earnings or capital.

From the economic standpoint, an investment statute is effective in encouraging foreign investment when its provisions reduce nonbusiness risks, lower costs, or result in an increase in the net rate of return. To this end, tax concessions represent the major legislative effort to promote private investment. These concessions take three principal forms: relief from income and other taxes to "new and necessary industries," partial or complete exemption from duties on the importation of essential equipment and materials, and liberal depreciation allowances in the calculation of company taxes.

[14] For a recent list of investment laws, see *The Promotion of the International Flow of Private Capital, op. cit.,* Annex IV. Texts of investment statutes are also periodically available in U.S. Department of Commerce, *World Trade Information Service.*
    Indicative of the objectives sought by the legislation, these statutes—some of which may relate to domestic private capital as well as foreign—are variously called "Industrial Incentive Law," "Pioneer Industries Law," "Export Industry Encouragement Law," or "Production Development Law."

It is commonly believed that these concessions have provided some incentive to foreign capital. But their use can be overdone. For this type of legislation imposes costs on the government in the form of some loss of government revenue, new differentials in tax burden distribution, and additional burdens upon administrative facilities. A central issue is whether these revenue, equity, and administrative costs outweigh the advantages that the use of the incentives may afford to a developing country. In examining this question, a major study concluded that for many countries the tax system is relatively unimportant in inducing investment, compared with other factors impeding investment, and that tax relief seems to be of only secondary importance in creating conditions conducive to industrial growth, especially when the objective is to increase the level of new investment instead of merely to promote reinvestment.[15] Given the low utility of tax incentives, the costs of tax concessions may commonly outweigh the advantages.[16]

The provision of tax holidays or reduced rates of taxable income is effective, of course, only when the investment yields substantial taxable profits. The assistance provided by tax exemption is, in fact, inverse to need: as long as a firm experiences losses

[15] Jack Heller and Kenneth M. Kauffman, *Tax Incentives for Industry in Less Developed Countries*, Harvard Law School, 1963, pp. 60–66.

[16] See also, Milton C. Taylor, *Industrial Tax Exemption in Puerto Rico*, Univ. of Wisconsin Press, 1957, pp. 143–149. Taylor concludes that tax exemption may serve as an irrational or purely psychological inducement in the sense that it may be instrumental in encouraging the initiation of new business, but there may be little relationship between the effect of the inducement or the need for the assistance and the amount of subsidy actually received. There is little evidence to indicate that tax exemption has been an important incentive leading to the expansion of existing Puerto Rican firms. It is also contended that many of the new firms that use labor-intensive methods of production would have come to Puerto Rico even without tax exemptions.

and needs assistance, it receives no income-tax subsidy; but the more successful and independent of aid it becomes, the more subsidy it enjoys.

Moreover, the foreign investor in a newly developing country is less likely to be attracted by the prospect of receiving an exemption after a profit is made than he is by being sure of a profit in the first instance. To raise profit expectations, the government may have to undertake additional public expenditures, particularly in providing public utilities, developing industrial sites, expanding labor training facilities, and furnishing statistical and information services. Governmental measures that increase labor productivity and help to stabilize the labor force are especially helpful in lowering the otherwise high marginal labor cost for a firm. With the same effect on the government's budget, these expenditures could be a more effective inducement for private investment than tax reduction. They would also reveal more directly the real cost of encouraging foreign investment. But governments have preferred the alternative of foregoing future tax revenue rather than incurring greater present expenditures.

Finally, it can be contended that a developing country might actually be offering excessive concessions to foreign capital. When confronting large foreign enterprises and competing among themselves for the short supply of foreign capital, small countries might well be providing more by way of inducement than is necessary—especially when the concessions do not affect the total of investment forthcoming, but only its intercountry allocation. Some types of foreign investment (for instance, those to secure a necessary raw material or mineral) would go to one developing country or another, regardless of inducements; but the foreign enterprise may "shop around" and attempt to secure the most favorable terms from each possible source of supply. Special concessions in this case have no appreciable effect in raising the total flow of international investment, but they can affect the allocation between one recipient country or another. Countries that are potential recipients compete among themselves, and the competing concessions will largely cancel out—to the benefit of no one country. Competitive tax subsidies among developing countries, for example, may result in a process in which few of the advantages but most of the disadvantages of tax subsidies would remain.[17] Negotiating independently, each developing nation offers greater concessions than it would if all the countries could act under a collective agreement regarding the maximum concessions that will be made. In this situation, there is a case for international discussion possibly leading to conventions or agreements that would eliminate the excessive competition.[18] It is to the interest of developing countries as a group that the tax treatment should be as uniform as possible, and that individual countries should not offer extra concessions except in agreement with the others.

Overconcessions are also made when, in order to avoid discriminatory policies, already existent investments are granted the same concessions that are necessary to encourage new capital. There is also the danger that the temporary preferential treatment offered by concessions will attract the quick, speculative type of foreign investment that makes no long-run contribution to the economy, but simply takes advantage of the concessions. Even for a desired foreign investment that initially has a high benefit-cost ratio, concessions may be extended for too long a time: if the benefits come within a short period of time, then

[17] *Ibid.*, p. 149.
[18] Nicholas Kaldor, "The Role of Taxation in Economic Development," E. A. G. Robinson, ed., *Problems in Economic Development*, Macmillan Co., 1965, p. 185; Dudley Seers, "Big Companies and Small Countries," *Kyklos*, Vol. 16 (1963), pp. 601–603.

prolongation of the concessions beyond this period is not justi-fied. The cost of "overencouraging" certain types of foreign in-vestment can be considerable. The problem therefore is not simply to consider the relative costs of different incentive devices, but also to devise sufficiently flexible instruments to allow selec-tivity in the conferral of concessions. The adoption of a selective investment statute, however, assumes that a necessarily high level of administrative capability exists to allow the conferring of broad discretionary powers on administrators who must be able to interpret the purposes of the law and its relationship to the country's development program.[19]

If the attraction of foreign investment to the country is one objective of an investment statute, another is to channel the in-vestment into fields of high priority within the country. By a denial of concessions or absolute prohibition, developing coun-tries now commonly screen foreign capital away from certain sectors of the economy that are reserved for public enterprise or domestic capital. Governmental grants of permits, licenses, leases, and concessions are important means of controlling the acquisi-tion and the extent of rights of foreigners in the country's natural resources. In many countries, authorization or official approval is not granted for foreign investments in the traditional areas of mining, plantations, and public utilities which are now reserved for national capital, either exclusively or by prescribing a share in ownership-control for nationals. Instead of supporting a con-tinuation of the historical pattern of foreign investment, develop-ing countries have shifted their emphasis to the encouragement of foreign capital in industries that process agricultural products, manufacture for export, or produce import substitutes. More and more the channeling of foreign capital appears predicated on a

[19] Heller and Kauffman, *op. cit.*, pp. 50–56.

desire to stimulate industrialization, exercise sovereignty over natural resources, avoid the granting of monopoly positions to foreign enterprises, and protect domestic competitors.

Beyond the negative controls of outright exclusion, the positive inducements to attract foreign investment into desired channels fall into three main categories: (1) tax exemptions or privileges for "approved investments," (2) a tariff structure that induces "tariff factories" to replace imports and that provides high protection on the final stages of production while reducing or removing tariffs on imported components,[20] and (3) the use of foreign exchange controls (especially multiple exchange rates and exchange licensing) in order to subsidize specific exports, favor the importation of necessary materials for approved investments, and allow a larger remittance of earnings on desired investments.

Although their effects may be indirect and not readily apparent, import restrictions and exchange controls are now extremely important in determining the pattern of foreign investment. For the effects of a differentiated tariff structure and multiple exchange rates are equivalent to those of a scheme of subsidies and taxes, affecting the rate of return on foreign investment. When the country imposes prohibitive tariffs, or other import restrictions, against foreign manufactures, the foreign manufacturer may be induced to escape the controls against his product by establishing a branch plant or subsidiary behind the tariff wall. Although the protection would have little effect in attracting supply-oriented industries, the inducement may be significant for the creation of "tariff factories" in market-oriented industries. It is particularly effective in encouraging the final

[20] The use of tariff differentials and the resultant degree of protection are discussed more fully in Chapter 7, section 10.

stages of manufacture and assembly of parts within the tariff-imposing country when there is an import duty on finished goods while raw materials or intermediate goods remain untaxed.

Turning to the "distribution effect," we are now interested in how regulatory measures may affect the contribution of the foreign investment to local income. This contribution depends on the value of total output attributable to foreign investment and the proportionate share of local participation in the value of that output. Tax measures—consisting mainly of taxes on income and profits and export duties—are, of course, the major policies for reducing the share of the gross domestic product accruing to nonresidents. Under double-taxation agreements, the investee country receives the first share of profits taxation. To raise the share of local participation, however, additional measures are also now taken to control the operation of the foreign investment. Thus, many of the developing countries require domestic partnership with the foreign investors and stipulate that a percentage of the capital in certain industries should be locally owned. The employment and training of nationals is also frequently sought by requiring a certain percentage of the labor force of foreign-owned enterprises to be composed of nationals, or by designating that a fixed percentage of the payroll should go to nationals. Minimum wage requirements and social welfare benefits are also designed to ensure a certain return to domestic labor from the operation of the foreign enterprise. There may also be an insistence on the local production or purchase of components and supplies. Finally, there are commonly restrictions on the amount of profit that can be earned or limitations on the distribution of profits.

All these measures are intended to give domestic factors of production a larger share of the total value of the foreign enterprise's output. This intention, however, may conflict with the objective of attracting foreign investment in the first place. If domestic partnership limits the management and control of the enterprise, labor legislation is onerous, and allowable profits are not sufficiently attractive, then foreign investment will not be forthcoming, and the concessions previously discussed will be of no avail. It is difficult to determine just when measures aimed at increasing the share of domestic income are more than offset by a loss in total income resulting from a decline in the inflow of foreign capital; but at some point, policies designed to raise the benefit-cost ratio may result in no benefit whatsoever as foreign investment ceases.

Special attention should be given to the third kind of effect of foreign investment measures—that on the balance of payments. If the development program is not to be constrained by a shortage of foreign exchange, policies must be instituted to ensure that the deficit is as small as possible and that the remaining irreducible deficit is accommodated by external financing. It is therefore important to analyze how policies affecting external private investment might lessen the pressure on the recipient country's balance of payments.

The initial inflow of foreign capital provides foreign exchange, and this is a benefit. But as noted previously, the outward flow of interest, profits and dividends may require balance of payments adjustments that involve some cost. The return flow of capital is a charge on domestic real income that has to be transferred abroad either by increasing exports, decreasing imports, or receiving additional capital from overseas. To avoid or reduce this cost, local equity participation is frequently required. Many developing countries also exclude foreign investments that will not contribute to an increase in exports or a replacement of imports, allowing entry only for investments which it is believed will earn sufficient foreign exchange to service their own transfers. Through exchange controls and taxation, the developing country may also limit the maximum transferable return on foreign capital, by restricting the transfer of profits to some percent of direct investment capital per annum, or by allowing earnings up to some percentage of registered foreign capital to be remitted at a lower official exchange rate and the remainder at only a higher free market rate. More severe exchange restrictions are generally applied to the repatriation of capital. A number of countries also attempt to limit transfer of income abroad by imposing a tax on dividends paid to nonresidents. By these means of an absolute ceiling on income and capital transfers, unfavorable exchange rates, and increased taxation, the host country seeks to encourage the reinvestment of profits rather than the withdrawal with consequent pressure on the balance of payments.

On the surface, these measures seem sensible; but when examined more closely, they too are subject to some criticism. As previously noted in connection with foreign aid, an investment may ease the balance of payments even if it does not occur in an export or import-replacing industry. What ultimately matters for the balance of payments is the productivity of investment and the impact of the investment on the total use of resources; the concern with the direct stimulation of exports or direct replacement of imports is a policy of misplaced concreteness.

The emphasis on reinvestment of profits may also be short-sighted. If the initial investment is of value in itself, but the foreign investor does not wish to reinvest his profits in the country, then an attempt to force him to do so is more likely to result simply in a smaller inflow of foreign investment instead of any additional contribution from the reinvestment of profits. There is then a loss to the economy equal to the amount by which real national income would have risen from the investment less the real value of dividend payments abroad. Those firms that will not be deterred by the reinvestment requirement will be precisely those that would expect reinvestment to be profitable anyway, and reinvestment would occur without the governmental requirement.

Moreover, while the insistence on reinvestment does reduce the immediate demand for foreign exchange to pay dividends abroad, it raises, at the same time, the amount of foreign investment on which further dividends may be earned and transferred in the future. The equity interest of the foreigner is increased, without new funds flowing in from abroad. If the intangible benefits—the managerial and technical assistance—from the original investment are realized within a short period of time, then the continued expansion of the foreign enterprise through retained earnings ceases to make any special contribution to the economy.[21] But the ploughing back of profit is tantamount to new foreign investment which expands the base on which profits may be made and causes the country's foreign service charges to become ever greater as the foreign equity increases. It may therefore be submitted that to restrain the rise in foreign service charges, the developing country should attempt to have as much of the subsequent expansion as possible be financed from local equity sources. Alternatively, instead of encouraging further expansion of the initial investment, the host country may find it more desirable in the interests of diversification of the economy to encourage the investment of profits in other activities in the economy. To the extent that the initial investment gives rise to future investment elsewhere in the economy, the benefits of foreign investment become more widespread.

[21] Edith T. Penrose, "Foreign Investment and Growth of the Firm," *Economic Journal*, June, 1956, pp. 220–235; "Some Problems of Policy Toward Direct Private Foreign Investment in Developing Countries," *Middle East Economic Papers*, 1962, pp. 135–136.

Out of concern for the "balance of payments effect" and also the "distribution effect," many countries have attempted to secure local equity participation from the very beginning of the investment by excluding the foreign investor in certain industries unless the investment is in the form of a joint international business venture. *Ceteris paribus,* an equity joint venture does allow more positive "distribution" and "balance of payments effects" than would 100 percent foreign ownership, but these advantages should not be overemphasized. There are also several disadvantages which may combine in certain cases to make it undesirable to encourage or enforce an equity joint venture.

If a foreign investor believed it was advantageous to participate in a joint venture, he would seek its establishment without the requirement of a foreign investment law. To the potential investor, the requirement cannot encourage more foreign investment than would have been forthcoming without the requirement; it can only operate in the direction of discouraging foreign investment. A joint venture will not be attractive to the foreign investor when the foreign enterprise has adequate capital and does not need local equity capital, there is no need to have a local partner to supply local knowledge, or when the participation of a local partner would affect the freedom of operation of an internationally integrated company. Given the foreign investor's disinclination to engage in a joint venture, the developing country's insistence on this form of investment will simply diminish the inflow of foreign capital.

From the standpoint of the recipient country's interests, there are also conditions under which the joint venture cannot be considered as the preferred form of foreign investment. To require domestic participation is, of course, to tie the amount of foreign investment to the amount of domestic investment that will be forthcoming; even if the foreign investor were willing to invest in a joint venture, the foreign investment will be lost if domestic investors do not respond. Assuming there is adequate response, there is still a problem connected with the means of financing the domestic participation. If, on the one hand, local savings do exist, and these are mobilized by local participation in the foreign investment, the result may simply be to replace domestic investment which would otherwise have been made; the joint venture then has an opportunity cost by way of the foregone domestic investment. If, on the other hand, a significant supply of local savings is not already existent, but the joint venture presents an attractive opportunity for investment and the local investor borrows the necessary funds, then the joint venture has simply led to credit creation and inflationary financing of the local equity participation; this, in turn, will induce imports which are uncovered by an inflow of foreign exchange. The joint venture might also arise through the acquisition of a pre-existing domestic firm—in this case, actual or potential competition will be diminished, and an undesirable concentration of economic power may result. To the extent that joint ventures tend to predominate in large-scale enterprises, there is also less scope for the imitation of the joint venture's production techniques elsewhere in the economy; the external economies from a large-scale joint venture may thus be less than from a number of smaller scale foreign enterprises which in the aggregate involve no greater amount of foreign equity than is present in the single large-scale joint venture.

6. Finally, the true alternative to the joint venture is not complete foreign ownership but rather no foreign equity participation at all. To the host country, the advantage of a joint venture is the acquisition of the intangible benefits and the nonmonetary transfer of resources associated with foreign investment without

incurring the costs of 100 percent foreign equity. But along a scale of different forms of foreign investment, the equity joint venture is only one of several alternative arrangements for securing the international transfer of technology and the acquisition of managerial skills. At one extreme on the scale is the foreign investment without local participation and without a time limit on its duration. This may be modified by a requirement that after the initial foreign investment, any subsequent expansion of the enterprise must come through local participation, in order to reduce the proportion of foreign equity over time; or a limited time duration may be imposed, after which the foreign enterprise must be sold to local investors. The joint venture extends this principle by limiting the amount of foreign equity and securing local participation at the outset. Compared with the alternative of a time limit on foreign investment and the eventual bringing of the foreign investment under local ownership and control, the joint venture is clearly less costly, insofar as the equity shares of the foreign enterprise will appreciate, and the repatriation of the sales proceeds imposes a foreign exchange burden.

If, however, the foreign know-how, managerial talent, and training facilities could be acquired without the foreign equity from the start, the developing country would then completely escape the costs of foreign financial involvement. To this end, contractual devices involving engineering and construction agreements, technical services agreements, management contracts, or license or franchise arrangements may be superior to the equity joint venture.[22] These contractual devices provide an extremely flexible means of directly transferring specialized technical and

[22] For an exposition of contractual devices, see generally, United Nations Economic and Social Council, *op. cit.*, chap. I.

managerial knowledge of a proprietary nature from a foreign enterprise, which is the outstanding—and the early—benefit of foreign investment, without the higher costs—which mount over time—of a foreign equity interest.

7. In the light of development planning, it is significant that not only is a new pattern of international investment emerging, but also that the developing countries are seeking a less costly mix of public and private foreign capital and public and private technical assistance. Instead of overemphasizing the institution of an equity joint venture, the less developed countries might be better advised to seek the following mix: for the securing of foreign exchange—foreign public sources of capital that can supply funds in the form of long-term low-interest loans and grants-in-aid; for the stimulation of the private sector—the relending of these funds to domestic enterprise through intermediate credit institutions, such as local development banks or domestic finance corporations;[23] for technical knowledge and business methods—more extensive use of contractual devices with foreign supplying enterprises. Through such a combination of public foreign capital with management contracts or technical collaboration agreements, the developing country may obtain both the capital and the technical, managerial, and training services at a lower cost than by insisting on an equity joint venture. The higher rate of

[23] For an elaboration of the role that these institutions can perform in providing long-term finance to private industry, see generally, Shirley Boskey, *Problems and Practices of Development Banks*, Johns Hopkins Press, 1959; W. Diamond, *Development Banks*, Johns Hopkins Press, 1957; Diamond, "Development Finance Companies," *Finance and Development*, June, 1965, pp. 97–102; Raymond F. Mikesell, *Public Foreign Capital for Private Enterprise in Developing Countries*, Essays in International Finance No. 52, Princeton University, August, 1966.

return required for a direct equity investment is in essence a payment for foreign knowledge, and if this can be acquired through contractual devices while the foreign capital is received from governmental sources at a low rate of interest, then there is a distinct advantage in shifting the emphasis to management and service contracts. If developing countries are attempting to depart from the traditional pattern of private foreign investment, so too is there a compelling need to seek new methods of foreign partnership to gain the benefits of "jointness" at reduced cost. The potentialities for thus combining local ownership with technical assistance from private foreign enterprise and financial aid from public sources can become of considerable practical importance.

7

Commercial Policy

1. Commercial policy comprises another major area of international economic policy that should be reconsidered in the light of development programming. This involves the controversial issue of whether the traditional case for free trade—convincing as it may be on the grounds of maximizing world production efficiency under static conditions—is relevant to the structural and dynamic problems of poor nations.

In popular and political discussions, the economics of development often degenerates into the "economics of discontent"—so that a protective commercial policy is advocated as a means of attaining the "superior way of life of an industrial society," or increasing "national power through self-sufficiency," or "becoming less dependent on foreigners." These are, however, noneconomic objectives, and while they may be valued for their own sake, they do not constitute an economic case for protection as a means of increasing real income. We shall be concerned here with only the economic arguments for protection.[1]

Economic arguments for protection arise once we ask whether free trade is the optimal policy when the conditions of production efficiency are considered in terms of intertemporal optimality, instead of for only a single time period, and when the concern is with national gains, instead of mutual gains from trade. More pointedly, it may be contended that a protective commercial policy will strengthen a development program by enabling the poor country to acquire a larger share of the gains from trade, increase its rate of capital formation, and promote the industrialization of its "infant economy." In support of these contentions, several specific arguments favoring trade restrictions are commonly advocated.[2] This chapter appraises the analytical validity of these arguments and their relevance for development programming. Although we shall refer only to tariffs, much of our discussion could apply equally well to exchange controls, multiple exchange rates, or quotas.

2. The belief that a poor country can alter the distribution of the gains from trade in its favor, and thereby directly raise its real

[1] On the noneconomic arguments, see Harry G. Johnson, "Tariffs and Economic Development," *Journal of Development Studies*, October, 1964, pp. 6–7, 11–13; Jagdish Bhagwati, "The Pure Theory of International Trade: A Survey," *Economic Journal*, March, 1964, pp. 70–75.

[2] The inappropriateness of relying on commercial policy to maintain external balance has already been discussed in Chapter 4. We also do not give any emphasis to the possibilities of using commercial policy to alter the internal distribution of income. Analytically interesting as this argument is, the redistribution effects of a tariff are not likely to have much practical bearing on the rate of development, and a redistribution of income can more appropriately be effected through the use of domestic fiscal policy.

income, is based on the terms of trade argument for protection. An expected deterioration in their terms of trade is a common concern of poor countries. This pessimism rests partly on an extrapolation of the alleged secular deterioration in their terms of trade, and partly on the expectation that future improvements in primary production, together with a low-income elasticity of demand for primary products will lower the prices of the poor country's exports relative to its imports.[3] It is argued that restrictions on exports or imports may result in a rise in export prices or a fall in import prices, so as to forestall the anticipated deterioration or bring about an improvement in the terms of trade.

This argument, it should be noted, does not assert that if a primary-producing country expects a future deterioration in its terms of trade or fluctuations in its export prices and export earnings, it should impose industrial protection in order to transfer, in advance, resources from the primary-producing export sector to the import-competing industrial sector. Even if the country's comparative advantage in primary production is expected to decline in the future, it does not follow that the country should forego the present gains from trade that can still be realized as long as there is a current comparative advantage in such production. Only if the future competitive adjustment to secularly changing comparative advantage cannot be relied upon, and some advance planning is required for the transfer of resources out of exports, is there a need for government intervention. Even then, industrial protection may be only a "second-best" solution compared with alternative domestic policy measures to stimulate such a transfer. Similarly, even though primary exports may be subject to greater variability of earnings than industrial exports, it does not follow that average earnings in primary production are

[3] Raúl Prebisch, "Commercial Policy in the Underdeveloped Countries," *American Economic Review, Papers and Proceedings*, May, 1959, pp. 261–264.

necessarily lower than they would be in industrial production, and that real income over the cycle would be enhanced by protection. Although cyclical fluctuations in export receipts have undesirable repercussions on a country's development program, their adverse effects are more appropriately avoided by stability measures than by protective trade policies.[4]

Properly interpreted, the terms of trade argument has merit when cast in the form of the optimum tariff argument. This argument rests on the condition that if a country has monopoly or monopsony power in world markets and can thus influence its terms of trade, the marginal terms of trade will diverge from the average terms of trade, and a distortion in international markets will arise under free trade between the foreign rate of transformation and the domestic rate of transformation in production. For under free trade, it is the average rate of transformation that is equated to the marginal rate of substitution in consumption and domestic rate of transformation. There is then a case for an optimum tariff to offset this distortion and equate the domestic rate of substitution and the domestic rate of transformation with the foreign rate of transformation. Instead of behaving as a perfect competitor, the country may impose a tariff that makes the *marginal* terms of trade (marginal revenue) equal to its marginal rate of transformation (marginal costs), in contrast to the free trade situation in which the terms of trade (that is, the *price* of exports in terms of imports) are equated to the marginal rate of transformation (Fig. 2).[5]

[4] The problem of export stabilization is discussed in Chapter 9, section 7.

[5] T. Scitovsky, "A Reconsideration of the Theory of Tariffs," *Review of Economic Studies*, Summer, 1942, pp. 95–98; Gottfried Haberler, *A Survey of International Trade Theory*, rev. ed., Princeton Univ. Press, 1961, p. 53; James E. Meade, *Trade and Welfare*, Oxford Univ. Press, 1955, chap. XVII; M. C. Kemp, "The Gain from International Trade," *Economic Journal*, December, 1962, pp. 814–818.

This argument is analytically valid. As classical economists recognized, a country that can exploit a monopoly or monopsony position can trade on better terms by appropriately taxing its exports or imposing a tariff on its imports. But for poor countries the practical relevance of this argument is only slight. Few, if any, of these countries can exercise sufficient monopoly or monopsony power to bring about an international transfer of real income through improvement in their terms of trade. This is especially difficult in view of alternative sources of supply for foodstuffs on the part of importing countries, the capacity of advanced industrial nations to develop synthetics as substitutes for natural raw materials, and the relatively small size of any one poor country's domestic market for a particular import. A tariff is most effective in improving the tariff-imposing country's terms of trade when the foreign offer curve is inelastic,[6] but the foreign offer curve that confronts any single poor country will normally be elastic, with less imports being demanded and less exports supplied as the price of imports rises. The greater is this elasticity, the more will the volume of trade decrease as a result of a tariff.

[6] It is sometimes argued that a tariff will at one and the same time improve the terms of trade, protect import-competing industries, and raise the real earnings of the factor used relatively intensively in producing importables. If, however, the foreign offer curve is inelastic, these objectives are likely to be contradictory. For then the terms of trade may improve so much that the domestic price of imports falls in the tariff-imposing country, with a consequent reduction in the domestic production of importables and a redistribution of earned income towards the factor used relatively intensively in producing exportables. Harry G. Johnson, "Income Distribution, The Offer Curve, and the Effects of Tariffs," *Manchester School of Economic and Social Studies*, September, 1960, pp. 223–224, 230–232; L. A. Metzler, "Tariffs, the Terms of Trade and the Distribution of National Income," *Journal of Political Economy*, February, 1949, pp. 1–29. Metzler notes in particular that if a primary producing country faces an inelastic foreign demand, it may not succeed in either stimulating domestic manufacturing or raising labor's share of income by imposing a tariff. *Ibid.*, pp. 19–28.

The problem then becomes one of calculating the optimal tariff rate, or more precisely, the optimal import and export duties. An optimal import or export duty is one that maximizes the gain from improved terms of trade minus the loss from a smaller volume of trade; and this duty will be lower, the greater is the elasticity of the foreign offer curve.

However, even if we assume the existence of sufficient monopoly or monopsony power, and ignore the practical difficulties of calculating an optimal tariff, the terms of trade argument is still limited severely by its dependence on price-elasticities of demand and supply at only a given moment of time. The conclusion may be quite different if it is recognized that a short-term gain may be easily offset by subsequent changes in elasticities. It is also possible for an initial improvement to be later counteracted by the retaliation of other countries, or by an increased demand for imports resulting from the government's expenditure of the tariff proceeds, or from an internal redistribution of income. If these dynamic effects are not taken into account, the terms of trade argument may be misleading, and may be given more weight than it merits in the context of development.

3. The second category of protection arguments concentrates on the need to increase investment. An improvement in the terms of trade can be one source of capital formation if the extra income is saved, but there are also other means by which commercial policy can contribute to capital accumulation.

One way is by increasing the savings ratio through controls on imports of consumer goods. The objective of greater investment will not be realized, however, if consumption expenditure merely shifts from imports to domestic products. A reduction in consumption expenditure—not a mere change in its composition —is needed for an increase in saving.

This requirement applies even if the importation of consumer goods is controlled in order to be replaced directly by imports of capital goods. Only if there is also a corresponding act of domestic saving will the new capital imports be a net contribution to capital formation. If the import restrictions do not lead to a reduction in consumers' expenditure, but simply to a switch of spending from imported consumer goods to domestic commodities, the increase in home consumption will draw domestic factors away from capital construction or maintenance. Home consumption simply rises at the expense of domestic investment, and the imports of capital goods are offset by the reduced domestic investment, so that there is no increase in total net capital formation. Barring an increase in voluntary saving, an increase in net investment could then come about only through the forced saving that results from inflation when the local purchase of imported capital goods is financed through domestic credit expansion.

The effectiveness of protection as a means of increasing investment is thus contingent upon a complementary domestic policy of mobilizing additional saving. Even if import restrictions allow more imports of capital goods in place of consumption goods, it is ultimately an increase in voluntary or compulsory saving that makes for the net contribution to capital formation.[7]

In connection with this argument, proponents of import controls frequently maintain that import restrictions will not reduce the total volume of imports but only alter their composition from consumer goods to capital goods. But this assumes that protection has no adverse effects on exports. If, however, the protection of import-competing industries tends to attract resources away from export industries, exports will be handicapped. Considera-

[7] This basic principle has been emphasized by Ragnar Nurkse, *Problems of Capital Formation in Underdeveloped Countries*, Basil Blackwell, 1953, pp. 112–116.

tion must also be given to the fact that for peasants who have the alternative of subsistence production or production of cash crops for export, the incentive to produce export crops may be highly dependent upon an aspiration to consume imported goods. The denial of imports may then reduce the incentive of peasants to produce for the market. Moreover, when the policies of protection and promotion of import-competing industries result in higher internal costs, the maintenance of exports becomes extremely difficult. Even if they are not directly designed to do so, the import restrictions may thus have adverse indirect repercussions on exports and result in a reduced capacity to import, although only a change in the composition of imports was intended.

To increase domestic investment, it might also be thought that it is justified to protect capital-intensive industries which yield high profits that will be ploughed back into an expansion of the industry. This policy amounts, of course, to a tax on consumers, and there is a consumption loss to be set against the gain in domestic production. If the domestic production is inefficient, as it is likely to be under the shelter of protection, it would be better to avoid such inefficiency and to use domestic taxation policies to raise the level of savings—assuming that the country has the capacity and administrative ability to impose additional taxes, and that the taxes do not, in turn, introduce other distortions entailing a real cost.

4. The foregoing argument relates to an increase in the domestic savings ratio, but protection may also be advocated as a means of capital formation through its attraction of foreign investment. A general proposition of neoclassical trade theory is that commodity movements are a substitute for international factor movements. Protection may then stimulate factor movements in place of commodity trade, since protection has the effect of increasing the relative scarcity of the scarce factor in the tariff-imposing country, thereby raising the factor's real return and making profitable an international redistribution of the factor.

Accordingly, for a poor country in which capital is the scarce factor, a tariff imposed on a capital-intensive industry may induce an inflow of foreign capital.[8] When the tariff is imposed, the price of the capital-intensive product rises relatively to the price of the labor-intensive product, and factors move out of the labor-intensive industry into the capital-intensive industry. There will then be, at constant factor prices, an excess supply of labor and an excess demand for capital. The marginal product of labor must therefore fall, and the marginal product of capital must rise.[9] In response to this higher marginal product of capital in the capital-poor country, capital may then be attracted from the capital-rich country where marginal products have remained constant.

This argument depends, however, on several restrictive assumptions. It assumes that production functions are identical in all countries, and that capital is perfectly mobile and will respond to a change in marginal product. But differences in production functions are undoubtedly pronounced between poor and rich countries; because of these differences, the tariff may not make capital movements profitable. It is also unrealistic to ignore other determinants of foreign investment besides a differential in the

[8] This argument is analyzed fully by R. A. Mundell, "International Trade and Factor Mobility," *American Economic Review*, June, 1957, pp. 331–335.

[9] In the case of a tariff on a capital-intensive industry, the ratios of labor to capital rise in both the capital-intensive and labor-intensive industries. If the production functions are subject to constant returns to scale, then the marginal productivities of factors depend only on factor proportions, so that in this situation the marginal product of capital rises and the marginal product of labor falls.

return on capital. The argument also precludes any change in the terms of trade. If, however, the tariff should improve the terms of trade, the price of the labor-intensive export commodity may increase relatively to the capital-intensive import commodity, and the marginal product of capital would then not rise.

Even if all the assumptions are granted, and capital does move until its marginal product is equal in both countries, the tariff will still have unfavorable effects which the capital movement can only alleviate, but not eliminate. As a result of the tariff, the marginal product of labor will fall, and real wages will be lower than in the pretariff situation. This is because the capital inflow will be largely absorbed in an expansion of the output of capital-intensive importables and can never succeed in raising the capital-labor ratio in each industry to its pretariff level. Only if the assumption of constant returns to scale is replaced by an assumption that external economies of scale exist in the production of capital-intensive importables, so that the marginal product of capital falls at a slower rate than it would in the absence of such economies, would it be possible for the tariff to attract a sufficiently greater supply of capital to allow the new equilibrium to be established with a higher marginal product of labor.[10]

A less sophisticated but more realistic case for protection as a means of attracting foreign investment is simply the old-fashioned appeal for "tariff factories." When a poor country imposes prohibitive tariffs, or other import restrictions, against foreign manufacturers, the inflow of direct foreign investment may increase as the foreign manufacturer is induced to escape the import controls by establishing a branch plant or subsidiary behind the tariff wall. But the tariff alone can not ensure a sufficiently high domestic demand for the product of the tariff factory; as long as

---

[10] Mundell, *op. cit.*, pp. 333–334.

the domestic market for the restricted import remains narrow, the necessary condition for the attraction of direct foreign investment will not be fulfilled. If, however, a former supplier of an import can be induced by the protection to come in and establish an industry behind the tariff, this may be the easiest way in which the country can gain not only capital, but also the technical knowledge and experience that are so necessary for the successful establishment of a new industry.

5. We may now examine the advocacy of protection in order to accelerate the growth of the "infant manufacturing sector." Gunnar Myrdal makes a challenging case for protection by maintaining that there are "four special reasons for industrial protection in underdeveloped countries—the difficulties of finding demand to match new supply, the existence of surplus labor, the large rewards of individual investments in creating external economies, and the lopsided internal price structure disfavoring industry."[11] These reasons are interrelated and may be interpreted as an extension of the infant industry argument to the "growing up" of the economy as a whole. In combination, they constitute an "infant economy" case for protection, and as such they have considerable appeal to a poor country. Nonetheless, a closer investigation of the arguments may temper this enthusiasm if it is realized that to be a guide to policy, the protection argument must be not only logically valid, but also supported by empirical evidence, not offset by practical qualifications, and superior to alternative domestic policies.

These other considerations limit the significance of even the time-honored infant industry argument. Temporary tariff pro-

[11] Gunnar Myrdal, *An International Economy*, Harper & Row, 1956, p. 279.

tection of an infant industry is supported on grounds that the existing comparative cost relations are irrelevant, insofar as after a certain period of time the initial production difficulties will have been overcome through practice, and the industry will then be able to produce at lower costs, through the full exploitation of economies of scale. The industry will thereby eventually acquire a comparative advantage.

This is a logically valid argument, but the scope of its applicability may be rather narrow. At best, the tariff can only be an instrument for channeling resources into specific industries; but it cannot create the capital or skills required by the industry at the outset. Before an industry can be protected, it must first be created.[12] Assuming, however, that this prior problem has been solved, the protected industry must still meet not only the "Mill test" of acquiring sufficient skill and experience to overcome an historical handicap, but also the "Bastable test" of realizing a sufficient saving in costs to compensate for the high costs of the learning period.[13] It is also necessary to be sure that the industry would not expand except with the aid of a tariff. On this basis, the case for a protective tariff is weak if there are only internal economies of scale—not external economies. For, even though there may be losses on early operations, if the future scale of output is sufficient to enable the current rate of interest to be earned on the initial amount invested in learning the job, the investment will be profitable for private enterprise. There is really no justifi-

[12] Nurkse, *op. cit.*, p. 105; A. O. Hirschman, *The Strategy of Economic Development*, Yale Univ. Press, 1958, p. 124. An essential conclusion of Hirschman's analysis of commercial policy is that infant industry protection should not be given before the industry has been established, but should become available, if at all, only afterwards.

[13] M. C. Kemp, "The Mill-Bastable Infant-Industry Dogma," *Journal of Political Economy*, February, 1960, pp. 65–67.

cation for state support when there are simply costs of growth as such, unless the profitability of an investment project is delayed for an especially long period, so that the risk element is particularly great for the individual investor and the degree of individual time-preference is unduly high, as compared with what may be appropriate from the point of view of the community.[14]

The learning process may, however, be external to the firm in the sense that all the knowledge and experience gained through "learning by doing," as the firm expands, is not appropriable, but instead can be freely tapped by other firms or industries. The social benefit would then exceed the private benefit of investment in learning industrial production techniques. There is thus a case for state support when the expansion of the aided industry would lead to this external productivity effect that is not allowed for in private cost calculations.[15]

When we limit the infant industry argument to these restrictive conditions, it remains a formidable task for any government to select the genuine infant industries, appropriately schedule their sequential appearance, and ensure that the governmental support is actually stimulating, within the protected industry, the type of activity that is the real source of an excess of social over private return. Instead of trying to impose selective tariffs of sufficient height to encourage particular industries, it may therefore

[14] William Fellner, "Individual Investment Projects in Growing Economies," *Investment Criteria and Economic Growth*, Center for International Studies, Mass. Inst. of Tech., 1955, pp. 125–130.

[15] Meade, *op. cit.*, pp. 256–257, 270–271. But, as will be discussed in section 9, the most appropriate form of governmental support should be a subsidy directed specifically to the learning process itself, rather than broadside protection or a subsidy on production in the infant industry; Johnson, "Optimal Trade Intervention in the Presence of Domestic Distortions," in *Trade, Growth, and the Balance of Payments: Essays in Honor of Gottfried Haberler*, Rand McNally, 1965, pp. 28–30.

be more expedient to place a uniform ad valorem tariff on the whole range of industrial products and then leave the selection to market forces.[16] This would avoid the overreaching of import substitution into all lines and would still allow specialization according to comparative advantage between industrial products.

6. Turning now from cost conditions to demand conditions, we may consider the proposal that protection is needed to create demand to match new supply. Whereas the infant industry argument maintains that the industry's present costs are too high, it might also be claimed that the demand for its product is too low, and that "one of the difficulties of industrial development in underdeveloped countries, and one of the great hindrances to giving real momentum to a development policy, is that internal demand must be built up simultaneously with supply."[17] It is thus argued that the unlikelihood, or "the exasperating slowness of any self-engendered process of 'natural growth'" calls for import restrictions that "afford a means of by-passing altogether this process of 'natural growth' and creating at once the necessary demand for a particular domestic industry."[18]

As stated, this argument is restricted simply to promoting the demand for import substitutes. Yet, aside from foreign exchange restrictions, there is no indication why this particular pattern of development is preferable to any alternative pattern. Even if the argument is extended to the "balanced growth" thesis, the particular emphasis on import substitutes is still unwarranted. For the balanced growth doctrine, as formulated by Nurkse, calls only for a balanced pattern of investment in a number of differ-

[16] Nicholas Kaldor, "Conferências sôbre desenvolvimento econômica," *Revista Brasileira de Economia*, March, 1957, pp. 28–29. But see Johnson, "Tariffs and Economic Development," *op. cit.*, pp. 13–19.

[17] Myrdal, *op. cit.*, p. 276.

[18] *Loc. cit.*

ent industries, including agriculture, so that people working with more capital and better techniques become each other's customers. It does not emphasize import-competing industries, and there is nothing in the doctrine itself to favor general protection for industry as contrasted with other policies designed to promote extensive investment. Indeed, Nurkse cautions that import restrictions should be used only sparingly, because they lead to costly and inefficient import-substitute production and have an adverse effect on real income. Further, Nurkse carefully stresses that the case for output expansion for the home market is clear only on the condition that the amount of resources is increasing at a sufficient rate—through population growth, capital accumulation, and the spread of knowledge—so that domestic output can expand without neglecting export production and giving up the benefits achieved through international specialization.[19]

Finally, it should be recognized that import restrictions are designed merely to replace imports—but this in itself is no guarantee of cumulative growth beyond the point that imports have been replaced. The problems involved in sustaining the development momentum may be quite different from those of initiating development, and other policies may be more appropriate to achieve a self-sustaining process of development.

7. A more cogent argument for industrial protection is that the establishment or expansion of an industry will yield external

[19] Ragnar Nurkse, "International Trade Theory and Development Policy," Howard S. Ellis, ed., *Economic Development for Latin America*, St. Martin's Press, 1961, pp. 251–254, 257–258; "The Conflict between 'Balanced Growth' and International Specialization," *Lectures on Economic Development*, Faculty of Economics, Istanbul University, 1958, pp. 177–180; *Patterns of Trade and Development*, Wicksell Lectures, Almqvist & Wiksell, 1959, pp. 41–48 (reprinted in *Equilibrium and Growth in the World Economy. Economic Essays by Ragnar Nurkse*, Harvard Univ. Press, 1961, pp. 314–322).

economies, thereby giving rise to a divergence between social and private returns. This divergence is of especial concern to a poor country in connection with the problem of allocating savings among alternative investment opportunities. The market evaluation of comparative advantage may not conform to the investment criterion of social profitability, and governmental support of the industry that yields external economies may then be advocated to correct the market mechanism.

To meet this problem, the linear programming approach to development planning attempts to include a number of nonmarket (but quantifiable) phenomena by using accounting prices in evaluating the allocation of resources. By this method, the optimal pattern of trade is determined simultaneously with the optimal allocation of investment. This approach does not, however, necessarily support protection. The objective of efficiency in trade is not superseded by the principles of development programming. On the contrary, the programming approach to resource allocation may show that the country's development policies are actually overemphasizing import-substitution and neglecting the potential gains from trade.[20]

Neoclassicists recognized that as an industry's scale of output expanded, the firms within the industry might benefit from a shift downward in their cost curves as a result of "external technological effects." These external technological economies affect a firm's output via changes in its production function.[21] If the price of the product of the expanding industry falls as its output

[20] For a detailed discussion, see Hollis B. Chenery, "Comparative Advantage and Development Policy," *American Economic Review*, March, 1961, pp. 33–48.

[21] Jacob Viner, "Cost Curves and Supply Curves," reprinted in American Economic Association, *Readings in Price Theory*, Richard D. Irwin, Inc., 1952, pp. 217–220; James E. Meade, "External Economies and Diseconomies in a Competitive Situation," *Economic Journal*, March, 1952, pp. 54–67.

increases, firms in other industries which use the product of the expanding industry as an input will also realize lower production costs; this may be termed an "external pecuniary economy," and will affect profits of firms in other industries.[22]

If production costs are lowered for firms in other industries, for technical or pecuniary reasons, as the result of an expansion in output of the protected industry, the social cost is less than the private cost of production. In this situation, private profitability understates the social desirability of an expansion of the protected industry; market forces would lead to a less than optimal output of commodities whose production involves external economies. Or, if investment in one sector increases the profitability of investment in another sector via increases in demand, market forces will again not necessarily lead to optimal investment decisions.

External economies are commonly believed to be more important in the industrial sectors than in primary production, so that their omission from the market mechanism is likely to bias resource allocation against manufacturing. The argument of ex-

[22] T. Scitovsky, "Two Concepts of External Economies," *Journal of Political Economy*, April, 1954, pp. 146–151. The lowering of production costs is only one of the possible instances of pecuniary external economies. As Scitovsky notes, expansion in industry A may also give rise to profits (1) in an industry that produces a factor used in industry A, (2) in an industry whose product is complementary in use to the product of industry A, (3) in an industry whose product is a substitute for a factor used in industry A, or (4) in an industry whose product is consumed by persons whose incomes are raised by the expansion of industry A.

For a thorough survey of the various interpretations of "external economies," see John S. Chipman, "A Survey of the Theory of International Trade: Part 2, The Neo-Classical Theory," *Econometrica*, October, 1965, pp. 736–749; Bela Balassa, *Economic Development and Integration*, Centro De Estudios Monetarios Latinoamericanos, Mexico, 1965, pp. 133–153; D. W. Pearce and S. G. Sturmey, "Private and Social Costs and Benefits: A Note on Terminology," *Economic Journal*, March, 1966, pp. 152–157.

ternal economies, as related to a poor country, might therefore
be broadened to support general protection for industry by claiming that the profitability of any single industry is a function of
the total number and diversity of industries in the economy. Cost
reductions in a single industry may be especially dependent upon
the economies of conglomeration when a large number of industries are all "conglomerated" close together in the same locality.[23]
More generally, interindustry external economies may stem from
the complementarity of industries on the side of costs, reinforc-
ing the "balanced growth" doctrine which stresses complementarity on the side of demand.[24] By supporting these interindustry
relationships, protection to facilitate the growth of a range of industries or an entire industrial complex may then allow each industry to become profitable, whereas investment in each of the
separate industries considered in isolation might be unprofitable.

Although the external economies argument is formally correct, modern proponents of protection are less careful to qualify
it than were the neoclassicists.[25] Myrdal, for instance, believes
that external economies are realizable in import-competing indus-

---

[23] Meade, *Trade and Welfare, op. cit.*, p. 258.

[24] Cf. Jacob Viner, "Stability and Progress: The Poorer Countries'
Problem," D. C. Hague, ed., *Stability and Progress*, St. Martin's Press,
1958, pp. 56–57.
These interactions are also related to the "linkages" discussed by
Hirschman, *op. cit.*, chap. 6.

[25] Alfred Marshall, *Principles of Economics*, 8th ed., Macmillan Co.,
1920, pp. 226, 271, 317–318, 615, 808; Allyn Young, "Increasing Returns
and Economic Progress," *Economic Journal*, December, 1928, pp. 528 ff.;
Jacob Viner, *Studies in the Theory of International Trade*, Harper & Row,
1937, pp. 480–482; H. S. Ellis and W. Fellner, "External Economies and
Diseconomies," *American Economic Review*, September, 1943, pp. 493–
511; Meade, *Trade and Welfare, op. cit.*, chap. XVI; Marcus Fleming,
"External Economies and the Doctrine of Balanced Growth," *Economic
Journal*, June, 1955, pp. 241–256; H. W. Arndt, "External Economies in
Economic Growth," *Economic Record*, November, 1955, pp. 192–214.

tries, and he is sanguine about the government's ability to estimate these external economies within a dynamic "national calculus."[26] Actually, what is essential is a calculation of the *net* external economies—that is, gross external economies *minus* external diseconomies—for all possible *alternative* investment opportunities. Insofar as investment funds are limited in any development program, the emphasis on import-competing industries must depend on an assumption that the net external economies realizable are greatest in import-competing industries. There is, however, no a priori reason why this should be so; external economies might be substantial in the export sector, or domestic industries, or in public overhead capital.

It is also necessary to distinguish whether the external economies are reversible or irreversible—that is, whether the gains to other enterprises continue even after protection is withdrawn and output in the formerly protected enterprise is reduced. For, if they are reversible, the protection must then be permanent, rather than merely temporary, to keep the reversible external economies utilized. The case of irreversible external economies can be considered as merging with the infant industry situation that requires only temporary intervention, but this does not apply to reversible external economies.

8. Finally, it is claimed that protection of industry in a poor country is justified because the structure of internal costs and prices tends to be lopsided between industry and agriculture in a way that disfavors industry. An early version of this argument was stated by Manoilesco who maintained that the advantage of international trade exists only for industrial countries—identified as the rich countries—and not for countries whose imports con-

[26] Myrdal, *op. cit.*, pp. 276–277.

sist of industrial articles and whose exports are agricultural products—identified as the poor countries.[27] Believing that industry is superior to agriculture as shown by a great difference between the average income per head of an agricultural worker and that of an industrial worker, Manoilesco advocated protection to facilitate the transfer of workers from low-productivity agriculture to high-productivity industry. Myrdal and others restate the argument in modern form: They claim there is a wide gap in real wages between industry and agriculture, but that the social costs for labor in industry are actually lower than the money wages insofar as wages in the manufacturing sector exceed the marginal product of labor in the agricultural sector. They therefore advocate trade controls to compensate for the gap in labor costs between industry and agriculture.[28]

In a more rigorous fashion, Professor Hagen demonstrates that when there are large differentials in factor returns in different sectors because of imperfect factor markets, real income can be increased by factor redistribution.[29] The consequence of a structural disequilibrium in the factor market is an inefficient allocation of factors between agriculture and industry. In effect, production occurs on an inferior transformation curve within the maximum possible production frontier, and a suboptimal position is selected on the inferior transformation curve because private costs of production exceed social costs. If the distortion in factor allocation is removed by protecting the importa-

[27] Mihail Manoilesco, *Theory of Protection and International Trade*, English edition, P. S. King, 1931. Also, Bertil Ohlin, "Protection and Non-Competing Groups," *Weltwirtschaftliches Archiv*, 1931, pp. 30–45.

[28] Myrdal, *op. cit.*, pp. 277–278; W. A. Lewis, "Economic Development with Unlimited Supplies of Labour," *Manchester School of Economic and Social Studies*, May, 1954, pp. 185–186.

[29] E. E. Hagen, "An Economic Justification of Protectionism," *Quarterly Journal of Economics*, November, 1958, pp. 496–514.

ble manufacturing industry that has to pay the higher factor price, real income might then be raised relatively to the free trade situation. Given that the marginal product of labor is higher in the industrial sector than the agricultural sector, but that industrial wages exceed agricultural wages for labor of equal quality, it is argued that industry should be protected to overcome the excessive wage differential and bring private costs in line with social costs.

There is merit in this argument—provided that the increase in the aggregate cost to buyers of the protected product is less than the increase in income to the factors which shift to the protected industry. The wage differential must also be due to non-economic causes that make the industrial wage rate exceed the agricultural wage rate by a margin larger than can be attributed to the disutility or higher economic costs incurred by labor in the industrial sector.[30] Although the entire wage differential cannot be so explained, some of the differential may be due to trade union activity, social legislation, or political and humanitarian considerations on the part of employers. These may cause a genuine distortion, with the industrial wage rate being above the alternative opportunity cost of labor in agriculture.[31]

[30] The empirical evidence used by Hagen is criticized by Anthony Y. C. Koo, "An Economic Justification of Protectionism: Comment," *Quarterly Journal of Economics*, February, 1961, pp. 133–144. Hagen has also been criticized for superimposing dynamic elements on static analysis: A. Fishlow and P. A. David, "Optimal Resource Allocation in an Imperfect Market Setting," *Journal of Political Economy*, December, 1961, pp. 534–535.

[31] Jagdish Bhagwati and V. K. Ramaswami, "Domestic Distortions, Tariffs, and the Theory of Optimum Subsidy," *Journal of Political Economy*, February, 1963, pp. 47–48. Bhagwati and Ramaswami offer eight reasons for the existence of a wage differential between the industrial and agricultural sector, only four of which involve genuine distortions. The differential does not represent a distortion if it reflects a preference be-

Even though such a genuine distortion supports government intervention, we should, however, recognize, as Hagen does,[32] that the "first-best" policy would combine free trade with a subsidy per unit of labor used in industry, equal to the difference between the higher unit labor cost in industry and the lower labor cost in agriculture.

Another variant of the factor disequilibrium argument relies on the existence of disguised unemployment in the agricultural sector.[33] If the concept of disguised unemployment is interpreted strictly, it means that beyond a certain number of workers, the marginal productivity of labor is zero in agriculture. And when some labor is withdrawn from agriculture, output can still be maintained without any change in organization or in cooperant factors. The marginal product of the surplus labor is not enough for its own support, but the institutional arrangement of the family farm, in which the unit of production is also the unit of consumption, allows the members of the household to share in the total product, receiving approximately the average product. When the marginal product of labor is less than the average product, the marginal workers are being subsidized by the rest of the peasant community. Nonetheless, to induce the excess workers to transfer to industrial employment from agriculture, the industrial wage must exceed the marginal product of labor in agriculture, and be at least equal to the average product in agriculture. Even if the actual wages are equal in the industrial and agricultural sectors, the market wage diverges from the true social cost of labor. For the marginal productivity of labor in ag-

---

tween occupations by the wage earners, a rent on scarce skills, a return on investment in human capital, or a return on investment in the cost of movement from the rural to the industrial sector.

[32] Hagen, *op. cit.*, pp. 510–511.

[33] *Ibid.*, p. 514.

riculture is zero, or at least below the average product (which sets the minimum transfer wage for industrial employment), while the cost to industrialists of hiring the surplus labor is considerably higher. In such a situation, labor is overvalued for the industrial sector, and the ratio of social cost to money cost is lower in industry than in agriculture. It is therefore claimed that a better utilization of domestic resources can be achieved if secondary industries are protected in order to offset the divergence between private money costs and true social marginal costs.

This appeal to the existence of disguised unemployment is, however, a tenuous foundation for a protection argument. At most, disguised unemployment applies to peasant or self-employed labor working on small farms, not to plantation labor, and not to thinly populated countries. It may also be only a seasonal phenomenon: there may be no excess of labor supply over labor requirements at the planting and harvest seasons. Rarely is conclusive evidence offered to show that there actually is in agriculture a substantial amount of labor that could be released with no effect on production, if other measures are not taken. To be sure, the measurement of disguised unemployment is difficult, but one might at least observe whether the labor resources of the poor countries actually behave as if there were considerable unemployment. According to Professor Schultz, experience in several countries demonstrates that "programs based on disguised unemployment have not performed as expected: instead of labor resources responding to an increase in the money supply or to new industries in the way that one would have expected if there were considerable underemployment, workers act as if the marginal productivities of laborers in agriculture and in other fields are about the same."[34] Schultz also maintains that he knows of

[34] T. W. Schultz, *The Economic Test in Latin America*, New York State School of Industrial and Labor Relations, Cornell University, Bulletin 35, August, 1956, pp. 14–15.

no evidence for any poor country anywhere that would suggest that a transfer of even some small fraction, say, five percent, of the existing labor force out of agriculture, with other things equal, could be made without reducing production.[35] Several others have also questioned the notion of disguised unemployment,[36] and the earlier estimates of the amount of disguised unemployment now appear to have been exaggerated. Even Nurkse, who originally emphasized the concept of surplus farm labor, states that "much of the surplus labor that may exist in subsistence agriculture is not readily available for other uses unless it is released through changes in agricultural organization. Such changes are a major undertaking and cannot be lightly taken for granted."[37] But what is clear, and of most significance, is that the productivity of labor is generally low in all activities—nonagricultural as well as agricultural. It may therefore be more appro-

[35] T. W. Schultz, "The Role of Government in Promoting Economic Development," L. D. White, ed., *The State of the Social Sciences*, Univ. of Chicago Press, 1956, p. 375.

[36] N. Köstner, "Comments on Professor Nurkse's Capital Accumulation in Underdeveloped Countries," *L'Egypte Contemporaine*, No. 272, 1952; Doreen Warriner, *Land Reform and Economic Development*, National Bank of Egypt, Cairo, 1955, pp. 25–26; Jacob Viner, "Some Reflections on the Concept of Disguised Unemployment," *Indian Journal of Economics*, July, 1957, pp. 17–23; Gottfried Haberler, *International Trade and Economic Development*, National Bank of Egypt, Cairo, 1959, pp. 25–27; Harry T. Oshima, "Underemployment in Backward Economies: An Empirical Comment," *Journal of Political Economy*, June, 1958, pp. 259–264.

[37] Ragnar Nurkse, "Stabilization and Development of Primary Producing Countries," *Kyklos*, 1958, pp. 261–262. Again, in his Istanbul lecture (p. 200), Nurkse maintained that "Some of the underdeveloped countries do have potential domestic resources available for capital construction. But it may be very hard for them to mobilize these resources, and it may be impossible to mobilize them without resorting to coercive methods. Even the necessary labor is not always available for construction: as a rule, it can be released from the land only through changes—and possibly revolutionary changes—in agricultural organization."

priate to conclude with Professor Viner that "there is little or nothing in all the phenomena designated as 'disguised unemployment,' as 'hidden unemployment,' or as 'underemployment' which insofar as they constitute genuine social problems would not be adequately taken into account by competent, informed, and comprehensive analysis of the phenomenon of low productivity of *employed* labor, its causes, its true extent, and its possible remedies."[38]

"Disguised unemployment" has also been interpreted as meaning that labor-time is employed up to the point where its marginal product is zero, but that too many laborers are contributing this labor-time. Some underemployed workers could then be removed with no reduction in total output—provided that the remaining workers worked a longer day to fulfill the original total number of hours.[39] If, for example, in a family of six, each member works only 5 hours a day on the family holding, one member could be considered in "disguised unemployment" if the other members would only work 6 hours a day to maintain the total of 30 hours' work a day. But to induce the remaining workers to make up the total, there may have to be some reorganization of production and the provision of economic incentives. The transfer of the "disguised unemployed" is then not costless.[40] If the remaining workers have to be provided with manufactured consumers' goods in exchange for their food surplus, there is a social cost represented by the extra resources required for the production of these incentive consumers' goods. There is an additional social cost when increased investments in

or increased output per hr.

[38] Viner, *op. cit.*, p. 23.

[39] A. K. Sen, *Choice of Techniques*, Oxford Univ. Press, 1960, pp. 13–15; Hla Myint, *The Economics of the Developing Countries*, Hutchinson, 1964, pp. 86–87.

[40] Myint, *The Economics of the Developing Countries*, *op. cit.*, pp. 87–90, 161.

housing and equipment are required for those removed from the land. And expanding employment in the industrial sector will also lead to an extra demand for and consumption of food which is a significant social cost in a country with a limited supply of food. Thus, even if total output can be maintained in the agricultural sector after underemployed workers are transferred to the sheltered industrial sector, this transfer process should not be considered as "socially costless."

Even assuming for argument's sake that disguised unemployment does exist, it still does not follow that industrialization through protection is the best solution. The mere existence of surplus manpower cannot be taken to mean that these individuals are either available or qualified to be permanent industrial laborers. We must distinguish between the simple existence of surplus laborers and the process of actually transferring the surplus labor into productive employment as efficient and fully committed industrial workers. This raises all the complex problems of creating and disciplining an industrial labor force.

The most significant effect of surplus labor in agriculture is low productivity, but the basic remedy for this, as Nurkse emphasizes, is capital formation, not industrialization as such.[41] Disguised unemployment constitutes simply an "investible sur-

---

[41] In Nurkse's words, "Some writers argue that since the problem is *agricultural* over-population, the cure is to transfer labor from agriculture to industry. Even though industrialization is a normal consequence of development, this view is in my opinion superficial. The effect of over-population is low productivity, for which capital formation, not industrialization as such, is the basic economic remedy. In what particular fields the capital is applied depends on many things including foreign trade opportunities and domestic income elasticities of demand. Often it is the category of public overhead facilities that claims the biggest share in a poor country's investment program. Often it is here that surplus farm labor can best be used: in building roads, railroads, schools, power plants and irrigation works." Nurkse, "Excess Population and Capital Construction," *Malayan Economic Review*, October, 1957, p. 8.

plus" which can be applied in various investment outlets. The labor need not be transferred from agriculture to industry, but might be better directed to other capital-formation projects—not the least of which might be the construction of rural overhead capital and other capital projects which can help transform the traditional structure of agricultural production.

Instead of resorting to offsetting tariffs, other measures might be more effective in directly stimulating labor mobility. Disguised unemployment cannot be attributed to any deficiency of demand; it is instead due to real causes such as land shortage, capital deficiency, and the lack of skills and organization which would be needed to utilize the underemployed labor in other activities. When occupational mobility is restricted by institutional and cultural barriers, extra-economic measures are required. In general, labor mobility might be better encouraged by public investment in overhead capital, education and training, land tenure reforms, and other policies that remove the social and institutional barriers to mobility.

Moreover, even if the private cost in agriculture is too low because wages are depressed, and in industry the private cost is too high compared with what it would be if the disguised unemployed competed freely in the labor market, the exact opposite may exist in the capital market.[42] It is generally true that rates of interest are considerably higher and capital is more overvalued in the agricultural sectors of poor countries than in the industrial sectors, so that the private return on capital invested in agriculture is less than the social return. The essential question, therefore, is whether manufacturing costs as a whole are overstated

---

[42] Hla Myint, "Infant Industry Arguments for Assistance to Industries in the Setting of Dynamic Trade Theory," R. F. Harrod and D. C. Hague, eds., *International Trade Theory in a Developing World*, Macmillan Co., 1963, p. 178.

relatively to agricultural costs. This depends on the relative capital-labor ratios in the two sectors and the relative sizes of the wage and interest rate differentials between the two sectors. It is then likely that the counterbalancing effects of the higher interest rate in agriculture and the higher capital-labor ratio in industry may more than offset the overvaluation of labor in industry. When due attention is given to capital, it is quite possible that the ratio of social cost to private cost is higher in industry than in agriculture.

Further, the marginal productivity of capital and the capacity to absorb capital may well be greater in agriculture, because of the scarcity of complementary factors which industrial capital would require in order to be successful, especially the shortages of certain raw materials and the lack of managerial ability and labor skills. These scarcities create bottlenecks in industrial production and bring about a sharp decline in the marginal productivity of capital. Capital absorption in industry is also constrained by the need to avoid inflation and balance of payments disequilibrium.

The basic question therefore remains—whether, when all the direct and indirect costs of protection are evaluated, the increase in national product that is expected from the encouragement of industry will constitute a net gain. This decisive issue certainly cannot be resolved by simply claiming that "manufacturing industry represents, in a sense, a higher stage of production," or that "the productivity of manpower in industry tends to be considerably greater than in the traditional agricultural pursuits."[43] This is to beg the question by introducing an irrelevant comparison between the efficient manufacturing of an advanced country and the inefficient agriculture that presently exists in a poor country.

---

[43] Myrdal, *op. cit.*, p. 226.

In itself, primary production cannot be identified as a cause of poverty; the relative concentration on primary production is merely an associative—not causative—characteristic of poverty. The high ratio of agricultural population to total population is a consequence, rather than a cause, of poverty. Where the agricultural population is poor, the nonagricultural population serving the agricultural sector will be small and also poor. Where agriculture is highly productive, the nonfarm population will be large and also prosperous.[44] Thus, since it is the low productivity in agriculture that is significant, it must be demonstrated that protectionist policies to encourage industry, rather than alternative policies to raise agricultural productivity, would result in the allocation of the poor country's scarce resources to their socially most productive use.

9. Even if the foregoing arguments constituted a valid case for aid to industry, the appropriate means for providing such assistance should be through subsidies rather than tariffs. It is true that the free trade case, as derived from the principle of comparative advantage, assumes an equality of the marginal social rate of substitution among goods with the marginal social rates of transformation among them, in both domestic production and foreign trade. In our earlier analysis of comparative costs in Chapter 2, we assumed that the private and social marginal rates of substitution and transformation were equal (as in Fig. 2, for example). If, however, there is a divergence between the private and social rates of substitution or transformation, then exceptions to the free trade conclusion arise. Thus, as we have seen in the

---

[44] Jacob Viner, *International Trade and Economic Development*, The Clarendon Press, 1953, pp. 45–50; Simon Kuznets, *Economic Change*, W. W. Norton, 1953, pp. 222–225.

optimum tariff argument, when world market prices diverge from relative opportunity costs in international trade, an optimum tariff can offset this international distortion and equate the domestic price ratios facing producers and consumers with the marginal rates of transformation between commodities (relative opportunity costs) in international trade. But it is important to recognize that if these divergencies are in domestic production or factor use—instead of in foreign trade—so that domestic prices do not reflect domestic opportunity costs (the marginal rate of transformation in domestic production), the appropriate remedy is a tax or subsidy on domestic production or factor use, rather than a tax or subsidy on international trade.[45] When it is a divergence between domestic price ratios and domestic rates of transformation that is to be corrected, a tariff will itself introduce a new divergence between either the marginal rate of substitution in domestic consumption or the marginal rate of transformation in domestic production and the marginal rate of transformation in foreign trade: the tariff might then possibly result in a net economic loss compared with the free trade situation.[46] An optimum subsidy is then superior to restricted trade.

[45] Bhagwati and Ramaswami, *op. cit.*, pp. 44–50; Johnson, "Tariffs and Economic Development," *op. cit.*, pp. 8–11; Johnson, "Optimal Trade Intervention in the Presence of Domestic Distortions," *op. cit.*, pp. 9–30.

A subsidy might be considered a type of protection because it encourages directly some domestic industries at the expense of others, but unlike the tariff, it does not create a disparity between the home market and foreign prices of the affected commodities.

[46] Given unusually restrictive conditions with respect to elasticities of home demand and supply, a tariff may allow the increase in producers' surplus (or government revenue) to be greater than the loss in consumers' surplus that results from the tariff. Even under these conditions, however, as long as a tariff entails some consumption cost, the tariff is inferior to a subsidy when it is a matter of offsetting a domestic distortion. This is rigorously proved by Bhagwati and Ramaswami, *op. cit.*, pp. 44–47.

Thus, aside from the optimum tariff and capital formation considerations, the foregoing arguments come down to arguments for subsidies as superior to a tariff policy.[47] For the case of an infant industry in which the social rate of return exceeds the private rate of return, or the social rate of discount is less than the private interest cost, the appropriate policy is subsidization of the investment in the learning process of the infant industry. For the case of external economies in manufacturing, the appropriate policy is again a subsidy on the activity giving rise to the externalities, so as to remove the divergence between the higher monetary private cost and the lower real social cost of production in the industry. And similarly, the case of a distortionary wage differential between the agricultural and industrial sectors calls for a subsidy per unit of labor used in industry equal to the difference in unit labor cost prevailing in industry and the true marginal opportunity cost, rather than a tariff protecting the output of the industry.

10. Although the foregoing sections have pointed out a number of theoretical qualifications to the various arguments for protection, the actual consequences of protection in practice are even more indicative of the limitations of protection. In most of the less developed countries, development planning has concentrated on industrialization via import-substitution, and import restrictions have been relied upon to implement such a program. It can be argued, however, that this strategy has been excessively costly and has had deleterious repercussions for resource allocation in the economy as a whole—in direct contrast to the claims

[47] From a world point of view, however, the terms of trade argument is also a "second-best" argument; international lump-sum transfers would be superior.

of the theoretical arguments that protection would bring about a more efficient allocation of development resources.

From the historical record, it is readily apparent that the extensive use of trade controls has been induced more by balance of payments considerations than by the theoretical arguments for protection. The latter may have furnished convenient rationalizations for a restrictive commercial policy, but the real cause has commonly been the pressure on the developing country's balance of payments. As continuing pressure has been exerted on the balance of payments, the developing country has met successive balance of payments crises by imposing quantitative restrictions over a wide range of imports. What has been said of Latin American countries is common to other developing countries: Ad hoc balance of payments measures, temporary to begin with, have become permanent in most cases and more general in their scope, giving rise to a form of protectionism which has been characterized by extemporaneousness, lack of autonomy (since it is primarily motivated by external causes), extremely high levels of indiscriminate application, with the basic objective being import substitution at any cost, regardless of which industries it is most expedient to develop and how far the process should be carried.[48]

In the face of continuing inflationary forces that have placed a premium on all imported goods and have simply induced another ad hoc round of import controls, it has been impossible to sustain an effective and selective protectionist policy, in accordance with the theoretical arguments for protection.[49] As long as inflationary monetary and fiscal policies have been pursued in combination with an unwillingness to devalue, the extensive re-

[48] Santiago Macario, "Protectionism and Industrialization in Latin America," *Economic Bulletin for Latin America*, March 1964, p. 61.

[49] See Myint, "Infant Industry Arguments for Assistance to Industries in the Setting of Dynamic Trade Theory," *op. cit.*, pp. 189–190.

sort to import restrictions has become self-justifying because of the increased incentives to import and the greater difficulties of exporting. In the actual context of inflation, chronic balance of payments difficulties, and fixed exchange rates, the results of protection have been quite different from those to be expected of a rational protectionist policy.

To the extent that tariffs have been embedded among the quantitative restrictions, they have strongly favored the domestic substitution of consumer goods in practically all of the developing countries. In part, this has been due to the easy appeal of restricting most severely "luxury" and "semi-luxury" imports for balance of payments reasons. Even more significantly, the developing countries have employed a differentiated tariff structure: The rates of import duty have been differentiated by stage of production, with low tariff rates on raw materials or partially processed materials, higher rates on semifabricated goods, and still higher rates on the finished product. Higher rates have also been set on consumer goods than capital goods, and on "nonessential" than "essential" consumer goods.

It is most important to realize that this "cascading" or "escalation" of tariff rates by production stages makes the *effective* rate of protection of value added in the production process that produces the final good greater than the *nominal* commodity tariff rate on the finished commodity.[50] A tariff on a finished

---

[50] For a fuller discussion of the theoretical implications of escalation in tariff rates, see C. L. Barber, "Canadian Tariff Policy," *Canadian Journal of Economics and Political Science*, November, 1955, pp. 523–525; Johnson, "Tariffs and Economic Development," *op. cit.*, pp. 19–24; "The Theory of Tariff Structure, With Special Reference to World Trade and Development," H. G. Johnson and P. B. Kenen, *Trade and Development*, Librairie Droz, Geneva, 1956, pp. 9–29.

Johnson offers a proof, in terms of an input-output system, that the effective rate of protection will be higher than the nominal tariff rate if

good is equivalent to a subsidy on its output, and a tariff on an input into the production process is equivalent to a tax on output; the lowering or elimination of tariffs on imported inputs has therefore the same effect as increasing the tariff on the output of the finished good. By maintaining lower tariff rates on inputs (raw materials, intermediate goods, and capital goods) than on finished products, the developing countries have thereby increased the degree of effective protection given to goods at successive stages of the production process: The tariff level as a percentage of value added by the domestic producer has been much greater than the tariff level as a percentage of final price. If, for example, there is an ad valorem duty of 20 percent on a final product, and raw materials and intermediate goods which constitute 50 percent of the value of final output are admitted duty free, then the nominal 20 percent tariff on the final price of the commodity provides an effective degree of protection equal to 40 percent of the value added to the product through domestic manufacture (that is, 20 percent on the 50 percent of value added, since the imported inputs are available to the domestic processor free of duty). To generalize: the greater the ratio of low-duty imported inputs to the value of the high-duty final product, the more the effective level of protection on the fabrication process exceeds the nominal tariff rate on the final fabricated commodity.

Further, while import restrictions have fallen most heavily on consumption imports, and the differential tariffs have favored the domestic fabrication of low-duty imported inputs into the

---

the weighted-average tariff rate on imported inputs is lower than the tariff rate on the output. See also W. M. Corden, "The Tariff," A. Hunter, ed., *The Economics of Australian Industry*, Melbourne Univ. Press, 1963, p. 197 f.; Corden, "The Effective Protective Rate, the Uniform Tariff Equivalent, and the Average Tariff," *Economic Record*, June 1966, pp. 200–218.

high-duty finished consumer goods, the developing country has failed to impose sufficiently strong domestic measures to prevent demand from simply switching from imports to domestic substitutes. The result has been greater pressure of domestic demand on the home output of consumer goods, and the unplanned growth of domestic consumer-goods industries providing the final stages of manufacturing for the products that are subject to quantitative restrictions or high tariffs.

This overencouragement of the domestic manufacture of import substitutes has had a high cost in terms of its waste of resources. In view of the developing country's narrow domestic market, which prevents exploitation of economies of scale in the production of importables, the prevalence of technological inefficiencies, and the monopolistic market structures that are sheltered behind high protection, we may readily understand why the domestic prices of importables have been much higher than foreign prices. The excess cost of protected production, however, has been even greater than that shown by domestic prices being above world market prices: the high level of effective protection given by differential tariffs has allowed the domestic cost of value added in the domestic fabrication process to exceed the foreign cost by substantially more than appears from merely nominal tariff rates on commodities or from the excess of domestic price over the foreign price.

The use of protection to foster industrialization has also failed to absorb much of the underemployed labor. A relatively capital-intensive technology has been used in the import-competing sector—stimulated in part by the differential tariffs and preferential exchange rates that have kept the price of imported capital goods relatively low, and in part by the high tariffs on finished goods that have attracted "tariff factories" which have simply duplicated the capital-intensive techniques of production that are familiar to the advanced foreign enterprise. Despite the growth of the import-replacement sector, the problem of under-employed labor has remained as pressing as ever in the densely populated countries.

Moreover, in most countries, the use of protection to replace imports has not succeeded in realizing a net saving of foreign exchange. For in following a policy of "industrialization from the top downwards," most of the developing countries have concentrated domestic activity on the assembling of imported components and the final stages of manufacture. This has meant that the import content of investment has been very high as imports of intermediate materials and capital goods have increased,[51] and the high import-intensity of the process of import-replacement has even led, in many countries, to imports rising at a faster rate than the growth of national product.

While import-replacement in any one industry is a once-for-all occurrence, there still remains the problem of sustaining the industrialization momentum beyond the point of import-replacement. Even on an industry by industry basis, the future scope for continuing import-substitution has now become extremely limited. Having already replaced the technologically simple consumer manufactures, many of the less developed countries would now have to turn to the replacement of manufactured intermediate inputs and capital goods. But production in these remaining import industries would involve more complex technology, increasingly capital-intensive techniques, and a progressively smaller domestic market in relation to the minimum efficient units of production. Further substitution in this direction would therefore be extremely difficult, and the excessive cost of protection would become progressively higher.

Finally, it is important to realize that protectionist policies

[51] See Alfred Maizels, *Industrial Growth and World Trade*, Cambridge Univ. Press, 1963, pp. 70, 145–161, 174, 266.

have conflicted seriously with the strategic roles that agriculture and exports must have in the development process. Policies that have subsidized importables have necessarily imposed a levy on agriculture and exportables.

From the experience of development programs, it is clear that a poor country cannot afford to neglect its agricultural base. Higher agricultural productivity is necessary to supply food for an expanding urban sector and the growing population; to supply raw materials for domestic industry; to create a "marketable surplus" in the agricultural sector and thereby a demand for non-agricultural commodities; to provide additional foreign exchange earnings; and to contribute to capital formation. And all this cannot be simply a once-for-all accomplishment, but must be cumulative, with a *growing* food surplus, etc., as the industrial sector expands.[52] In short, the rate at which nonagricultural sectors can expand depends, ultimately, on the rate of increase in agricultural supplies, and a country's rate of development must be restrained when its agricultural base is neglected.

The lagging agricultural sector now constitutes a major obstacle to accelerated development in most of the less-developed countries. The average annual rates of growth in the supplies of agricultural materials and foodstuffs have been declining over the past decade, and an agricultural bottleneck has caused disappointments in one development program after another.[53]

That agricultural output has been disappointing at the same time as import substitution policies have been pursued is no mere coincidence. For the attempt to industrialize via import-substitution has had severely restrictive effects on agriculture. Urban ex-

---

[52] Myint, *The Economics of the Developing Countries, op. cit.*, p. 88.

[53] For empirical evidence, see Food and Agriculture Organization, *The State of Food and Agriculture*, 1964; United Nations, *World Economic Survey, 1964, Part I*, New York, 1965, chap. 1, pp. 253–258.

ploitation of agriculture has only too often materialized, and agriculture has been heavily taxed by the complex of policies used to promote import-replacement. Even more inhibiting than the direct taxation of agriculture have been the indirect levies imposed through higher prices of industrial inputs for agriculture, price controls on agricultural products, the neglect of investment in agriculture, and the diversion of resources into the home production of importables.

These repercussions have been adverse not only for agriculture producing for the home market, but also for agriculture producing staple primary products for export. Such exports have been taxed under the guise of terms-of-trade considerations, and a large part of the proceeds from exports obtained through export duties, discriminatory exchange rates, and the activities of the government marketing boards has been diverted to industrial development. The rise in home consumption of foodstuffs, especially in the industrial urban sector, has also limited the export surpluses of foodstuffs. And those countries that export nonfood staples and import foodstuffs have attempted to become more self-sufficient in food by diverting agricultural resources from their traditional exports.

More generally, the wide range of import controls, together with the maintenance of an overvalued exchange rate, have discriminated heavily against the developing countries' exports. While the policy of industrialization through import-substitution has subsidized the imports of intermediate inputs, it has had the effect of taxing exports. The protection of importables has had effects equivalent to a tax on exports: by raising the production costs of exports through an increase in the prices of factors that are used in both the export and import-competing sectors, and by increasing the cost of imported inputs for exports.

At the same time as the home cost of producing exports has

risen, the developing country's unwillingness to adjust its over-valued exchange rate has also kept the foreign price of its exports high, holding back export flows that might otherwise have been achieved. In addition, the highly profitable sheltered market for importables has attracted scarce capital and entrepreneurship away from the export sector. And the limited financial and human resources of the government have also been concentrated on an inward-looking industrialization program, to the neglect of export promotion. Under these conditions, it has been difficult to maintain a competitive position even for export commodities for which world demand has grown, and several of the developing countries have experienced a decline in the proportionate share of the world market for their key export commodities. When its exports have thus lagged, the developing country has had either to retrench on investment for the home market or impose ever-tighter restrictions on imports.

Instead of realizing, however, that their import-substitution policies have reacted to the detriment of agriculture and exports, many of the poor countries have been prone to interpret the slow growth in export proceeds and in agricultural output as evidence that it is impossible to base their development on agriculture and exports. Instead of concentrating on efforts to raise agricultural productivity and promote exports, development plans have merely intensified their import-substitution policies, thereby further preventing an improvement in the performance of agriculture and exports. It is this self-justifying character of protectionist and import-substitution policies that has made it so difficult to shift the emphasis of development planning away from import replacement to the improvement of agriculture and exports. With progressive import-substitution, however, the implicit taxation of agriculture and exports has increased, and the waste of resources through the real excess costs of import substitution has increased over time. Indeed, it can be submitted that the costs of protection and the adverse effects of progressive import-substitution have actually cancelled out a large part or all of the gains in productivity that should have by now accrued through development plans.[54]

11. So far, our discussion has been concerned with only nationalist commercial policy. In a setting of regional systems of trade, however, the developmental effects of commercial policy may be more substantial. From the theory of economic integration, it may be argued that the establishment of a customs union could play a vital role in promoting a region's development.

When tariffs are removed among members of a customs union,[55] while an external tariff is retained, the development of the members might be accelerated in the following ways: (1) by increasing the gains from trade, (2) by promoting technical efficiency in existing industries, (3) by stimulating the creation of

[54] See Johnson, "The Theory of Tariff Structure, With Special Reference to World Trade and Development," *op. cit.,* pp. 28–29; Macario, *op. cit.,* pp. 78–83.

It is noteworthy that when a country is industrializing by means of protectionist and import-substitution policies, it is even possible that technical progress in the import-substitute industry, or accumulation of the factor used intensively in that industry, will actually reduce the country's real income, over a range of change set by the degree of protection. The increased waste of resources through the excess cost of protected production may more than absorb the increase in potential output per head. This has been demonstrated by Harry G. Johnson, "The Possibility of Income Losses from Increased Efficiency or Factor Accumulation in the Presence of Tariffs," *Economic Journal,* March, 1967, pp. 151–154.

[55] We are concerned here with the complete removal of tariffs on intraregional trade. The alternative of a preferential tariff association involving only a partial reduction of tariffs among regional trading partners is considered in Chapter 9, section 9–10.

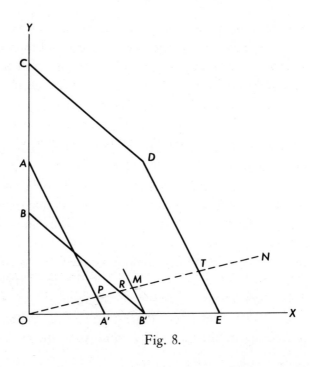

Fig. 8.

new industries, and (4) by improving the region's terms of trade.

The analytical framework for this reasoning can be summarized diagrammatically.[56] Consider two countries, A and B, each capable of producing two commodities, X and Y. Assume a linear production possibility curve for each country as depicted in Fig. 8, where AA' represents the maximum possible combinations of X and Y that can be produced in A, with its given factor supply and given techniques of production, and BB' represents the maximum possible production combinations of X and Y in B, with its given resources and techniques. Together with its production possibilities, let each country's demand conditions deter-

[56] H. Makower and G. Morton, "A Contribution Towards a Theory of Customs Unions," *Economic Journal*, March, 1953, pp. 44–45.

mine its consumption point in isolation as P in A, and R in B. For simplicity, P and R lie on a straight line through the origin, indicating that the consumption pattern is the same in A and B.

a. If A and B now form a customs union the total consumption amounts of X and Y for the two units acting as a single producing area will be greater than the sum of the consumption amounts when A and B acted in isolation. This can be readily seen by aggregating the production possibilities AA' and BB', giving CDE in Fig. 8 ($AC = OB$, $B'E = OA'$). The coordinates of the customs union's consumption point T are greater than the sum of the coordinates of P and R.[57] Thus, when the commodity substitution rates differ in A and B, and there is not complete specialization in isolation, it is possible to gain from acting as a single producing area and having intraregional trade: within the customs union there can be more efficient production and hence a higher real income than would be possible if each country remained isolated.

b. This gain may be even greater than that depicted if each country had previously failed to achieve in isolation an optimal allocation of its resources or full employment, but is able to do so through formation of the union. Malallocation or unemployment of resources in A would mean that production and consumption were not at P on the production possibility curve, but to the left of P along OP (assuming the same consumption pattern); similarly, the production and consumption point in B would be not at R but to the left of R along OR. To the extent

[57] Proof: Draw $B'M$ parallel to $A'P$, intersecting ON at M.

$$OA' = B'E \text{ (by construction)}.$$
$$OP = MT.$$

Total consumption after union $= OT$. Pre-union consumption $= OR + MT$. Therefore, post-union consumption is greater than pre-union consumption by the amount RM.

that the consumption points in isolation are to the left of P and R, the coordinates of the union's consumption point T would be *pro tanto* superior. If the union creates more internal competition so that marginal firms are forced to improve their methods of production, and resources are reallocated from less efficient to more efficient firms, then economic integration will improve the technical efficiency of existing industries.

c. If now, in addition, the union imposes a protective tariff on imports from nonunion countries, then new import-competing industries might be created within the union. If the stimulation of the new industry is not at the expense of a previously existing industry, but comes from an increase in domestic saving or new foreign investment, it will mean an outward shift in the production possibility curve. Thus, if Y is B's import commodity, and a new industry producing Y is established in B, the production possibility curve of B will shift out along the Y axis.

d. Finally, the outside tariff might be used to improve the region's commodity terms of trade. Acting in combination, A and B will have stronger bargaining power than if they acted as separate tariff areas, and the region may be able to use this power to raise its own duties on trade with the outside world or to induce outsiders to reduce their duties on their trade with the area. This bargaining power will be more effective in improving the terms of trade the more elastic is the region's reciprocal demand for outside products, and the less elastic is the reciprocal demand of the outside world for the region's exports. The formation of a customs union might also turn the terms of trade in favor of the union if the intraunion trade is sufficiently large and of such a composition that it reduces the demand within the union for outside imports or reduces the outside supply of the union's exports.

Although the foregoing considerations indicate that the

establishment of a customs union might raise the level of development of the region, these theoretical possibilities may not be so significant in practice. Regarding the first possibility of an improved international division of labor, we must note that, unlike the initial situation assumed for Fig. 8, the pre-union situation of prospective members is not one of isolation but, on the contrary, involves high dependence on foreign trade. The formation of a customs union will therefore not only create trade among the members but may also cause some of the existing trade between the members and nonmembers to be replaced by trade within the union. When the liberalization of regional trade has this "trade-diverting effect,"[58] the international division of labor will be worsened to the extent that the outside source of supply is actually a low-cost source and its product becomes higher priced within the union because of the outside duty. The consequence is an uneconomic diversion of output from the low-cost outside source to the high-cost source within the union. World output is reduced, and real income is lowered.[59]

In contrast, if in facilitating trade among members, the union

[58] Jacob Viner, *The Customs Union Issue*, Carnegie Endowment for International Peace, 1950, pp. 48–52; James E. Meade, *The Theory of Customs Unions*, North-Holland Pub. Co., 1955, chap. II.

[59] Following Viner, this conclusion ignores the effect of expanded consumption of previously taxed importables and assumes that consumption within the union is unaffected by changes in relative prices brought about by the union. Even though the production effect may be trade-diverting, the consumption effect may be trade-creating (greater quantities of commodities produced in other member countries are substituted for domestic goods because they become cheaper in the home market of each member country). See R. G. Lipsey, "The Theory of Customs Unions: Trade Diversion and Welfare," *Economica*, February, 1957, pp. 40–46; Johnson, *Money, Trade and Economic Growth*, *op. cit.*, chap. 3; C. A. Cooper and B. F. Massell, "A New Look at Customs Union Theory," *Economic Journal*, December, 1965, pp. 742–747.

replaces high-cost domestic production by low-cost production from another member, then the effect is one of "trade creation." This constitutes an economic shift of resources into more efficient production.

The expansion of trade within the union, therefore, will not necessarily increase the gains from trade—unless the expanded regional trade is from trade creation. Whether trade creation or trade diversion is likely to dominate depends on the pre-union level of tariff rates among the members, the level of post-union external tariffs compared with the pre-union tariff level, the elasticities of demand for the imports on which duties are reduced, and the elasticities of supply of exports from the members and foreign sources. Trade creation is more likely to result under the following conditions: the higher are each member's pre-union duties on the others' products; the more the members are initially similar in the products they produce but different in the pattern of relative prices at which they produce them; the lower is the "average" tariff level on outside imports as compared with the pre-union tariff level; and the less competitive are the products of the members with outside imports. Further, the sort of countries likely to gain more through forming a customs union are those doing a high proportion of their foreign trade with their union partners, and making a high proportion of their total expenditure on domestic trade.[60] Such considerations would indicate that when a customs union is composed of a small number

[60] When the union is formed, the tariff is taken off imports from the country's union partner, and the relative price between these imports and domestic goods is brought into conformity with the real rates of transformation. This tends to raise real income. On the other hand, the relative price between imports from the union partner and imports from the outside world are moved away from equality with real rates of transformation. This tends to reduce real income. Therefore, given a country's volume of international trade, a customs union is on balance more likely to raise real income the higher is the proportion of trade with the coun-

of poor countries the possible gains from new trade are likely to be less than they would be in a union composed of "sizeable countries which practice substantial protection of substantially similar industries."[61]

The second possible contribution of a customs union to development—an increase in the productive efficiency of existing industries—may have considerable appeal through the prospect of realizing economies of scale in the wider regional market. This is certainly a major argument, but it does assume that the optimum-sized plants are necessarily of a large size, and that the extent of the individual member's market is too small to sustain the large size plant. In many industries, however, technical economies can be exhausted by firms of only moderate size, and even relatively small and poor countries can have a number of firms of the minimum efficient size.[62] This is especially true for light industry in which fixed investment is only a small part of total

---

try's union partner and the lower the proportion with the outside world. Further, the union is more likely to raise real income the lower is the total volume of foreign trade; for the lower is foreign trade, the lower must be purchases from the outside countries relative to purchases of domestic commodities. R. G. Lipsey, "The Theory of Customs Unions: A General Survey," *Economic Journal*, September, 1960, pp. 507–509.

[61] Viner, *The Customs Union Issue, op. cit.*, p. 135.

[62] But see Balassa, *op. cit.*, pp. 76–82, 87–107; T. Scitovsky, "Economies of Scale, Competition and European Integration," *American Economic Review*, March, 1956, pp. 71 ff. Scitovsky points out that an economy that is large enough to provide adequate domestic market outlets for the output of at least one optimum-sized plant in all industries producing final goods may still be sub-optimal if some of these plants need equipment, servicing, or other intermediate products, but provide too small a market outlet for some of these. The fact of industrial interdependence therefore makes the scale of output necessary for the full exploitation of economies of scale very much larger than might appear at first thought.

An analysis of the relationships between size of markets, scale of firms and efficiency is also provided in E. A. G. Robinson, ed., *Economic Consequences of Size of Nations*, St. Martin's Press, 1960, Part VI.

costs. Moreover, an individual member's market is not likely to be extended very much to the wider area of the union unless there is in the pre-union situation a high degree of rivalry for protected industries. There is also the complication that, regardless of the size of the consumer market, if the supply of productive factors is limited, then an industry that is expanding its output will encounter increasing unit costs as the price for its intensive factor rises. Unless the customs union results in a substantial increase in factor mobility among the members, it will not increase the "scale" of the "national" economy from the standpoint of production conditions, even if it does extend it in terms of the size of the protected market for sales.[63]

Finally, it should be realized that there may be more scope for a reduction in an industry's unit-costs, even without a customs union, through a closer approach to the least-cost combination of factors, and hence a downward shift in the entire cost curve, rather than in a movement along a falling cost curve as output expands. The essential point is that the presently low labor productivity results from other conditions besides a small scale of output—namely, inefficient entrepreneurship, unskilled labor, and lack of capital. A better combination of existing factors, an improvement in the quality of existing factors, and the introduction of cost-reducing innovations may all offer more of an increase in productivity than would result from the production of a larger output for a wider market.

The third possibility—the creation of new industries—may provide the largest potential source of gain from a customs union. In its early stages, the union may have more of an effect through the inducement of direct foreign investment to get behind the tariff wall than by a marked expansion in already established industries or the development of industrial products for export.

---

[63] Viner, *The Customs Union Issue, op. cit.,* p. 47.

If, however, the union should subsequently entail ever greater economic integration and coordination of economic, financial, and social policy, then sheltered and export industries might also be more readily created. A regional market might also provide the initial step towards industrial exports to nonmember countries by making production within the regional market more economical. Most importantly, common institutional arrangements within the union may facilitate a regional development program which avoids the wastes of "watertight" compartments of industrialization and the uneconomic multiplication of new industries which otherwise result from independent industrialization programming by each country.

The last possibility—an improvement in the region's commodity terms of trade—rests on the presumption that the demand by members of the union for imports from outside countries will be reduced, or that the supply of exports from the union will be reduced, or that the bargaining power of the members will be increased. But this depends on whether the poor countries, even within a customs union, could exercise sufficient monopolistic or monopsonistic power to influence their terms of trade by raising duties on their trade with the outside world, or by inducing outside suppliers to supply their goods more cheaply. Unless the members of the union are the chief suppliers on the world market or constitute a large part of the world market for their imports, the effects on the terms of trade will be negligible.[64]

While the theory of economic integration has been limited mainly to analyzing static efficiency conditions, the prospect of realizing dynamic gains through new investment and a change in the pattern of investment is of greater significance for a union

[64] If instead of assuming constant costs, as Viner does, we allow for increasing costs, then trade diversion might turn the terms of trade against the outside country. This improvement in the terms of trade of the member countries will reduce the loss borne by the members due to trade diversion.

among developing countries. Where the objective is accelerated development for the members of the region, the dynamic gains over the longer run may prove more important than the short-period welfare gains through a reallocation of a given amount of resources. The case for a customs union rests ultimately on a belief that these dynamic gains will be realized and will more than offset any possible welfare loss through trade diversion. The case is also strengthened when a customs union is compared with the existing system of trade restrictions among less developed countries—which is the immediately relevant comparison—rather than with the nonexistent situation of universal free trade. Insofar as regional import-substitution involves less loss than national import-substitution policies,[65] and avoids the excessive costs of compartmentalized industrialization in every country, a customs union would be superior to an intensification of national restrictive policies.

The argument that integration can bring about a more rational location of industry implies, of course, that industrial production will expand in a member country that has an intraunion comparative advantage in those industries, while another member country will have to suffer a contraction in its industrial sector. The member countries are certainly unlikely to benefit equally, and some will be only too prone to believe that other members are gaining at their expense.[66] When manufacturing in-

---

[65] The argument that economic integration may enable member countries to protect a given amount of industry at a lower real cost in terms of income foregone is systematically presented by C. A. Cooper and B. F. Massell, "Toward a General Theory of Customs Unions for Developing Countries," *Journal of Political Economy*, October, 1965, pp. 461–476; also, Balassa, *op. cit.*, p. 83.

[66] Sir Roy Harrod has remarked that "A regional free-trade area might increase inequality inside the region; . . . It should not, however, be assumed that an increase of inequality is necessarily bad, provided that the

dustry becomes highly localized within one country in the union, other members are likely to revert to the old argument and contend that if they too had been able to adopt tariff protection against their partners, they would also have been able to attract industry. A nonindustrialized member country may further complain that in buying from an industrialized partner, instead of importing from the outside, it is losing revenue equal to the duty on outside manufactures. And, with a common external tariff, member countries no longer have the discretionary power to use variations in the tariff for the purpose of adjusting their national revenues to their own requirements. The internal strains that arise from uneven development among the member countries may make it extremely difficult to preserve the union. Some of the inequalities can be mitigated through a system of public finance transfers among members, a regional development bank, encouragement of free factor movements, regional policies for the location of industry, the pooling of overhead costs of public serv-

---

least favored become just a little better off; an increase in inequality may be justified if it is the best way of getting quick progress in the region as a whole." Harrod, in a review of Sidney Dell, *Trade Blocs and Common Markets*, Knopf, 1963, published in *Economic Journal*, December, 1963, p. 708.

A typical reaction to such a view as Harrod's is that of Miguel S. Wionczek, who quotes Harrod and then maintains that "If, as appears to be the case, the integration program founded exclusively on the freeing of trade and on the laissez faire policy within the union cannot ensure reciprocity of union benefits for all participants, such a program is doomed to failure. Extremely underdeveloped countries have had such regrettable experiences in their relations with the rest of the world, based on the false principle of equality, that it would be vain to try to induce them to enter into new agreements, this time regional ones, in which they would run the risk that inequality within the area would become even more pronounced." Wionczek, *Latin American Economic Integration*, Praeger, 1966, pp. 9–10.

ices, or coordination of development policies. But all this requires a union sufficiently strong to pursue these measures and
distribute the gains more evenly.

Thus, while there are potential benefits to be derived from a
customs union, especially the dynamic gains over the longer run,
the immediate benefits should not be overestimated. And, aside
from the political and administrative difficulties, due attention
must be given to the possible undesirable economic consequences,
particularly if the union becomes highly sheltered and inward-
looking. If a union is to be effective, it must be a strong one—
and most proposals for regional integration among the less developed countries have not yet shown this promise of sufficient
cohesion.

12. The general conclusion that emerges from the foregoing
discussion is that the power of commercial policy to accelerate
the development of poor countries is likely to be exaggerated. The
specific arguments for protection must be highly qualified, their
costs not underestimated, and the advantages of alternative policies not ignored. We have emphasized especially the inappropriateness of tariffs to remove domestic distortions in commodity
or factor markets. Above all, we have noted the excessive cost of
protection in practice, the debilitating effects on exports and agriculture, and the presently severe limitations of attempting to
industrialize through import-substitution. Some of the objectives
sought by a positive commercial policy may be better realized in
the context of a customs union, but the practical effects are still
unlikely to be as influential as the proponents of a customs union
claim.

Of far greater importance to a poor country than the control
of its foreign trade is the fundamental problem of how to achieve
a more extensive "carry-over" from its export sector to other

sectors of the domestic economy. Most poor countries have been able to attain a secular increase in their exports, but this has not succeeded in transmitting development. Unlike the situation in some other countries, the growth in the export sector of a poor country has not propelled the rest of the economy forwards. Instead of limiting our attention to the narrow issue of commercial policy, we should now proceed to examine the broader problem of whether, and by what means, development might yet emerge from trade.

8

Development Through Trade

---

1. Dominating all the issues discussed in the preceding chapters is the ultimate question of whether there is a conflict between the gains from trade and the gains from growth. Can foreign trade have a propulsive role in the development of a country? Or, on the contrary, are the dictates of international trade incompatible with the requirements for accelerated development? To the extent that classical and neoclassical economists offered a judgment on this problem, they held that foreign trade could make an impressive contribution to a country's development. Trade was considered to be not simply a device for achieving productive efficiency; it was also an "engine of growth."[1]

There have, however, always been dissenters from this op-

---

[1] D. H. Robertson, "The Future of International Trade," reprinted in American Economic Association, *Readings in the Theory of International Trade*, Blakiston Co., 1949, p. 501.

timistic view—as varied as List, Lenin, and Manoilesco. With the present concern for poor countries, the critics are now more numerous, and their arguments are far more challenging.[2] At the theoretical level it is frequently contended that the conclusions from the static equilibrium analysis of traditional trade theory are irrelevant for interpreting the problems of development which are inherently dynamic. And in the historical context, it is argued that international trade has actually operated as a mechanism of international inequality—widening the gap in the levels of living between rich and poor countries. The policy implications of these theoretical and historical arguments are that, even if there is some cost in sacrificing the gains from international specialization, the poor countries will still realize a net gain by way of inducing a higher rate of development if they follow policies of import replacement and deliberate industrialization. It is maintained that, instead of waiting for the transmission of development through trade, the poor countries would be better off if they directed their own development towards an expansion of output for their domestic markets. Just as the theory of the "big push" for a domestic economy minimizes the importance of fulfilling marginal conditions in favor of achieving a series of big discontinuous "jumps,"[3] so too is it claimed, in terms of the

[2] There are, of course, differences of emphasis in the various arguments. See H. W. Singer, "The Distribution of Gains between Investing and Borrowing Countries," *American Economic Review, Papers and Proceedings*, May, 1950, pp. 473–485; United Nations, Economic Commission for Latin America, *The Economic Development of Latin America and Its Problems*, New York, 1950, *passim*; Gunnar Myrdal, *Rich Lands and Poor*, Harper & Row, 1957, *passim*.

[3] P. N. Rosenstein-Rodan, "Notes on the Theory of the 'Big Push,'" H. S. Ellis, ed., *Economic Development for Latin America*, St. Martin's Press, 1961, pp. 57–73; Benjamin Higgins, *Economic Development*, W. W. Norton, 1959, pp. 384–396.

international economy, that the gains from trade are of only secondary significance compared with the achievement of the gains from growth.

Neither the traditional case for development through trade nor the rival interpretation, however, has been presented in a systematic manner. In this chapter we shall therefore sort out the basic arguments and attempt to clarify the fundamental issues of disagreement. We shall first restate the classical position, appraise the opposing view that international trade has inhibited the development of poor countries, and then suggest alternative reasons why—in spite of their expansion in exports and increased capacity to import—the poor countries have not been able to realize a more significant "carry-over" from external trade to internal development.

2. The problem of the gains from trade versus the gains from growth can be stated as follows: When a country specializes according to its comparative advantage and trades at the international exchange ratio, it gains an increase in real income. As noted in Chapter 2, this gain is tantamount to an outward shift in the country's production frontier, even if the economy operates under the constraints of fixed amounts of resources and unchanged techniques of production. By increasing its income, the country would also increase the domestic resources potentially available for capital formation. But there still remains the question of whether some other pattern of resource allocation, different from that governed by comparative advantage, might not lead to an even greater outward shift in the production frontier over time. Although the resource allocation associated with trade might conform to requirements for production efficiency in a single period, it is possible that another initial allocation would conform more closely to the multiperiod, not merely single-period, requirements for production efficiency. In other words, there may be a domestic misallocation of resources, from the standpoint of maximizing output over time, even though there is optimal allocation from the standpoint of achieving the gains from trade in each single period.[4]

Such a possible conflict between the gains from trade and the gains from growth was not envisaged in traditional trade theory. Although the dynamic aspects of trade were not central in classical and neoclassical thought, there was nonetheless some recognition, particularly in classical theory, of the dynamic and growth-transmitting aspect of trade above and beyond the static gains from international specialization.[5] In this interpretation, the gains from trade were entirely consistent with the gains from growth; indeed, the latter could be expected to increase *pari passu* with the extension of foreign trade.

John Stuart Mill was exceptionally clear on this. Trade, according to comparative advantage, results in a "more efficient employment of the productive forces of the world," and this may

---

[4] This argument simply extends to an open economy the analogous problem of defining an efficient program of capital accumulation for a closed economy. It has been demonstrated that perpetual one-period efficiency can be inefficient over longer periods. The multiperiod requirements for achieving the maximum production frontier in a closed economy are discussed in R. Dorfman, P. A. Samuelson, R. M. Solow, *Linear Programming and Economic Analysis*, McGraw-Hill, 1958, chap. 12.

[5] Several references of this nature can be cited: in particular, David Ricardo, *Principles of Political Economy and Taxation*, London, 1817, chap. VII; J. S. Mill, *Principles of Political Economy*, London, 1848, Book I, chap. X, sec. 1; Book III, chap. XVII, sec. 5; Book IV, chap. II, sec. 1; Alfred Marshall, "Memorandum on the Fiscal Policy of International Trade," *Official Papers*, The Macmillan Co., 1926; Marshall, *Money, Credit, and Commerce*, The Macmillan Co., 1923, appendix J, sec. 8, 10; F. W. Taussig, *Some Aspects of the Tariff Question*, Harvard Univ. Press, 1915, chap. III.

be considered the "direct economical advantage of foreign trade. But," emphasizes Mill, "there are, besides, indirect effects, which must be counted as benefits of a high order." One of the most significant "indirect" dynamic benefits, according to Mill, is "the tendency of every extension of the market to improve the processes of production. A country which produces for a larger market than its own, can introduce a more extended division of labour, can make greater use of machinery, and is more likely to make inventions and improvements in the processes of production." Another important consideration, "principally applicable to an early stage of industrial advancement," is that "a people may be in a quiescent, indolent, uncultivated state, with all their tastes either fully satisfied or entirely undeveloped, and they may fail to put forth the whole of their productive energies for want of any sufficient object of desire. The opening of a foreign trade, by making them acquainted with new objects, or tempting them by the easier acquisition of things which they had not previously thought attainable, sometimes works a sort of industrial revolution in a country whose resources were previously undeveloped for want of energy and ambition in the people: inducing those who were satisfied with scanty comforts and little work, to work harder for the gratification of their new tastes, and even to save, and accumulate capital, for the still more complete satisfaction of those tastes at a future time."[6]

Mill also showed his awareness of the special conditions in poor countries by observing that trade benefits the less developed country through "the introduction of foreign arts, which raise the returns derivable from additional capital to a rate corresponding to the low strength of the desire of accumulation; and the importation of foreign capital which renders the increase of pro-

[6] Mill, *op. cit.*, Vol. II, Book III, chap. XVII, sec. 5.

duction no longer exclusively dependent on the thrift or providence of the inhabitants themselves, while it places before them a stimulating example, and by instilling new ideas and breaking the chain of habit, if not by improving the actual condition of the population, tends to create in them new wants, increased ambition, and greater thought for the future."[7]

Considering the classical economists more generally, Hla Myint has distinguished three different theories of international trade in classical thought: the "vent-for-surplus" theory, the static comparative costs theory, and a dynamic "productivity" theory.[8] The "productivity" theory links development to international trade by interpreting trade as a dynamic force which, by widening the extent of the market and the scope of the division of labor, permits a greater use of machinery, stimulates innovations, overcomes technical indivisibilities, raises the productivity of labor, and generally enables the trading country to enjoy increasing returns and economic development.[9] These gains correspond to Mill's "indirect effects, which must be counted as benefits of a high order."

[7] Mill *op. cit.*, Vol. I, Book I, chap. XIII, sec. 1.

[8] Hla Myint, "The 'Classical Theory' of International Trade and the Underdeveloped Countries," *Economic Journal*, June, 1958, pp. 317–337. The emphasis on the "vent-for-surplus" theory may be overdone, for as Professor Haberler has observed, the vent-for-surplus (if it is not part and parcel of the productivity theory) may be interpreted as simply an extreme case of differences in comparative costs—a country exporting commodities for which it has no domestic use. If, however, this extreme situation exists, it does make trade appear doubly productive and desirable. Gottfried Haberler, *International Trade and Economic Development*, National Bank of Egypt, 1959, p. 9, n. 1. Cf. R. E. Caves, "'Vent for Surplus' Models of Trade and Growth," R. E. Caves, H. G. Johnson, P. B. Kenen, eds., *Trade, Growth, and the Balance of Payments: Essays in Honor of Gottfried Haberler*, Rand McNally, 1965, pp. 95–115.

[9] Myint, *op. cit.*, pp. 318–319.

This conception of the impact of trade emphasizes the supply side of the development process—the opportunity that trade gives a poor country to remove domestic shortages and to overcome the diseconomies of the small size of its domestic market. Of major benefit is the opportunity that trade offers for the exchange of goods with less growth potential for goods with more growth potential, thereby quickening the progress that results from a given effort on the savings side.[10] An obvious example is the opportunity to import capital goods and materials required for development purposes. Perhaps of even more value than the direct importation of material goods is the fundamental "educative effect" of trade. A deficiency of knowledge is a more pervasive handicap to development than is the scarcity of any other factor. Contact with more advanced economies provides an expeditious way of overcoming this deficiency. The importation of technical know-how and skills is an indispensable source of technological progress, and the importation of ideas in general is a potent stimulus to development. Not only is this vital for economic change in itself, but also for political and socio-cultural advances which may be the necessary preconditions of economic progress. By providing the opportunity to learn from the achievements and failures of the more advanced countries, and by facilitating selective borrowing and adaptation, foreign trade can help considerably in speeding up a poor country's development. As Mill emphasized, "It is hardly possible to overrate the value in the present low state of human improvement, of placing human beings in contact with persons dissimilar to themselves, and with modes of thought and action unlike those with which they are familiar . . . Such communication has always been and is

---

[10] J. R. Hicks, *Essays in World Economics*, Oxford Univ. Press, 1959, p. 132.

peculiarly in the present age, one of the primary sources of progress."[11]

Classical economists also noted the effects of trade on the domestic factor supply, especially on capital accumulation. The capacity to save increases as real income rises through the more efficient resource allocation associated with international trade. And the stimulus to investment is strengthened by the realization of increasing returns in the wider markets that overseas trade provides. Further, by allowing economies of large-scale production, the access to foreign markets makes it profitable to adopt more advanced techniques of production which require more capital; the opportunities for the productive investment of capital are then greater than they would be if the market were limited only to the small size of the home market.[12]

For these several reasons, the traditional conclusion has been that international trade stimulates a country's development. Above and beyond the static gains that result from the more efficient resource allocation with given production functions, international trade also transforms existing production functions and induces outward shifts in the production frontier. The dynamic benefits of trade can be summarized as meaning, in analytical terms, that a movement along the production frontier in accordance with the pre-existing comparative cost situation will tend to push the production frontier upwards and outwards.[13]

[11] Mill, *op. cit.*, Vol. II, Book III, chap. XVII, sec. 5.

[12] Hicks, *op. cit.*, pp. 183–185.

[13] Haberler, *op. cit.*, p. 14. Haberler emphasizes in particular four ways in which trade bestows dynamic benefits upon a developing country: the provision of the material means of development in the form of capital goods, machinery and raw and semifinished materials; access to technological knowledge, skills, managerial talents and entrepreneurship; the receipt of capital through international investment; and the stimulating influence of competition (pp. 10–15).

Thus, when they are properly interpreted in their dynamic sense, the gains from trade do not result merely from a once-over change in resource allocation, but are continually merging with the gains from growth. And if trade increases the capacity for development, then the larger the volume of trade the greater should be the potential for development.

3. The foregoing analysis, however, indicates only what could be or what ought to be—not necessarily what has been or is. Indeed, the historical experience of numerous poor countries reveals considerable growth in their foreign trade, but only a slow rate of domestic development. In contrast with what would be expected from classical analysis, the practical question therefore now arises why external trade has induced comparatively little internal development in poor countries.

True, the optimism of the classicists has been vindicated in many cases: International trade did have a propulsive role in the development of a number of countries that are now among the richest in the world. In the case of Britain, development was fostered by the export trade in woolen manufacture and cotton textiles; for Sweden, it was the timber trade; for Denmark, dairy produce; Canada, wheat; Australia, wheat and wool; Switzerland, lace-making and clock-making; Japan, silk. In many historical cases of successful development the importance of international trade is clearly confirmed—and not only for countries that exported industrial products, but also for primary product exporters. At the same time, however, that some countries which were poor a century ago have developed through foreign trade, other countries have still remained poor until the present day, notwithstanding an expansion in their foreign trade.

It is apparent that after a poor country became part of the international economy, its production did increase, but mainly in the direction of production for export. For the poor countries, international trade has frequently been much cheaper and easier than internal trade, and their devotion to international specialization has often been much easier and earlier than specialization among regions within their own countries.[14] A marked secular expansion in exports from the poor countries has consequently been the outstanding result of their integration into world markets. As they entered the international economy, their production for export grew, frequently at an increasing rate and generally at a rate greater than population growth. The variety of exports also became more extensive as more revenue crops were produced and new commodities were established.

On the demand side, this expansion in exports of foodstuffs and raw materials was induced by the growth of richer countries. Their demand for imports of primary products increased as their industrial output rose, their population increased, real income grew, and consumption standards changed. While their demand for primary products rose, the richer countries followed their own comparative advantages in industry and allowed the specialization in primary production to occur overseas.

On the supply side, the movement of resources within the country and the increase in factor supplies also raised the output of exports. External contacts caused a shift of the resources of land and labor away from subsistence production into the production of revenue crops for exchange. In part, there may initially have been some compulsion to earn cash income when the government imposed direct taxes. The movement in this direction persisted, however, because of the desire to improve standards of living and to consume commodities which the subsistence sec-

[14] K. E. Berrill, "International Trade and the Rate of Economic Growth," *Economic History Review*, April, 1960, p. 352.

tor did not produce. As the imports of manufactured goods increased, another tendency, although of less significance, was the displacement of handicraft workers, and their movement into the export sector. The internal movement of resources has thus been directed towards export production.

Over the longer run, the main contribution to an expansion of exports has come from an increase in factor supplies and technological progress. Owing to the transference of public health measures from the rich countries, the death rate has fallen, and in the absence of a commensurate fall in the birth rate, the population and labor force have grown rapidly. The increasing demand for primary products has also pushed out the extensive margin of land cultivation. For some of these products, it has been relatively easy to duplicate simple techniques of production in the extension of cultivation. For other products, an inflow of capital has come from overseas and has concentrated directly on the development of primary products for export, or else has gone into public overhead capital to facilitate the expansion of exports. Productivity also increased when the direct foreign investment brought with it foreign enterprises that operated under efficient management and with advanced production techniques. To provide an adequate supply of plantation or estate labor, a considerable immigration of labor also occurred in some countries.

These changes in factor supplies may be summarized as having been export-biased. For most poor countries, we may also infer that, because of the nature of their export products, the income elasticity of demand for imports has been greater than for their exportables, and the income effect has been export-biased. Thus, the effects on the production side and consumption side have been on balance export-biased. Even for those cases in which, on the consumption side, the effect may have been import-biased, the net effect is still likely to have been export-biased, insofar as the export-bias in production has probably been sufficiently greater than the import-bias in consumption. Expansion in production has been proportionately greater in the direction of exportables, and this has not been neutralized or reversed on the consumption side.

Nonetheless, despite this increase in exports, the development process has not caught hold in many poor countries. We return to the fundamental question—why has this growth in the export sector not carried over to other sectors and propelled the rest of the economy forwards?

4. Critics of the traditional view that trade will transmit development answer this question at two levels—first, by denying the relevance of the conclusions of traditional trade theory, and, secondly, by contending that historically the very forces of international trade have impeded the development of poor countries.

As for the criticisms at the theoretical level, we have already attempted in Chapter 2 to counter the claim that the comparative cost doctrine is irrelevant for problems of economic change. We have seen that it is a relatively simple exercise to incorporate different types of factor growth, technological progress, and changes in the structure of demand into the classical theory of comparative advantage. Although we have done this with the method of comparative statics, short of an explicitly full dynamic theory, this has still carried us a considerable way in interpreting changes in the comparative cost structure. By no means must the conclusions derived from the theory of comparative advantage be limited to a "cross-section" view and a given once-for-all set of conditions; the comparative cost doctrine still has validity among countries undergoing differential rates of development.

Another criticism is directed against the "factor-price equalization theorem" derived from neoclassical theory. This theorem states that, under certain conditions, free international trade is a perfect substitute for complete international mobility of factors and is sufficient to equalize, in the trading countries, not only the prices of products, but also the prices of factors.[15] Against this proposition, however, it is argued that in reality the international distribution of income has become more unequal. And some, like Myrdal, would contrapose against the factor-price equalization theorem a theory of "cumulative causation" or a "cumulative process away from equilibrium in factor proportions and factor prices, engendered by international trade."[16]

This criticism is, however, highly overdrawn. Proponents of classical theory have never claimed that international trade will actually equalize real wages or real per capita income levels among the trading countries. Far short of this, the contention of classical theory is simply that the real income of each country will be higher with trade than without trade.

Even if the criticism is levelled at only the special factor-price equalization theorem, it is still excessive. For it attributes much more importance to the theorem than did its expositors, who recognized its highly restrictive assumptions and hence never maintained that equalization will actually hold or that the theorem is a valid empirical generalization.[17]

The expositors of the factor-price equalization theorem were

[15] P. A. Samuelson, "International Trade and the Equalization of Factor Prices," *Economic Journal*, June, 1948, pp. 163–184.

[16] Gunnar Myrdal, *An International Economy*, Harper & Row, 1956, p. 225; Myrdal, *Rich Lands and Poor, op. cit.*, chap. 11.

[17] P. A. Samuelson, "International Factor-Price Equalization Once Again," *Economic Journal*, June, 1949, p. 182; James E. Meade, *Trade and Welfare*, Oxford Univ. Press, 1955, pp. 332–333. For a review of various statements of the theorem, together with many bibliographical references, see Richard E. Caves, *Trade and Economic Structure*, Harvard Univ. Press, 1960, pp. 76–92; J. Bhagwati, "The Pure Theory of International Trade: A Survey," *Economic Journal*, March, 1964, pp. 29–32.

careful to indicate the limits of the theorem's applicability by emphasizing its dependence on a very special set of assumptions—namely, the existence of perfect competition in all markets, constant returns to scale in the production of each commodity, identical production functions in all countries, and incomplete specialization in all countries (each commodity is produced in all countries). It need not then come with any surprise that factor returns have failed to reach equality between rich and poor countries when factor endowments have been so different that complete specialization has occurred, or economies of scale have led to complete specialization, or production functions have been dissimilar in different countries because of differences in technical knowledge and in the quality of factors, or impediments to trade have existed—when, in short, the restrictive conditions of the theorem have been so clearly violated in reality.

Moreover, we should distinguish between factor-price equalization as inferred from the static model and the inequalities in factor prices which have actually resulted from the historical operation of dynamic forces and changes in the world economy. Only by confusing the static and dynamic problems can it be argued that international trade, instead of equalizing factor prices, has increased the differences. For, in the dynamic setting, trade has been but one of many variables affecting factor prices; it is, therefore, illegitimate to single it out from other dynamic changes as having been the cause of increased inequalities.

Finally, the failure to have even a tendency towards factor-price equality, let alone full equality, does not mean that measures which bring the economy closer to a fulfillment of the assumptions underlying the theorem might not be effective in diminishing the inequalities, or that trade might not still contribute to a poor country's development. Only by misinterpreting the factor-price equalization theorem, and ignoring all the other dynamic benefits of trade, can the absence of equal factor prices be construed as indicating that trade makes no contribution to development.

5. We may now examine whether historical experience shows that international trade has operated to the detriment of the poor country's development. Unlike the Marxists or others who concentrate on the unfavorable effects of imperialism or colonialism, the modern critics do not base their historical critique on any notion of "deliberate exploitation" by the advanced countries. Instead, the emphasis is simply on the free play of international market forces. As argued by Myrdal, "market forces will tend cumulatively to accentuate international inequalities," and "a quite normal result of unhampered trade between two countries, of which one is industrial and the other underdeveloped, is the initiation of a cumulative process towards the impoverishment and stagnation of the latter."[18]

There appear to be three main strands in the argument supporting this conclusion. It is alleged that development has been retarded by first, the unfavorable effects of international factor movements; second, the international operation of the "demonstration effect"; and third, a secular deterioration in the terms of trade. Before offering an alternative explanation of why the poor countries have not succeeded in deriving a higher rate of development from their foreign trade, we should first appraise this historical interpretation.

The effects of international factor movements, it is claimed,[19] have been adverse in creating a highly unbalanced structure of production. It is maintained that the inflow of foreign capital has developed only the country's natural resources for export, to the

[18] Myrdal, *An International Economy, op. cit.*, pp. 55, 95.

[19] See, among other sources, *Ibid.*, pp. 27–29, 57–59, chap. 5; Jonathan V. Levin, *The Export Economies*, Harvard Univ. Press, 1960, pp. 4–10, 201–202.

neglect of production in the domestic sector. Foreign enterprises have transformed the export sector into the most advanced part of the economy, but this imported western capitalism has not penetrated very far into the indigenous economy. Foreign investments, it is said, have become to a high degree economic enclaves, and even when the enclaves have been large, as in mining or the plantation system, they have seldom been integrated into the local economy, but have remained attached to the interests of a metropolitan state. The result has simply been the creation of a "dual economy" in which production is export-biased, and the export sector remains an island of development surrounded by a backward low-productivity sector.

One version of the dualistic character of poor countries emphasizes the "factor proportions problem" or the "technological dualism" associated with the differences in factor endowment and techniques of production in the advanced "industrial" sector and the backward "pre-industrial" sector.[20] The advanced sector is composed of plantation or other large-scale commercial agriculture, mines, oilfields or refineries which produce for export,

[20] For a detailed analysis of this two-sector model, see R. S. Eckaus, "The Factor Proportions Problem in Underdeveloped Areas," *American Economic Review*, September, 1955, pp. 539–565; H. Leibenstein, "Technical Progress, the Production Function and Dualism," *Banca Nazionale del Lavoro Quarterly Review*, December, 1960, pp. 3–18; International Labour Office, *Employment Objectives in Economic Development*, Geneva, 1961, pp. 27–32.

Features of "dualism" are also stressed in Lewis' model of a high-wage capitalist sector and a low-wage noncapitalist sector: W. A. Lewis, "Economic Development with Unlimited Supplies of Labour," *Manchester School of Economic and Social Studies*, May, 1954, pp. 139–191; "Unlimited Labour: Further Notes," *Ibid.*, January, 1958, pp. 1–32.

A sociological interpretation is presented by J. H. Boeke, *Economics and Economic Policy of Dual Societies*, Institute of Pacific Relations, 1953. For a contradiction of Boeke's thesis, see B. Higgins, "The 'Dualistic Theory' of Underdeveloped Areas," *Economic Development and Cultural Change*, January, 1956, pp. 99–115.

and large-scale manufacturing, while the backward rural sector is dominated by peasant agriculture, handicrafts, and small-scale industry producing for a local demand. Methods of production in the advanced sector are capital-intensive, and technical coefficients are relatively fixed, whereas in the backward sector production is labor-intensive and the factors of production may be combined in variable proportions. It is contended that the result of this dualism has been that capital, especially foreign capital, flowed into the advanced sector to produce mineral and agricultural products for export markets, but the rate of investment in this sector and labor employment opportunities in the capital-intensive activities did not keep pace with population growth. For lack of alternative employment opportunities, the increasing population therefore had to seek employment in the traditional, variable-coefficient sector. But after a point all available land was cultivated by labor-intensive techniques, and with continuing population growth, disguised unemployment became inevitable in the rural sector. Furthermore, whatever technological progress occurred was biased towards the capital-intensive, fixed-coefficient sector, and the introduction of labor-saving devices diminished still further the capacity of the advanced sector to absorb the population growth. Under such conditions of technological dualism, an expansion in exports may have induced investment and stimulated technological progress in the advanced sector, but it was ineffectual in removing the disguised unemployment or stimulating investment in the backward sector.

It is also argued that foreign-owned plantation and mining enterprises and foreign trading firms have frequently acquired monopsony and monopoly positions.[21] As laborers, the natives

[21] Hla Myint, "An Interpretation of Economic Backwardness," *Oxford Economic Papers*, June, 1954, pp. 154–155.

have confronted the monopsonistic power of foreign plantations and mining concerns. As peasant producers, they have faced a small group of exporting and processing firms with monopsonistic power in buying the native crop. And as consumers, they have had to purchase imported commodities from monopolistic sellers or distributors of these commodities.

Further, it is said that the stimulating income effects of foreign investment have been lost through income leakages abroad.[22] Not only has there been a drain of profits and interest to the capital-exporting countries, but the poor countries have also had to import from the richer countries the capital equipment associated with any investment that has been induced by a growth in exports. The implication is that a given amount of investment in the poor country has generated a much smaller amount of income than the same amount of investment would have generated in a more advanced and less dependent country.

It is also believed that the immigration of unskilled labor into poor countries has reinforced the dualistic structure of their economies. In some countries which were at one time sparsely inhabited, the mass immigration of labor into plantations and mines allowed the supply of labor to remain elastic at the conventional low-wage rate. In other countries, labor emigration to richer countries has not been sufficient to exert an upward pressure on wages.

6. This critical interpretation of the historical impact of international factor movements has become part of the ideology of economic development in many countries. In contradiction, however, much can be said against such a view of the development-retarding effects of the international migration of capital and

[22] Singer, *op. cit.*, p. 475.

labor. The following counterarguments readily suggest themselves.

First, regarding the inflow of capital, we should recognize that since foreign trade has accounted for a large share of governmental revenue, the governments of many poor countries have actually pursued policies designed to attract foreign investment to their export sectors in order to promote their export trade. Moreover, in many instances the chief beneficiaries of foreign investment have been not the foreign investors but groups within the recipient country.[23] For a number of export crops, the production by small holders has also become possible only because of the opportunity to imitate plantation examples and to locate near large-scale enterprises producing the same crop and providing marketing facilities (as in the case of bananas) or furnishing processing services (sugar cane).

What is most significant, however, is that foreign investment, regardless of its character, has not been competitive with home investment. There is no reason to believe that if there had not been foreign investment, a poor country would have generated more domestic investment; or that, in the absence of foreign entrepreneurs, the supply of domestic entrepreneurs would have been larger. We need not resort to any notion of unbalanced international forces to explain the limited amount of domestic investment and the lack of domestic entrepreneurship: the explanation is apparent in all the domestic obstacles asso-

---

[23] In the case of British foreign investment in Argentina, for instance, it has been concluded that British investors dominated in the less profitable enterprises, while the really great fortunes accrued to native Argentinos from the appreciation of land values and the profits of pastoral enterprise, commercial agriculture, and share-cropping. H. S. Ferns, *Britain and Argentina in the Nineteenth Century*, Oxford Univ. Press, 1960, pp. 489–490.

ciated with narrow domestic markets and the absence of cooperant factors in sufficient quantity and quality—the very
impediments that made foreign capital and technical resources
turn away from the domestic towards the export sector.

Much of the criticism is thus misplaced, once it is recognized
that the relevant comparison is not between the pattern of resource utilization that actually occurred with international factor
movements and some other ideal pattern, but between the actual
pattern and the pattern that would have occurred in the absence
of the capital and labor inflow. As Nurkse observes, "even 'unbalanced' and unsteady growth through foreign trade was surely
much better than no growth at all."[24] If foreign capital and the
power of foreign enterprise had resulted in a deliberate diversion
of resources from domestic production to the export sector, the
argument would be more serious. The real choice, however, was
not between using the resources for export production or for domestic production, but between giving employment to the surplus resources in export production or leaving them idle. A
considerable margin of surplus productive capacity in the form
of both surplus land and surplus labor, over and above subsistence
requirements, allowed production of cash crops for export markets without reducing subsistence output.[25] And over the longer
run, the increase in export production was in the form of net
additions to output made possible by the utilization of previously

[24] Ragnar Nurkse, "The Conflict between 'Balanced Growth' and International Specialization," *Lectures on Economic Development*, Faculty
of Economics (Istanbul University) and Faculty of Political Sciences (An-
kara University), 1958, p. 167. A similar conclusion, based on several historical examples of colonial development, is expressed by W. K. Hancock,
Wealth of Colonies, Cambridge Univ. Press, 1950, p. 39.
[25] Hla Myint, *The Economics of the Developing Countries*, Hutchinson, 1964, p. 44.

idle resources and growth in factor supply, not by a withdrawal from the domestic sector.[26]

Similarly, the complaint about the economic power of foreign enterprises does not demonstrate that development would have been more rapid in the absence of foreign enterprise. All that it implies is that the native's real income might have risen more if he had sold and bought in more competitive markets. But without the impetus from outside, the spread of the exchange economy would have been severely limited in the first place. The power of foreign enterprises can also be exaggerated by overlooking the fact that, on the supply side, the native generally had a reservation price in terms of alternatives between subsistence production, cash cropping, and wage earning.

As for the argument concerning leakages of income abroad, this has simply meant that the secondary round of income effects from an increase in exports would have been larger if there had not been the leakages. The relevant argument, therefore, is for reducing the overseas drain, not for restricting international investment. Without the capital inflow, the initial expansion in exports would have been much smaller. Again, the main impetus to the growth of an exchange economy has come from outside, and as the subsistence sector has diminished and the monetary sector has grown, so has the effectiveness of the multiplier process increased. The leakages can also be exaggerated: As exports rose, the demand for local labor and materials increased, sources of taxation expanded, some of the profits were retained and reinvested locally, and by taxation and profit-sharing arrangements the government controlled some of the profit outflow. In many cases, the net payments abroad of interest, dividends, and branch

[26] Hla Myint, "The Gains from International Trade and the Backward Countries," *Review of Economic Studies*, Vol. XXII (2), No. 58, (1954–55), p. 133.

profits have been only minor in relation to the net geographical product of these countries. Consideration should also be given to the fact that the growth in exports from the poor countries was induced by the growth of income in rich countries, and in this sense some of the secondary investment that resulted from an initial increase in demand in the rich countries actually occurred as foreign investment in the poor countries.

Regarding the effects of labor immigration, we should note that in many countries the low-wage policy for labor in mines and plantations depended more on the persistence of a migrant labor system than on mass immigration. The existence of a casual labor force, migrating back and forth from the subsistence sector to the mines and plantations, allowed the maintenance of a low-wage policy. The ability to secure additional labor in the export sector at the conventional low-wage rate rested ultimately, however, on the low productivity in the subsistence sector. And a switch-over from a low-wage, low-productivity pattern to a high-wage, high-productivity pattern in mines and plantations would have required not merely the raising of wages, but also the heavy investment expenditures, in both material and human capital, involved in converting a casual labor force into a stabilized labor force on a permanent basis.[27]

For those countries that depended on immigration for an adequate labor supply, the immigration did at least remove the potential barrier of labor scarcity in countries that were sparsely populated, and acted as a permissive condition for the expansion of their exports. Nor should other positive benefits be ignored: in many instances, an entrepreneurial class has emerged from an originally immigrant group; expatriate merchants and traders

[27] Myint, *The Economics of the Developing Countries, op. cit.*, pp. 59, 67–68.

have frequently been responsible for the domestic financing of industries. As for the more general problem of population pressures, one cannot believe that less immigration or any realistic amount of emigration would have been sufficient to remove this problem, in view of the high rates of natural increase due to medical advances.

The over-all contention regarding the effects of factor movement is that the economy of the poor country has suffered a type of structural disequilibrium through its "export bias." But there is some ambiguity as to whether this is meant to imply an absolute overexpansion in the exports of primary products, or merely a relative overexpansion as compared with domestic output. If interpreted in the absolute sense, it implies that the expansion in exports was at the expense of domestic output, and that the economy would have developed more rapidly if exports had been less. Actually, however, there is no convincing evidence that export production was at the expense of home output. And, in view of the comparative cost structure and the essential roles that agriculture and exports must have in the development process, it is difficult to understand how development could have been accelerated by a reduction in exports. If, however, "export bias" implies that the expansion in exports was too rapid relative to growth in domestic output, then it is merely another way of stating the general problem of the lack of carry-over from the export sector to the rest of the economy. "Dualism," or "export bias," or "lack of carry-over," is not an explanation of why the process of derived development has been arrested; instead, it is simply a statement of the problem.

7. In addition to the adverse consequences of international factor movements, it has also become common to claim that the international operation of the "demonstration effect" has been a handicap for the poor country. It is argued that the demonstration of advanced consumption standards in rich countries has excessively raised the propensity to consume in the poorer countries and has thereby limited capital accumulation. But this effect is easily exaggerated. The emulation of consumption patterns of rich countries could be expected to be strong only for countries which imported secondary products and had a significantly large urban population. Insofar as the imports of some poor countries consisted mainly of foodstuffs and primary products, and the urban component of most populations was small until recently, the demonstration effect was weak.[28]

Moreover, all the relations between rich and poor countries have, in a sense, demonstration effects. Even if one of these effects —that on the propensity to consume—is considered to have been deleterious, the net result of the other effects may have more than offset this. To the extent that the demonstration effect operates in favor of raising the consumption of imported commodities, it operates *pari passu* on the incentives to work and to produce more. Classical economists stressed the incentive side of the demonstration effect, and from the standpoint of accelerating development, this may well outweigh the effect on the consumption side. When the transition to an exchange economy has not been completed, the demonstration effect stimulates more effort to create a marketable surplus of agricultural products, since the ability to purchase new types of consumer goods depends on money in-

[28] The "international demonstration effect" was first applied to Western European countries in connection with the postwar dollar shortage problem; see W. F. Stolper, "A Note on the Multiplier, Flexible Exchanges and the Dollar Shortage," *Economia Internazionale*, August, 1950, pp. 772–773. Although the demonstration effect may be significant for relations between Western Europe and the United States, it is much weaker for poor countries.

come. Extension of the exchange economy entails greater specialization and increased production, and, eventually, additional saving. The general point is that the demonstration effect tends to stimulate the "aspiration to consume" as well as the "propensity to consume" and as long as it affects the aspiration to consume, it may actually lead to greater effort and more production. Indeed, emulation of the urban area by the rural areas has been a contributing element to development in rich countries, and it need not be less favorable simply because it operates internationally.

A demonstration of advanced technological standards has also paralleled the demonstration of advanced consumption standards. In many cases, peasants have been able to adopt a crop introduced and demonstrated by foreign-owned plantations, and in other instances home industries have developed to copy foreign goods. More generally, the demonstration of superior productive techniques in rich countries acts as a constant stimulant to the spread of technology.

8. The third major criticism of international forces rests on the contention that there has been an international transfer of income from the poor to the rich countries through a secular deterioration in the commodity terms of trade of the poor countries. We have already considered in Chapter 3 the thesis that the commodity terms of trade between industrial and primary producing countries shifted in favor of industrial countries, allegedly because monopolistic elements in their product and factor markets allowed these countries to retain the benefit of their technical progress in the form of rising factor incomes, while in primary producing countries the gains in productivity have been distributed in price reductions. We saw that the statistical foundations for this claim are extremely weak, and that the analytical reasoning is unconvincing. It is difficult to entertain seriously the argument that the slow pace of development has been due to a worsening in the terms of trade. Even more extreme is the assertion that the case of "immiserizing growth" through a deterioration in the terms of trade has actually occurred. No evidence has been offered that the restrictive conditions necessary for this result have prevailed.

We may also observe that even if the commodity terms of trade had deteriorated, the basic difficulty would have been not the external change in prices, but the failure to have had sufficient internal resource flexibility. If domestic resources were mobile, the distribution of resources would tend to shift from export industries to home-market industries when the commodity terms of trade deteriorate. By inducing shifts in production and in the distribution of resources, a change in the terms of trade would tend to reverse or counteract itself. In other words, changes in the terms of trade are apt to be "washed out" in the long-run.[29]

9. Although we conclude that international market forces did not inhibit development, we are nonetheless left with the question of why the classical optimism regarding development through trade has not been vindicated for the poor countries. We must still explain why the gains from trade have not led to more substantial gains from growth. If the expanding export trade constituted the primary change in the economy, why did it not have more penetrative power and induce more significant secondary changes elsewhere in the domestic economy?

[29] Ragnar Nurkse, *Patterns of Trade and Development*, Wicksell Lectures, Almqvist & Wiksell, 1959, pp. 60–61 (reprinted in *Equilibrium and Growth in the World Economy. Economic Essays by Ragnar Nurkse*, Harvard Univ. Press, 1961, pp. 333–334). Also, C. P. Kindleberger, *The Terms of Trade*, John Wiley, 1956, pp. 305–308, 311–312.

Instead of seeking an answer in the allegedly unfavorable effects of international trade, we may find a more convincing explanation in the differential effects of different exports, and in the domestic market conditions of the poor country. For, although the initial expansion of the export sector is potentially favorable for development, the actual scale and rapidity with which this stimulus is transmitted to other sectors will depend not only on the rate of export growth, but also on the character of the country's export-base,[30] and on the degree of domestic market imperfections, interpreted in a wide sense. The export stimulus to development will therefore differ among countries, with the exports of some countries giving more of a stimulus to development than others.

In the first instance, an increase in export production has a direct effect on the growth of the economy, but in addition there are secondary changes elsewhere in the economy which are ex-

---

[30] Some essentials of an export-base theory of regional economic development have been discussed by A. F. W. Plumptre, "The Nature of Political and Economic Development in the British Dominions," *Canadian Journal of Economics and Political Science*, November, 1937, pp. 489–507; D. C. North, "Location Theory and Regional Economic Growth," *Journal of Political Economy*, June, 1955, pp. 249–251; C. M. Tiebout, "Exports and Regional Economic Growth," *Journal of Political Economy*, April, 1956, pp. 160–164; North, "Agriculture in Regional Economic Growth," *Journal of Farm Economics*, December, 1959, pp. 943–951.

The "staple approach" to economic history, often applied by Canadian economic historians, also focuses upon the stimulating role that staple exports have in the process of development; see, for example, K. Buckley, "The Role of Staple Industries in Canada's Economic Development," *Journal of Economic History*, December, 1958, pp. 439–450; R. E. Caves and R. H. Holton, *The Canadian Economy*, Harvard Univ. Press, 1959, pp. 30–47, 141–144, 387; M. H. Watkins, "A Staple Theory of Economic Growth," *Canadian Journal of Economics and Political Science*, May, 1963, pp. 141–158. But cf., E. J. Chambers and D. F. Gordon, "Primary Products and Economic Growth," *Journal of Political Economy*, August, 1966, pp. 315–332.

tremely important in determining to what extent development can be stimulated through foreign trade. Some of these secondary consequences can be associated with the different forms of the production functions of particular export commodities.[31]

One consequence is that, with the use of different input coefficients to produce different types of export commodities, there will be different "backward linkage" effects. An expansion in the output of some exports may induce an expansion elsewhere in the economy in industries supplying inputs to the export sector. For other exports, however, the input coefficients may be such as to provide little opportunity for the emergence or growth of other sectors in the economy.

The use of different factor combinations to produce different export commodities will also affect the distribution of income. In broad terms, the relative shares of profits, wages, interest and rent will vary according to whether the export product comes from mining, plantation agriculture, or peasant farming. We would expect, for instance, from the different types of organization of the tin and rubber industries, that the ratio of profits to wages would be higher for tin than for rubber. And, given the same increase in exports in the two industries, the direct effect of the tin industry on employment and personal income will be smaller than for the rubber industry. When the export commodity is produced by both peasants and plantations, or by both pri-

[31] For discussions of the importance of production functions to economic development, see R. E. Baldwin, "Patterns of Development in Newly Settled Regions," *Manchester School of Economic and Social Studies*, May, 1954, pp. 161–179; Baldwin, "Export Technology and Development from a Subsistence Level," *Economic Journal*, March, 1963, pp. 80–92; Dudley Seers, "An Approach to the Short-Period Analysis of Primary-Producing Economies," *Oxford Economic Papers*, February, 1959, pp. 6–9; Caves and Holton, *op. cit.*, pp. 41–47; Boris C. Swerling, "Some Interrelationships between Agricultural Trade and Economic Development," *Kyklos*, Vol. XIV, No. 3 (1961), pp. 377–379.

vate mines and company mines, the internal distribution of the export income will also differ according to the relative shares of the output produced by each type of organization.

Along with the variation in the domestic distribution of export income, the structure of demand and saving propensities are also likely to differ among poor countries. By favoring groups with a higher propensity to consume domestic goods than to import, the resultant distribution of income from some export commodities is more effective in raising home demand. If income increments go to those who tend to save large portions, then the export sector may also make a greater contribution to the financing of growth in other sectors. And the investment which the savings make possible may be more productive in one economy than another. To the extent that variations in conditions of demand, and in the supply and utilization of saving, are related to the type of export production, different export industries vary in their influence on the development process.

This emphasis on the nature of the export commodity's production function extends beyond the "factor proportions problem" (discussed in section 5). In affecting the distribution of income, the pattern of consumption, and the use of savings, the nature of the production in the export sector has implications other than those of technological dualism. Even the conditions of technological dualism are highly special and do not exist to the same extent in different poor countries. Not all types of exports can be characterized as being produced under capital-intensive and fixed-coefficient conditions; the degree of capital intensity and factor substitutability varies from commodity to commodity. Moreover, even if all the exports of different countries were produced with a high capital-labor ratio and did not provide much employment to labor, other industries that are linked to exports might still differ in capital-intensity and factor-substitutability among the various countries.

A significant implication of the "factor proportions problem," however, is that the degree to which modern processing techniques are used in export production is important in determining the extent of the "carry-over" from exports. For the machine processing of raw materials or foodstuffs for export raises supply requirements, increases employment, and creates income in other activities supporting the export sector, such as the supplying of materials, tools and implements, transportation, and construction. Insofar as output of the export industry becomes an input for other industries, processing activities also provide "forward linkages."

The degree to which the various exports are processed is also highly important in determining external economies: The processing of primary-product exports by modern methods is likely to benefit other activities through the spread of technical knowledge, training of labor, demonstration of new production techniques that might be adapted elsewhere, and the acquisition of organizational and supervisory skills. It also increases the scope for innovations in the export sector. Thus, when the processing of primary-product exports by modern methods sets in motion a chain of further modern sector requirements and provides external economies, the export sector may, in Rostow's terminology, play a strong role as the leading sector in the take-off into self-sustained growth.[32]

In contrast, even though it may have the highest growth rate in the economy, the export sector will provide only a weak stimulus if its techniques of production are the same as those already in use in other sectors, and if its expansion can occur by a simple widening of production without any change in production functions. The ability to expand export production without introduc-

[32] W. W. Rostow, *The Stages of Economic Growth*, Cambridge Univ. Press, 1960, pp. 39, 56.

ing new techniques of production has been a feature of some peasant export sectors. In some cases, when the export crop was a traditional crop, the growth in export output was achieved simply by bringing more land under cultivation with the same methods of cultivation used in the subsistence sector. In other instances, when new export crops were introduced, their success as peasant export crops was determined by the fact that they involved simple methods of production that did not differ markedly from the traditional techniques used in subsistence agriculture.[33] When the export expansion of peasant crops merely reproduced existing production conditions on a larger scale, the stimulus to development was less than it would have been if the expansionary process had entailed the introduction of new skills and more productive recombinations of factors.

The repercussions from exports also differ according to the degree of fluctuation in export proceeds. Disruptions in the flow of foreign exchange receipts make the development process discontinuous; the greater the degree of instability, the more difficult it is to maintain steady development. The larger the amplitude of fluctuation, the more disturbing the effects on employment, real income, government revenue, capital formation, resource allocation, and the capacity to import.

Fluctuations in retained proceeds from exports may also affect the internal distribution of income, and in different ways

[33] Myint, "The Classical Theory of International Trade and the Underdeveloped Countries," *op. cit.*, p. 321.

"The fact that peasant export production has not shown any technical improvements in the past does not mean that it is inherently incapable of improvement if adequate resources are ploughed back into it. The past pattern merely shows that these opportunities for improvements have been neglected because, with unused land easily available, it was so much easier to expand along existing lines than to try to introduce improved methods of production." Myint, *The Economics of the Developing Countries, op. cit.*, p. 52.

for different types of economies. For instance, it may be that in a peasant economy the middlemen have been able to maintain fairly constant rates of profits on the external prices of exports and imports by shifting the burden of cyclical adjustments on to the peasants, while in a mineral or plantation economy profits have borne more of the adjustment.[34] And when the impact of fluctuations in an export industry falls on wages or employment, the effects on labor's income will vary according to whether labor can shift into another export industry, domestic industry, or subsistence farming.

From a consideration of various characteristics of the country's export-base, we may thus infer how the strength of the stimulus from exports will differ among countries. In summary, we would normally expect the stimulus to be stronger under the following conditions: the higher is the growth rate of the export sector; the greater is the direct effect in the export sector on employment and personal income; the less the distribution of export income favors those with a higher marginal propensity to import; the more productive is the investment resulting from any saving of export income; the more exports expand through a change in production functions, rather than by a simple widening process; the more extensive are the externalities and linkages connected with the export sector; and the more stable are the export receipts retained at home.

If we have so far looked to the character of a country's export base for an indication of the strength of the export stimulus to development, we must now look to market conditions within the domestic economy for evidence of how receptive the economy is to the stimulus from exports. For, when intersectoral re-

---

[34] Myint, "The Gains from International Trade and the Backward Countries," *op. cit.*, pp. 132–133; Levin, *op. cit.*, pp. 186–193; Clark W. Reynolds, "Domestic Consequences of Export Instability," *American Economic Review*, May, 1963, pp. 93–102.

lationships are many and the response to an expansion in exports is rapid and extensive in scope, then even a weak stimulus can result in a significant carry-over. In contrast, when there are formidable domestic impediments to a transmission of the gains from exports to other sectors, then even a strong stimulus will have only slight penetrative power.

In connection with these domestic impediments, we can recognize that the pervasiveness of market imperfections has severely limited the carry-over from exports. The economies of poor countries are characterized by factor immobility, price rigidity, restrictive tendencies in both the factor and good markets, ignorance of technological possibilities, limited knowledge of market conditions, and few centers of entrepreneurship. All these imperfections handicap the achievement of intertemporal efficiency in the utilization of resources. Although the monetary sector of the economy has expanded, this does not mean that there is yet a well-articulated price system which promotes specialization and coordinates activities. Though local markets for the sale of surplus products have grown in volume and variety, and there has been a movement of labor into wage employment, the price system certainly does not operate as effectively as in a more advanced economy. The functions of the price system are narrowly constrained in an economy in which markets are local, subsistence production accounts for a substantial proportion of national product, and traditional rules and customary obligations prevail. There are then definite limits to the extent to which the price system can operate as an instrument for development.[35]

35 H. A. Innis, "The Penetrative Powers of the Price System," *Canadian Journal of Economics and Political Science*, August, 1938, pp. 299–319. But see Eric E. Lampard, "The Price System and Economic Change, A Commentary on Theory and History," *Journal of Economic History*, December, 1960, pp. 617–637.

Many of these inhibiting factors are a function of socio-cultural customs and institutions.[36] While economic change in itself, especially those change-inducing factors introduced through international contacts, may help to transform traditional customs and mores, there is still a need for indigenous forces of sociological and political development. When political and social policies have maintained conditions under which the traditional village system has persisted; when the value structure of the society has placed little emphasis on a concern about the future, or on man's mastery of nature; when even the government of the poor country has remained economically backward in the sense of being unable to formulate and administer economic policies—when all these hindrances to change have existed within the domestic economy, it is understandable why the stimulus from the export sector has not been sustained.

In terms of Rostow's schema, the failure of the export sector to have been a primary growth sector, setting in motion expansionary forces elsewhere in the economy, may be attributed in large part to the absence of the preconditions necessary for a take-off into self-sustained growth. While their exports rose, many poor countries at the same time had not yet experienced the second stage of growth—a transitional era when the politics, social

[36] The literature on development has given increasing attention to the cultural, social, and psychological factors which operate to inhibit development. See, for example, J. L. Saide, "The Social Anthropology of Economic Underdevelopment," *Economic Journal*, June, 1960, pp. 294–303; "Symposium on Economic Motivations and Incentives in a Traditional and in a Modern Environment," *International Social Science Bulletin*, Vol. VI, No. 3, 1954, pp. 369–476 (with bibliography); D. C. McClelland, *The Achieving Society*, D. Van Nostrand Co., 1961; R. Braibanti and J. Spengler, eds., *Tradition, Values and Socio-economic Development*, Duke Univ. Press, 1961; B. F. Hoselitz and W. E. Moore, eds., *Industrialization and Society*, UNESCO, 1963.

structure, and values of a traditional society are altered in such ways as to permit regular growth.[37]

No matter how strong the stimulus from foreign trade, it is essential that the prior development of the society and its economy should result in a positive and self-reinforcing response to it. If this necessary foundation exists, international trade can then release latent indigenous forces which can exploit, in turn, the stimulus from the export sector and produce further transformative effects throughout the economy. Unlike this favorable situation, however, the domestic economy of the poor country has remained fragmented and compartmentalized, the transference of resources from less productive to more productive employment has been restricted, and the linkage of markets and their subsequent extension have been handicapped. The secondary round of activities induced by an increase in exports has thereby been cut short, and the dynamic gains from trade have not been fully realized.

We thus conclude that the domestically-based obstacles to development have been of much greater significance than any external obstacles, and that if the internal handicaps had been less formidable, the stimuli from foreign trade would have been more effective in inducing responses favorable to technical progress, entrepreneurship, and capital accumulation.

If the penetrative power of foreign trade has been limited by domestic handicaps, instead of by the nature of international

---

[37] Rostow, *op. cit.*, chaps. 2–4. Although the economists concerned with economic development, and even the economic historians, have concentrated almost exclusively on the period of the "take-off" and the period of "self-sustaining growth," it is the earlier period of the emergence of the preconditions for development that is still most relevant for many poor countries. An understanding of this period is most important; yet it is the most difficult to explain and remains the least understood.

trade itself, there is a greater likelihood that the development through trade mechanism may yet be effective in poor countries, as it has been in many other countries. For if the obstacles are within the domestic economy, they are likely to be more amenable to change through suitable policy measures; and more immediate effects on the country's rate of development might be forthcoming than would be the case if the country had to await widespread transformation in the structure of international trade.

Mindful of the potential contribution that foreign trade can make to development, we have submitted that the basic international trade problem for a poor country is not so much how to control its trade, but rather how to achieve a more extensive carry-over from its export trade to its domestic economy. Many of the policy implications of the foregoing analysis thus center upon a reduction in the market imperfections. To accomplish this, alternative forms of economic and social organization are required. If the export sector is to be able to propel the rest of the economy forward, domestic policies must concentrate on diminishing the prevalence of semimonopolistic and monopolistic practices, removing restraints on land tenure and land use, widening the capital market, and making credit and marketing facilities more readily available. The economy must also be made more flexible through investment in transportation, communication, education, and manpower training. If the market imperfections are reduced, the development process may then be more readily established on an indigenous base within the society of the poor country.

If market imperfections are eliminated, and the internal economic structure becomes more flexible, the penetrative power of foreign trade can be greater. Modern production techniques can be diffused more widely. New skills can be created and transferred to domestic enterprises. Entrepreneurial activities can also be expanded, since entrepreneurship depends not only on individual abilities and motivations but also on a congenial environment for the individual. And investment can be greater, with a higher rate of plough-back of foreign exchange proceeds into the investment opportunities created by foreign trade. Insofar as this investment is directed to industries related to exports, the investment can be more productive than the short-run speculative type of investment that has been only too prevalent.

Thus, in the future for currently poor countries, as in the past for other countries, foreign trade may operate as an engine of growth transmission—provided there are latent indigenous forces of development that can be released through trade. The gains from trade can facilitate development, but they cannot be a substitute for the developmental forces that must necessarily be created within the domestic economy. And these forces cannot be viewed as comprising only the basic economic determinants of development, such as entrepreneurship, technical progress, and capital accumulation. For these proximate determinants are, in turn, related to the indirect noneconomic, but nonetheless highly strategic, influences of the society's political, social, and institutional organization. The merging of the gains from trade with the gains from growth rests ultimately, therefore, on the efficacy of domestic policy measures in producing sufficient social and political change, as well as economic change, to make the economy more responsive to the stimulus from trade.

10. Against the emphasis on removing domestic obstacles, however, it may be argued that, while this may be an appropriate consideration when the stimulus from exports is strong, it is scarcely relevant when exports do not provide much of a stimulus in the first place. Even though domestic obstacles may have accounted for the weak carry-over of exports in the past, when

export markets were expanding, it is now possible to contend that exports may no longer enjoy a strongly rising world demand and may not provide an adequate foundation for development. If exports cannot be relied upon to grow sufficiently, then foreign trade will be a weak transmitter of development even if the domestic obstacles are removed.

Focusing on this possibility, the less developed countries have become extremely concerned about their opportunities for expanding exports. After the disappointments of overreliance on "development through aid" and "development through import-substitution," many of the poor countries have become doubtful about the adequacy of foreign aid and disenchanted with import restrictions and multiple exchange rates as measures to foster protection and to cope with external disequilibrium.[38] Since the first session of UNCTAD, there has been a marked shift in emphasis away from policies that have an anti-trade bias towards the problems of achieving an expansion in exports. But, as interpreted by the great majority of developing countries in UNCTAD, the problem of export promotion is "externalized," in the sense that the developing countries attribute their inability to secure a sufficiently strong basis for development through trade to the protectionist policies of advanced countries and the restrictive rules of the General Agreement on Tariffs and Trade (GATT) and the International Monetary Fund (IMF).[39]

[38] The growing skepticism about trade and exchange controls as suitable policy instruments for development is conveniently traced by Margaret G. De Vries, "Trade and Exchange Policy and Economic Development: Two Decades of Evolving Views," *Oxford Economic Papers*, March, 1966, pp. 34–44.

[39] For a concise statement of this view, see United Nations, *Towards A New Trade Policy for Development*, Report by the Secretary-General of UNCTAD, New York, 1964; also, *Proceedings of UNCTAD*, Vol. I: *Final Act and Report*, United Nations, 1964, pp. 3–16.

The trade complaints of the less developed countries are now subsumed under the notion of the "widening trade gap." Extreme pessimism characterizes the developing countries' outlook for their traditional primary product exports. In spite of the rapid economic expansion in the industrial countries during the postwar period, the growth in exports of foodstuffs and industrial raw materials from the less developed countries to the industrial nations has been disappointingly slow. From 1950 to 1965, gross world exports increased by 130 percent, but exports from developing countries rose by only 50 percent; and instead of being nearly one-third of total world exports, as in 1950, the share of the developing countries' exports was only one-fifth in 1965. The poor export performance, it is said, has been due mainly to changes in the pattern of demand in the industrial importing countries; to technological developments that have reduced usage of primary materials per unit of output of manufactures, and substituted synthetic for imported natural materials in industry; and to the adoption of fiscal and protectionist policies by the advanced countries which restrict imports from the less developed countries.[40] Without special measures to support exports from the developing countries, these trends are not expected to reverse themselves. But while the less developed countries' capacity to import based on exports is growing only slowly, their development programs require a much higher rate of growth in imports. Even the presently low rates of development entail a widening gap in the balance of payments of the developing countries; if a higher growth target were to be achieved (say, the five percent target of the Development Dec-

[40] United Nations, *World Economic Survey, 1964*, New York, 1965, pp. 221–229; A. Maizels, "Recent Trends in World Trade," R. F. Harrod and D. C. Hague, eds., *International Trade Theory in a Developing World*, Macmillan Co., 1963, pp. 33–46.

ade), and trends in trade and aid were simply to continue as in the recent past, the gap would become even greater.[41]

It is therefore submitted that to avoid this gap and allow the fulfillment of development plans, there must be an expansion in exports, improvement in the terms of trade, and an increase in the flow of capital and aid. After having argued that in the past foreign trade had undesirable repercussions on the historical course of development, many spokesmen for the developing countries now argue that the present volume of trade is insufficient and the pattern of trade is unfavorable for achieving higher rates of development. Again, the onus is placed outside the less developed countries; to overcome the "widening trade gap," the less developed countries now contend that the commercial policies of developed countries need to be liberalized, a new international code of conduct in trade relations must be adopted by GATT, and the international monetary system should be reformed. Just as it was argued earlier that traditional trade theory lacked "relevance and realism" for developing countries, so too is it now claimed that the postwar international institutional arrangements embodying GATT and the IMF do not squarely meet the problems of newly developing

[41] In his report to the first session of UNCTAD, the Secretary-General of the Conference (Raúl Prebisch) estimated that the less developed countries' deficit in the balance of payments on current account will grow to $20 billion in 1970. Even if the net inflow of long-term capital and official donations from developed countries continued to rise at recent rates, the projected payments gap by 1970 would still be as much as $11 billion. See United Nations, *Towards a New Trade Policy for Development, op. cit.*, pp. 4–5; United Nations, *World Economic Survey 1962—Part I*, New York, 1963, pp. 6–9.

For alternative calculations that are not so large, but still substantial, see Bela Balassa, *Trade Prospects for Developing Countries*, Richard D. Irwin, 1964, pp. 93–97; *New Directions for World Trade*, Proceedings of a Chatham House Conference, Oxford Univ. Press, 1964, pp. 23–50, 161–212.

economies. And just as the gains from trade have allegedly been distributed historically in favor of the advanced countries, so too is it now asserted that the policies of international economic institutions are biased in favor of the more developed countries.

This call for international economic reform in order to promote "development through trade" now deserves the most serious consideration. We shall devote the next chapter to examining the major policy issues raised by the demand for reform of international trading arrangements and the international monetary system.

9

International Economic Reform

1. Dissatisfaction with the development record in most of the poor countries is leading to fresh emphasis on international economic action. Instead of continuing to rely on ad hoc national measures that have proved disappointing, the less developed countries are becoming increasingly sensitive to their export performance and are giving more recognition to the value of outward-looking policies for development. This shift of emphasis is, however, being coupled with a widespread demand by the less developed countries in UNCTAD for modifications of international trading arrangements under the General Agreement on Tariffs and Trade and for new international monetary arrangements. The novel—and, as we shall see, the most controversial—aspects of the UNCTAD proposals for international economic reform are the attempts to obtain an increase in aid through the use of commercial policy and to link development finance directly with international monetary reform.

This chapter appraises the various proposals of UNCTAD in terms of two overriding questions: Do GATT and the IMF actually inhibit the promotion and financing of an expansion in the trade of the developing countries? And would the remedial measures proposed by UNCTAD constitute the most efficient policies for allowing trade to make a greater contribution to the pace of development?

2. Following World War II, the IMF and GATT were intended to be the central international economic institutions that would provide a more adequate framework for a liberalized trade and payments system in the postwar world economy. While the Fund was designed to repair the disintegration of the international monetary system that had occurred in the thirties, GATT was intended to reverse the protectionist and discriminatory trade practices that had multiplied during the prewar depression years. In combination, the IMF and GATT were addressed primarily to a resolution of the difficult problems of how the advanced industrial countries might achieve at one and the same time the multiple objectives of full employment, freer trade, and stable exchange rates.

To an ever increasing extent, however, problems raised by the newly developing countries have been superimposed upon the Fund and GATT. Although both institutions have made some effort to adapt to the new set of development problems, the less developed countries remain dissatisfied.

Developing countries believe that the principles underlying GATT are especially unfavorable for them. As exemplified by UNCTAD, it is now argued that GATT imposes too heavy a burden of commitments on the low-income countries—that GATT exercises more of a negative role in policing trade than a positive role in promoting trade from less developed countries. Moreover, it is claimed that the liberalization of trade that has been achieved by GATT has been mainly to the advantage of the industrial countries, not the developing countries.[1] The latter, it is said, have not benefited from GATT because it is based on the "classic concept that the free play of international economic forces by itself leads to the optimum expansion of trade and the most efficient utilization of the world's productive resources; rules and principles are therefore established to guarantee this free play. . . . The free play concept is admissible in relations between countries that are strictly similar, but not between those whose structures are altogether different as are those of the industrially advanced and the developing countries."[2] Once it is recognized that all nations are not equal, and that the underdeveloped countries are in a special situation, then there is a need for "different attitudes from those prevailing in the past, and these attitudes should converge towards a new trade policy for development."[3]

3. Before turning to the specific recommendations of UNCTAD, we should first appreciate the extent to which GATT, in the course of its evolution, has given increasing attention to the problems of trade and development.

In the original General Agreement, the major provisions relating to less developed countries were contained in Article

[1] *Towards a New Trade Policy for Development,* Report by the Secretary-General of UNCTAD (Raúl Prebisch), United Nations, 1964, p. 27.

[2] *Ibid.,* pp. 28–29. For a similar view that the special conditions of newly developing countries justify a double moral standard in international trade, see Gunnar Myrdal, *An International Economy,* Harper & Row, 1956, pp. 288–292; Sidney Dell, *Trade Blocs and Common Markets,* Knopf, 1963, pp. 244–245; Thomas Balogh, "Notes on the United Nations Conference on Trade and Development," *Bulletin of the Oxford Institute of Economics and Statistics,* 1964–65, pp. 21–37.

[3] *Towards a New Trade Policy for Development, op. cit.,* p. 107.

XVIII. Although it is a general principle of GATT that protection should be exercised only by tariffs and not quantitative restrictions, Article XVIII provides an exception for countries "which can only support low standards of living and are in the early stages of development" by allowing them to impose quotas in order to protect infant industries or safeguard their balance of payments, if prior approval of the contracting parties is obtained. These countries are also allowed at any time to enter into negotiations for the modification or withdrawal of a tariff concession in order to promote the establishment of particular industries. Article XVIII also provides that whenever the exports of primary products from a less developed country are "seriously affected" by measures taken by another contracting party, the less developed country may invoke special consultation procedures, in the first instance bilaterally, but with the possibility of referring the matter to the contracting parties if no settlement is reached. The provisions of this article have been invoked largely in connection with the use of quota restrictions for balance of payments purposes—and by this means the developing countries have also been enabled to protect domestic industry.[4]

In addition, Article XXV confers broad powers upon the contracting parties to waive "in exceptional circumstances not elsewhere provided" in the Agreement any obligation undertaken by members. The granting of such a waiver requires an approving vote by two-thirds of the members; but this number has now been

---

[4] In contrast to the UNCTAD position, it could be argued that the exceptions allowed by GATT for the less developed countries have actually facilitated or even encouraged the policies of import-substitution and excessive protectionism that have proved costly to these countries. When combined with the IMF's attempt to maintain stable exchange rates, it is not surprising that the developing countries have resorted to a panoply of ad hoc domestic controls.

reached by the developing countries in GATT, provided they act in unanimity.

The principle of reciprocity in tariff negotiations has also been modified for developing countries. Although Article XXVIII specifies that tariff negotiations should be "on a reciprocal and mutually advantageous basis," this article further recognizes that "negotiations shall be conducted on a basis which affords adequate opportunity to take into account . . . the needs of less developed countries for a more flexible use of tariff protection to assist their economic development and the special needs of these countries to maintain tariffs for revenue purposes." This provision has been interpreted by some developed countries as implying that in tariff negotiations with less developed countries full reciprocity need not be sought. And the abandonment of the reciprocity principle as an obligation on developing countries was explicitly acknowledged in the Kennedy Round of tariff negotiations.

Finally, the most significant recognition of the trade problems of developing nations was given in 1966 when the GATT member governments added a new chapter on trade and development to the General Agreement. This chapter comprises three new articles. Article XXXVI, on principles and objectives, states that "there is need for a rapid and sustained expansion of the export earnings of the less-developed contracting parties; there is need for positive efforts designed to ensure that less-developed contracting parties secure a share in the growth in international trade commensurate with the needs of their economic development; there is need to provide in the largest possible measure more favorable and acceptable conditions of access to world markets for [primary] products, and wherever appropriate to devise measures designed to stabilize and improve conditions of world markets in these products, including in particular measures designed to attain stable, equitable, and remunerative prices; there is . . . need for increased access in the largest possible measure to markets under favorable conditions for processed and manufactured products currently or potentially of particular export interest to less-developed contracting parties"; and lastly, the principle is enunciated that "the developed contracting parties do not expect reciprocity for commitments made by them in trade negotiations to reduce or remove tariffs and other barriers to the trade of less-developed contracting parties."

Article XXXVII, on commitments, states that "the developed contracting parties shall to the fullest extent possible . . . (a) accord high priority to the reduction and elimination of barriers to products currently or potentially of particular export interest to less-developed contracting parties, including customs duties and other restrictions which differentiate unreasonably between such products in their primary and in their processed forms; (b) refrain from introducing, or increasing the incidence of, customs duties or non-tariff import barriers" on such products; (c) "refrain from imposing new fiscal measures, and in any adjustments of fiscal policy accord high priority to the reduction and elimination of fiscal measures, which would hamper, or which hamper, significantly the growth of consumption of primary products, in raw or processed form, wholly or mainly produced in the territories of less-developed contracting parties."

Article XXXVIII, on joint action, calls for collaboration among the contracting parties within the framework of the General Agreement and through other international arrangements, as appropriate, "to further the objectives set forth in Article XXXVI."

4. Although the foregoing articles are sympathetic to the special trade problems of the developing countries, these countries remain critical of GATT. For they still believe that the disposition in these articles are neutralized by other articles that benefit the advanced countries, that the actual results of tariff negotiations under GATT

have favored and will continue to favor the major industrialized countries, and that there is a need for more positive and definitive action.

Regarding the neutralizing measures that can be taken by developed countries, the less developed countries express particular concern over Article VI, which allows countries to resort to anti-dumping or countervailing duties to offset the use of subsidies on exports; Article XI, which allows an exceptional use of import quotas on agricultural products in conjunction with domestic agricultural stabilization programs that restrict agricultural production; and Article XIX, which contains an "escape clause" authorizing the withdrawal of concessions if, because of "unforeseen developments," they "cause or threaten serious injury to domestic producers." The elaboration of the doctrine of "market disruption" as a ground for restraining "damaging" exports from low-cost exporters is also of concern to developing countries. It is feared that agreements to avoid "market disruption," such as the Cotton Textiles Arrangement restraining exports of textiles from several developing countries, constitute a threat of restrictive action in respect to the whole range of potential manufactures from less developed countries.[5] In addition, it is claimed that exports from developing countries are particularly hampered by the escalation of tariff rates in the tariff structure of industrialized countries.

While GATT has allowed the developed countries to protect their home production of primary products against competition from less developed countries, the reduction of industrial tariffs that has occurred under GATT's bargaining procedures has been mainly applicable to commodities of interest to the developed countries. For the less developed countries have had little bargain-

[5] Secretariat of UNCTAD, "The Developing Countries in GATT," *Proceedings of UNCTAD*, Vol. V, United Nations, 1964, pp. 452–454.

ing power with which to negotiate, and the technique of negotiating a reduction in tariffs "on a reciprocal and mutually
advantageous basis" has, in practice, meant that the bargaining
has been dominated by the larger, developed countries. The most
substantial reductions in tariffs have been achieved only for manufactured products supplied mainly by the major industrialized
countries.[6] The Kennedy Round of trade negotiations, however,
proved more beneficial to the developing countries insofar as
negotiations for reduction of tariffs on nonagricultural products
were not on a commodity-by-commodity basis, but rather on a
linear across-the-board basis, and full reciprocity was not required
from less developed countries.

Most importantly, it is now contended that GATT does not
go far enough in promoting international arrangements that
would allow developing countries, while retaining their right to
control imports, to gain higher prices for their primary-product
exports and preferential treatment for their export of semimanufactured and manufactured products. The need for such affirma-
tive action is contrasted with the present articles of GATT, which
grant dispositions to less developed countries merely by way of
exceptions to the general rule. Even the new chapter on trade
and development is considered as only minimal: while it professes
some desired objectives, the problem remains to implement these;
also, other objectives sought by the developing countries are not
recognized. It is therefore still argued that new international insti-
tional arrangements are required for: "(a) a full recognition of
the significance of the problem of economic development for

[6] For a full discussion of the several tariff conferences conducted under
GATT, and the conclusion that these conferences have had greater significance for the trade between industrialized countries than for the trade of
underdeveloped countries, see Staffan B. Linder, "The Significance of GATT
for Under-Developed Countries," *Proceedings of* UNCTAD, Vol. V, *op. cit.*,
pp. 502–533.

world trade; (b) differentiation between countries of various levels of economic development and of different economic and social systems; (c) positive and deliberate action to promote exports of developing countries, overcoming the obstacles of agricultural protectionism and industrial discrimination, and providing for preferential treatment and other special measures of aid and encouragement."[7]

To this end, the Final Act of the first session of UNCTAD embodied a number of principles which the Conference recommended to govern international trade relations.[8] Three recommendations may be singled out as most significant:

a. "The expansion and diversification of international trade depends upon increasing access to markets, and upon remunerative prices for the exports of primary products. Developed countries shall progressively reduce and eliminate barriers and other restrictions that hinder trade and consumption of products from developing countries and take positive measures such as will create and increase markets for the exports of developing countries. All countries should cooperate through suitable international arrangements, on an orderly basis, in implementing *measures designed to increase and stabilize primary commodity export earnings, particularly of developing countries, at equitable and remunerative prices* and to maintain a mutually acceptable relationship between the prices of manufactured goods and those of primary products."[9]

b. "Whenever international measures to stabilize prices of primary products in relation to the prices of manufactured goods are inadequate, arrangements should be made on an equitable and universal basis, and without prejudice to the general level of

[7] Secretariat of UNCTAD, *op. cit.*, p. 469.

[8] *Proceedings of* UNCTAD, Vol. I: *Final Act and Report*, United Nations, 1964, pp. 18–25 (hereafter referred to as *Final Act*).

[9] *Ibid.*, pp. 19–20; italics added. The United States and the United Kingdom voted against the adoption of this principle.

financial aid to developing countries, to correct and *compensate for the deterioration in terms of trade and short-term decline in export earnings of countries exporting primary products,* with a view to facilitating the implementation of economic development plans and programmes."[10]

c. "International trade should be conducted to mutual advantage on the basis of the most-favored-nation treatment and should be free from measures detrimental to the trading interests of other countries. However, *developed countries should grant concessions to all developing countries* and extend to developing countries all concessions they grant to one another *and should not, in granting these or other concessions, require any concessions in return from developing countries. New preferential concessions, both tariff and non-tariff, should be made to developing countries as a whole and such preferences should not be extended to developed countries. Developing countries need not extend to developed countries preferential treatment in operation amongst them.*"[11]

Much of the demand for reform of international economic institutions in the interest of development focuses upon proposals for increasing and stabilizing primary export earnings and for preferential trading arrangements for the exports of manufactures from developing countries. These proposals now merit further examination.

5. The case for international action to increase and stabilize primary export earnings acquires special force from the contention that, without such action, the growth in primary exports will continue to be too slow to finance the import requirements of a

[10] *Ibid.,* p. 23; italics added. The United States and United Kingdom also voted against this principle.

[11] *Ibid.,* p. 20; italics added. Again, the United States and United Kingdom voted against this principle.

development plan, and the instability of export earnings will have adverse effects on development programming. The preceding chapter has already noted the sluggish growth in primary exports in connection with the "widening trade gap," and evidence can be cited to warrant a pessimistic view regarding the prospects of primary exports.[12]

In addition to the low rate of growth in the level of their primary export earnings, the developing countries are also disconcerted about the instability in their export revenue and short-period fluctuations in their terms of trade. It is not, however, possible to generalize on the degree of instability in primary export proceeds, nor the causes of fluctuations in export earnings. Although some empirical studies would indicate that these countries are subject to a much greater degree of instability in export proceeds than are the industrial countries,[13] several other studies find the degree of difference to be much less than commonly supposed.[14] One's conclusions, with respect to the instability in

[12] See UNCTAD, *Commodity Survey, 1966* (TD/B/C.1/23); United Nations, *Monthly Bulletin of Statistics*, November, 1966, pp. xxi-xxiv; Alfred Maizels, *Industrial Growth and World Trade*, Cambridge Univ. Press, 1963, chap. 5; Bela Balassa, *Trade Prospects for Developing Countries*, Richard D. Irwin, 1964, chaps. 3-4; FAO, *Agricultural Commodities: Projections for 1970*, Special Supplement to *FAO Commodity Review*, Rome, 1962.

[13] UNCTAD, *The Adequacy of Reserves of Developing Countries in the Post-War Period*, November 10, 1965, TD/B/34, pp. 1-3; United Nations, *World Economic Survey 1962*, Vol. I, New York, 1963, pp. 48-58; "Fund Policies and Procedures in Relation to the Compensatory Financing of Commodity Fluctuations," *IMF Staff Papers*, November, 1960, pp. 1-76.

[14] Alasdair I. MacBean, *Export Instability and Economic Development*, Harvard Univ. Press, 1966, chap. 2; Benton F. Massell, "Export Concentration and Export Earnings," *American Economic Review*, March, 1964, pp. 47-63; Michael Michaely, *Concentration in International Trade*, North-Holland Pub. Co., 1962, pp. 102-132; John D. Coppock, *International Economic Instability*, McGraw-Hill, 1962, chap. 5.

export proceeds, depends very much on the statistical method selected for correcting for trends, the coverage of countries and commodities, and the period examined. Perhaps the most reasonable conclusions from the various empirical studies are that the tendency for the developing countries as a group to have less stable export earnings is not as strong as some spokesmen for these countries have asserted; there is wide variation in the experience of different primary-producing countries; there is also considerable overlap in the experience of instability between rich and poor countries; for many of the developing countries, export quantum instability is more important than export price instability in determining instability in their export proceeds; there is no necessary relationship between the size of fluctuations in export earnings and a country's specialization in one or two primary exports (commodity concentration) or on one or two importing market areas (geographical concentration); and finally, for those individual countries that have experienced a high degree of export instability, the causes of the instability must be analyzed in terms of specific factors relevant to the individual country and its particular export products.

Although statements by UNCTAD tend to overemphasize and overgeneralize the degree of instability, nonetheless UNCTAD is calling attention to a real problem. The uncertainty and variability of export prices and earnings can certainly have adverse effects on the development program of a particular country when the country depends upon one or two primary-product exports which are peculiarly vulnerable to price fluctuations, and when the country's exports are large relative to its national product. For such a country, wide fluctuations in export receipts can disrupt the development program in various ways: There will be parallel fluctuations in the level of national income, savings, and investment; there may also be changes in the distribution of money incomes that are adverse for the development program; the induced variation in government revenue is likely to be substantial, since a large fraction of government revenue may be derived from taxation of foreign trade. Also, in the presence of uncertainty about future earnings, subsistence farmers may be discouraged from shifting-out of subsistence agriculture to reliance on cash crops. Finally, and most significantly, the pattern of investment will be distorted and its efficiency reduced if imports of necessary goods and materials must be restricted when export proceeds fall, or if there is overinvestment in the export sector when exports rise and the gestation period in production is long so that excess production capacity appears in the future.[15]

Some of these adverse effects could be mitigated if the developing country had "adequate" foreign exchange reserves or were the recipient of sufficient foreign capital to offset the fluctuations in export proceeds. But this is rarely true. And yet the traditional primary products account for more than 90 percent of the export earnings of the developing countries, and the fulfillment of development targets will continue to depend largely on the prices and volume of primary exports. To increase and stabilize the proceeds from these exports, UNCTAD has therefore called for trade liberalization policies by the industrial countries, an extension of international commodity agreements, and a greater amount of compensatory financing for shortfalls in export proceeds.

For some primary exports, the instability in foreign-exchange earnings can be attributed mainly to fluctuations in demand. To this extent, the maintenance of import demand through high and

[15] Cf. William C. Brainard and Richard N. Cooper, "Uncertainty and Diversification in International Trade," Cowles Foundation Discussion Paper No. 197, October 27, 1965, sec. 1; Clark W. Reynolds, "Domestic Consequences of Export Instability," *American Economic Review, Papers and Proceedings*, May, 1963, pp. 93–102; Michaely, *op. cit.*, pp. 107–119.

stable levels of employment in industrial countries is of prime importance, and the less developed countries rightly insist on the pursuit of expansionary policies and higher rates of growth in industrial countries.

In addition, there is merit to the UNCTAD argument that tariffs and quotas should be removed on imports of primary products into industrialized countries, in order to increase the share of imports from the developing countries in the total consumption of the advanced countries. Out of consideration for their domestic farm price-support schemes, many developed countries have imposed tariffs and quotas on primary products which compete with domestic production. As has been concluded by a committee of GATT,[16] trade in agricultural products is largely isolated from the operation of market forces, and the application of the provisions of GATT has therefore been extremely difficult. Some 30 percent of the primary products exported from less developed countries (excluding petroleum) compete directly with protected agriculture in the high-income importing countries, and the additional earnings from relaxations in import restrictions on these commodities could be quite significant.[17] But it is optimistic to expect any marked reduction in trade restrictions on agricultural trade before there is a change in the character of domestic farm programs that have given rise to import restrictions. Even though it may be politically unrealistic to expect any immediate and dramatic reversal of domestic agricultural policies and agricultural protectionism, the developing countries can legitimately complain about the adverse affects of these restrictions on their exports. In the interest of trade liberalization, UNCTAD fulfills a useful function

---

[16] Third Report of Committee II, GATT, *Basic Instruments and Selected Documents*, Tenth Supplement, Geneva, March, 1962.

[17] *New Directions for World Trade*, Proceedings of a Chatham House Conference, Oxford Univ. Press, 1964, pp. 46, 175; United Nations, *World Economic Survey 1963*, Part I, New York, 1964, chap. 5.

in focusing on this problem and applying constant pressure for the reduction of obstacles to agricultural trade.

On those tropical agricultural exports which do not compete with domestic production, tariffs and quantitative restrictions are negligible or nonexistent in most of the importing countries. But several advanced countries maintain substantial excise taxes on coffee, tea, cocoa, and sugar. When these excises operate in the elastic range of demand, their reduction would benefit the exporting countries. If, however, demand is inelastic, then it might be argued that the revenue collected from such taxes should be remitted directly to the poorer exporting country, or contributed by the tax-levying country to some foreign aid use.

6. Not all of the slow rate of growth in primary exports, however, can be attributed only to deficiencies in external demand. Low elasticities of supply and the domestic policies of a developing country—especially the protectionist import-substitution policies—may also limit the growth of exports of primary produce.[18] A country can ill-afford to overlook internal factors when its relative share of exports in the world market has declined in the face of a rise in world demand.[19]

[18] See, among others, Harry G. Johnson, *Economic Policies toward Less Developed Countries*, Brookings Institution, 1967, pp. 67–78; Hla Myint, *The Economics of the Developing Countries*, Hutchinson, 1964, pp. 153–155; Myint, *Economic Theory and Development Policy*, G. Bell and Sons, Ltd., 1967, pp. 8–11; GATT, *International Trade 1963*, Geneva, 1964, pp. 8–17; A. K. Cairncross, "International Trade and Economic Development," *Economica*, August, 1961, pp. 242–249.

[19] For the case of India, see Benjamin I. Cohen, "The Stagnation of Indian Exports, 1951–1961," *Quarterly Journal of Economics*, November, 1964, pp. 604–620; M. Singh, *India's Export Trends and the Prospects for Self-Sustained Growth*, Clarendon Press, 1964, pp. 150–174, 337–338; Bhabatash Datt, *et al., Economic Development and Exports*, World Press Private Ltd., 1962, pp. 194–211.

Even if the price elasticity of demand for a primary commodity is generally low on world markets, it may be high from any one supplier among alternative sources of supply. If the prices of substitute products in importing countries rise relatively to the price of the primary export, the volume of exports may also increase. A developing country may thus benefit to the extent that it improves its competitive position in export markets and acquires a cost advantage over substitutes by increasing productivity and restraining internal demand.

Since it is highly improbable that all primary products face unfavorable growth prospects, poor countries must also attempt to specialize as much as they can in exports with the highest growth prospects. This entails, of course, the difficult problem of reallocating resources. To shift, for example, from the production of a foodstuff export, which faces only a slowly rising demand, to an industrial raw material or mineral export, which has a more rapidly expanding demand, will require structural changes and greater mobility of resources. When the possibility of transformation in production exists, proper internal policies are still needed to increase resource flexibility and facilitate a better pattern of resource use. But instead of giving the necessary attention to promoting their primary exports, many developing countries have neglected agricultural production, imposed export controls and export duties, and have used the export sector to finance the domestic manufacturing sector. We have already laid considerable emphasis on the widespread discrimination against exports and the implicit levy on agriculture and exports as a result of policies involving import restrictions, inflation, overvalued exchange rates, and subsidization of import-substituting industries.[20]

It should therefore be recognized that, in addition to urging the liberalization of trade, the developing countries must also take

[20] See Chapter 7, section 10.

remedial action on their own to exploit fully their available opportunities and raise the level of their exports.

7. UNCTAD's insistence on market access for the developing countries' primary exports can be supported as a desirable way of increasing foreign-exchange earnings through an expansion of world trade, in conformity with market forces and efficiency in resource allocation. More controversial issues, however, are raised by UNCTAD's demand for the extensive use of international commodity agreements in order to attain "equitable and remunerative prices" for the primary exports of developing countries and to "maintain a mutually acceptable relationship between the prices of manufactured goods and those of primary products."[21]

International commodity agreements can take a variety of forms, but they essentially involve, either separately or in combination, the operation of a system of export quotas (as in the coffee agreement), an international buffer stock which operates within a range of prices (tin agreement), or a multilateral long-term contract which stipulates a minimum price at which importing countries agree to buy specified quantities and a maximum price at which producing countries agree to export a stated amount (as originally in the wheat agreement).[22]

---

[21] UNCTAD, *Final Act, op. cit.*, pp. 19–20, 26–29; also, *Towards a New Trade Policy for Development, op. cit.*, pp. 43–48, 55–58, 119–120.

[22] For details of various possible schemes, and an appraisal of their respective merits and demerits, see MacBean, *op. cit.*, chap. 12; J. W. F. Rowe, *Primary Commodities in International Trade*, Cambridge Univ. Press, 1965, Part IV; Gerda Blau, "International Commodity Arrangements and Policies," *FAO Monthly Bulletin of Agricultural Economics and Statistics*, September, 1963, pp. 1–9; Sir Sydney Caine, *Prices for Primary Products*, Hobart Papers No. 24, Institute of Economic Affairs, 1963; Nicholas Kaldor, "Stabilizing the Terms of Trade of Under-Developed Countries," *Economic Bulletin for Latin America*, March, 1963, pp. 1–7.

Regardless of the particular form of a commodity stabilization agreement, the objective of "stabilization" is ambiguous: "stabilization" may refer to the international price of an export commodity, producers' money income or real income, export earnings, or the purchasing power of primary exports over imports. An inescapable difficulty of a commodity control scheme is that in stabilizing one of these variables (for instance, price), it may at the same time destabilize another variable (for instance, export earnings).

It is, however, apparent from the emphasis that UNCTAD gives to the attainment of "equitable and remunerative prices" that the main objective is not simply to obtain stable export prices but to use commodity control schemes as instruments for increasing export prices. In drawing an analogy with the protection afforded agricultural producers in the developed countries through domestic price-support programs, the poor countries are clearly seeking similar protection for their primary producers through international price-support schemes with the hope of raising their level of export earnings and the purchasing power of their exports in terms of industrial imports. But while under a domestic price-support program the domestic consumers are in effect being taxed to support domestic producers, an international control agreement would in effect tax the consumers in the importing country for the benefit of the exporting country. The international agreement would be a means of transferring resources from the advanced importing country to the less developed exporting country. As such, aid would be provided in the guise of a commodity agreement. Indeed, the distinctive feature of an international agreement is precisely that it might raise the long-term trend of the developing country's export prices, improve its terms of trade, and thereby have the quality of giving aid to the exporting country.

If, in contrast, the objective were only to offset the domestic effects of instability in export prices, the developing country could utilize national policy measures—for example, marketing boards, stabilization funds, or variable export duties—without the need for an international agreement. For purposes of pure stabilization, internal policies may be used to break the link between export earnings and the level of domestic spending.[23] An official marketing board can limit the impact of export fluctuations on the domestic economy by paying a price to the producer that differs from the price which the board receives when it sells in the export market. Export duties can be on a sliding scale so that they are higher when the export price is high, and lower when the export price is low. More effective monetary and fiscal measures could also reduce instability.

Although it is one thing to compare a commodity agreement against alternative measures as a technique for offsetting the range of fluctuation in export prices around the trend, it is quite a different matter to view it as a means of raising the price above what is justified by the long-run average trend in supply and demand conditions. While its potential as a form of aid makes the use of an international commodity agreement appealing to the less developed countries, it is highly questionable whether in practice this would even be feasible, or desirable.

If the use of an international buffer stock scheme is contemplated, it can obviously be applied only to those primary products

[23] See MacBean, *op. cit.*, chaps. 10, 11; David Walker, "Marketing Boards," E. A. G. Robinson, ed., *Problems in Economic Development*, Macmillan Co., 1965, pp. 574–596; R. C. Porter, "The Optimal Price Problem in Buffer Fund Stabilization," *Oxford Economic Papers*, November, 1964, pp. 423–430; H. C. Wallich, "Stabilization of Proceeds from Raw Material Exports," H. S. Ellis, ed., *Economic Development for Latin America*, St. Martin's Press, 1961, pp. 356–357; P. T. Bauer and F. W. Paish, "The Reduction of Fluctuations in the Incomes of Primary Producers," *Economic Journal*, December, 1952, pp. 750–780.

that have the physical characteristics of being highly standardized in quality-grades and capable of being stored at not too high a cost over long periods without deterioration in quality. In terms of only technical practicality, the range of eligible primary commodities is narrow. The next question of financing the buffer stock fund is also a difficult one: The less-developed countries may have the greatest interest in initiating such a fund, but they are the least able to afford the burden of financial contributions, while the richer countries are the least willing to support a scheme that will raise the prices of their imports. Finally, to the extent that the buffer stock arrangement is designed to maintain the minimum price of the commodity above the long-run equilibrium price, it will be necessary to engage in the continual accumulation of stocks. To forestall the eventual exhaustion of financial resources, and collapse of the scheme, there would then have to be a downward adjustment in the operating range of prices (and abandonment of the higher price level desired by the producing countries), or else the buffer stock has to be supplemented by sufficiently effective export controls.

Once a commodity agreement must depend upon restriction of output or export quotas, the problems multiply—as the dismal historical record of control schemes abundantly indicates. To be effective, there must be comprehensive control of both actual and potential production: The producing countries in the agreement must supply the dominant part of exports and have some control over the potential supply. To ensure adequate policing of the export quotas, importing countries must also cooperate in discriminating against nonparticipating exporters. A common failing of an export-quota arrangement is its inability to secure or maintain full participation by all the producing countries: Some exporters are tempted to remain outside the agreement and benefit from the higher export prices without being restricted in the development of their own exports; if there is a redistribution of export quotas (as there must be when the pattern of production and trade changes with time), those countries required to reduce their share of world trade will be reluctant to remain within the agreement, and those countries that are the low-cost producers will be tempted to break away from the agreement with the expectation that they will gain more from the expansion of their own share of trade outside the agreement than they will lose from any possible fall in prices. An individual producing country must also have sufficient power to control the output of individual producers in accordance with changes in its quota allocation, or else it will face a heavy financial strain in accumulating excess stocks, and will again be tempted to evade the agreement. If importing countries agreed to import only from participants in the agreement, this would help maintain full participation by producing countries; but the more effective the agreement in raising price above the free market level, the less inclined will the consuming countries be to support the agreement. Finally, the agreement must be for a commodity for which substitutes do not exist and cannot be easily evolved; otherwise, the upward pressure on price will induce the importing countries to replace the commodity domestically with natural or synthetic substitutes (as could be expected for rubber, jute, cotton, vegetable oils, nonferrous metals). Only a very limited number of primary products possess the necessary demand and supply requisites for effective agreements with price-raising objectives, and even for these the estimated increase in export earnings is fairly small.[24]

Assuming that an agreement could be successfully negotiated and effectively administered, so that the export price rises to a higher level than would otherwise prevail, we must still ask whether the possible benefits will outweigh any unfavorable con-

---

[24] John Pincus, *Trade, Aid and Development*, McGraw-Hill, 1967, pp. 267–268; MacBean, *op. cit.*, pp. 295–297.

sequences. When the essential benefit of the agreement is the receipt of an increase in aid in the concealed form of a commodity agreement, we should be aware of the differences between this form of "disguised" aid and the alternative of an increase in "open" aid.

In contrast to all that has been said about rational criteria for the allocation of aid among countries, this approach would distribute aid merely on the basis of production of those commodities for which prices can be raised. There is then no reason to believe that the recipients of aid would be those countries that meet the criterion of "need" or "performance" or any other criterion beyond being a producer of the protected commodity. Not only is there a problem in having the wrong countries receive aid, but also a further complexity in having the wrong groups within the developing country be the beneficiaries of this form of aid. Unlike open aid, disguised aid through a commodity agreement would benefit directly the producers of the commodity. An additional step of intervention by the fiscal system is then necessary if the producers' gains are to be captured for support of the country's development program.

The commodity approach to aid also places the burden of aid more heavily on the larger importers—not necessarily those most able to bear it. And it does not allow the donor to exercise any influence over the disposal of its aid for development objectives. For these reasons, it would generally be more difficult to incorporate into a development program the gain from aid through a commodity agreement than is true for open aid.[25]

[25] For a similar conclusion that commodity agreements represent an inefficient and inequitable means of raising and allocating aid, see Mac-Bean, *op. cit.*, pp. 293–302; Little and Clifford, *op. cit.*, pp. 157–158; Thomas Balogh, *The Economics of Poverty*, Weidenfeld and Nicolson, 1966, pp. 111–117.

This approach to commodity agreements also stresses a deliberate improvement in the terms of trade, but this emphasis can easily be misdirected. As already noted in Chapter 2, a country's factoral terms or income terms of trade may be more significant than its commodity terms of trade. The attempt to raise long-run prices focuses, however, on an improvement in only the commodity terms of trade. If a country succeeds in increasing productivity, it may offset the deterioration in the price of its primary export. And a country may gain an increase in its foreign exchange earnings while its commodity terms of trade deteriorate.

It can, of course, be argued that an increase in open aid does not exist as a realistic alternative. Even if this were granted, however, we must still recognize other unfavorable consequences of commodity agreements.

It is especially important to realize that if the main cause of price changes is due to variations in supply rather than demand, the stabilization of price may at the same time destabilize export earnings. If, on the other hand, commodity receipts do increase, the immediate beneficiaries would be the producers of the commodity, and if their additional income is not to be simply dissipated in higher consumption, or capital flight, the government must have sufficient tax power to siphon off the benefit of higher export prices and channel the funds into development financing. Most significantly, the major disadvantage is the resultant misallocation of resources: If high-cost producers are sheltered, and the price is not related to cost of production, there is bound to be inefficient use of resources. And the misallocation of resources will intensify over time when the commodity agreement prevents equilibrating adjustments in supply and demand, subsidizes production of products for which demand is declining, freezes the pattern of commodity trade in defiance of changing comparative advantage, or revises the distribution of export quotas in terms of political considerations instead of economic criteria. It is certainly a dubious proposition that development can be furthered by protecting inefficiency and inhibiting the necessary shifts in production.

In summary, the case against international commodity agreements rests on the extremely disappointing historical record of such agreements, the fact that they are at best relevant for only a small number of primary commodities, and the difficulty in avoiding the adverse effects, which tend to outweigh any potential benefit.

It is therefore not surprising that increasing attention is being given to other policy measures that might stabilize export earnings. Among these measures, the proposals for compensatory financing schemes and the use of national stabilization policies are most significant.

8. A variety of compensatory financing schemes have been proposed in order to stabilize export earnings.[26] Details differ, but all the schemes relate to some special financial support to the developing countries in periods of low export earnings. Some proposals would entail grants or contingent loans (repayable only if export proceeds later rise) to cover a fall in export proceeds in accordance with some formula, while other schemes would provide loans which must be repaid within a certain time period, regardless of future export earnings.

Since 1963, the IMF has provided some compensatory financ-

---

[26] The most significant proposals are outlined in the following: United Nations, *International Compensation for Fluctuations in Commodity Trade*, Report by a Committee of Experts, New York, 1961; Organization of American States, *Final Report of the Group of Experts on the Stabilization of Exports Receipts*, Washington, D.C., 1962; UNCTAD, *Final Act, op. cit.*, pp. 14, 52, 138–140, 201–202.

ing to primary exporting countries.[27] If a member has a temporary shortfall in export receipts from a medium-term trend value, it is entitled to a compensatory drawing from the IMF equal to one tranche (25 percent of the member's quota) beyond its gold tranche.[28] The conditions of compensation are that the shortfall must be of a short-term character and largely due to circumstances beyond the member's control. Repayment must be made within a three- to five-year period. In 1966 the IMF extended the compensatory facility to permit outstanding compensatory drawings up to 50 percent of a member's quota, subject to the condition that outstanding drawings may not increase by more than 25 percent of the quota in any twelve-month period. The compensatory facility has also been separated from other drawing facilities of the Fund and does not affect the member's ability to participate in ordinary drawings in the various quota tranches. No change, however, has been made in the repayment system.

Although UNCTAD proposed an extension of the IMF's compensatory facility, it was still believed that the compensatory financing that could be provided by the Fund would remain too limited in amount and for too short a duration. Additional assistance was sought between the short-term balance of payments support of the IMF and the long-term basic type of foreign aid. It was therefore further recommended that the World Bank study

[27] IMF, *Compensatory Financing of Export Fluctuations*, Washington, D.C., 1963.

[28] The first session of UNCTAD adopted a recommendation calling for an increase in compensatory financing from 25 percent to 50 percent of a member's quota; the placing of compensatory credits entirely outside the structure of the gold and successive credit tranches, so that the drawing of compensatory credits would not prejudice a member's ability to make an ordinary drawing; and the exploration of ways to secure possible refinancing of compensatory financing obligations: UNCTAD, *Final Act, op. cit.*, Annex A.IV.17, p. 52.

the feasibility of a new scheme for supplementary financial measures which "should aim to deal with problems arising from adverse movements in export proceeds which prove to be of a nature or duration which cannot adequately be dealt with by short-term balance-of-payments support."[29]

Such a study was prepared by the staff of the World Bank,[30] and it has been supported in principle by various committees of UNCTAD. Believing that it is necessary to provide adequate insurance against disruption of development plans because of a shortfall of export proceeds from reasonable expectations, the study proposes a scheme for supplying supplementary finance when export proceeds fail—for reasons beyond the control of the developing country—to yield the anticipated amount of foreign exchange.

The essential features of the scheme are, in brief, as follows: The scheme is predicated on the assumption that the financing that it would provide would be supplementary to, and not a substitute for, the already existing basic forms of aid. Through consultation and collaboration, the international agency administering the scheme and the developing country would first reach an understanding upon a development program and a related set of development policies to be pursued by the country.[31] The assessment of this "policy package" would be flexible and pragmatic, but it is intended that the government of the developing country

[29] UNCTAD, *Final Act, op. cit.,* Annex A.IV.18, pp. 52–53.

[30] International Bank for Reconstruction and Development, *Supplementary Financial Measures*, Washington, D.C., December, 1965. For some objections to the study, however, see UNCTAD, *Report of the Committee on Invisibles and Financing Related to Trade*, April 23, 1966, TD/B/73, pp. 3–9.

[31] The UNCTAD resolution on supplementary finance proposed that the scheme be administered under the International Development Association (IDA) of the World Bank, and that "assistance should be on concessional and flexible terms."

should be committed to "good performance, rather widely conceived." This collaborative effort could also be instrumental in integrating the coordinating mechanisms among other international lending agencies and the recipient countries.

As part of a mutual understanding, there would be an agreed projection of "reasonable expectations" of export earnings over a period of years; normally this projection period would correspond to the country's plan-period of four to six years. Throughout the course of the agreement, both the policy package and projection of export earnings would be subject to regular review and, if necessary, to revision. There would also be agreement upon measures the government of the developing country would take to adjust to a possible shortfall in export earnings without disrupting its development program: First, any excess of export earnings above the agreed projection experienced earlier in the projection period, i.e., any "overage," would be applied against a subsequent shortfall; additional steps might then include use of the country's own reserves and drawings on the IMF. After other sources of financing are exhausted, the scheme would operate as a residual source of lending to cover the unexpected shortfall in export proceeds (net of accumulated "overages"), provided the shortfall is potentially disruptive to the country's development program, and has resulted for reasons beyond the country's control. Ordinarily, for ease of administration, the agency would calculate actual shortfalls and "overages" on the basis of one-year periods.

The supplementary financing is not intended to relieve the country of all the burden of adjustment, but rather to allow the adjustment process to be compatible with continuation of the development program. It is to be noted that no arbitrary statistical formula would be used to determine the shortfall from some "export norm"; instead the shortfall would be related to "reasonable expectations" of export earnings. Moreover, as long as the country has been acting within the mutually understood frame of reference, all unexpected shortfalls would be considered as beyond the country's control, and the agency would then provide the necessary financing to offset the shortfall with certainty and "all deliberate speed." It is conservatively estimated that the financing entailed by such a scheme would be some $300 to $400 million a year; the bulk, if not all, of the financing would come from the developed countries. Members would have to reimburse the scheme to the extent that initial shortfalls are followed by "overages" during the same projection period. The net deficit over the entire projection period that was financed by the agency would be transferred into long-term indebtedness, and the terms of repayment to the agency would be tailored to the debt-servicing capacity and other relevant factors of the country.

Although technical and administrative details remain to be worked out, some broad criticisms of the scheme immediately suggest themselves. It is clear that its operational significance would depend heavily on the determination of "reasonable expectations" of the level of export revenue, the meaning of "disruption of development programs," the choice of indicators of "good performance," and the separation of internal factors from external factors in identifying the causes of the shortfall. According to how these crucial concepts were interpreted and measured, a country's eligibility for supplementary financing would be significantly affected. Moreover, the countries that would benefit would be those whose export prospects were interpreted as "good" but turn out to be disappointing, while nothing would be done for those countries whose export prospects were expected to be "poor" and actually turn out so. Similarly, a country that has a fairly satisfactory absolute level of export proceeds but is subject to instability in export revenue would benefit, while another country with a less adequate absolute level of export revenue but with less instability, would benefit less. The scheme would also meet the problem of external imbalance from only the side of a fall in exports; but for many countries the pressure on the balance of payments may instead be coming from a rise in imports or the strain of debt servicing. Nor is the shortfall considered in real terms; unexpected changes in import prices are neglected. Finally, the scheme is addressed to only the problem of fluctuations in export revenue. It does nothing to remove uncertainty about export prices, and to this extent the social costs of price fluctuations would remain even though export proceeds were not allowed to fall below "reasonable expectations."

But most of these criticisms are asking the scheme to meet other problems beyond that for which it is designed. Judged simply by whether it is a practicable way of helping developing countries overcome unpredictable export shortfalls, and carry on well-prepared development programs without disruption, the scheme does have considerable attraction.

Unlike other measures that would stabilize only export prices, a scheme of supplementary financing would directly take account of fluctuations in the volume of exports as well as price fluctuations. And since, for many countries, the instability in total export proceeds stems more from quantity fluctuations than from changes in price,[32] this is highly important.

The developing country's task of planning would clearly be eased if it could rely on a definite level of export proceeds for a number of years ahead: While long-term basic aid would be related to an expected decline in a recipient country's export earnings, supplementary financing would provide funds when exports fail to yield the expected amount of foreign exchange for reasons beyond the control of the developing country. And by having

[32] MacBean, *op. cit.*, pp. 46–57.

the assistance have a direct impact on the public finances of the country, instead of affecting the prices received by producers (as under an international commodity agreement), there may be a greater contribution to the development of the economy.

Indeed, by associating the problem of primary exports with a country's development program in general, a scheme of supplementary financing properly shifts the emphasis away from the overly narrow concern with individual commodities to the more significant relationship between the country's balance of payments and its development program. If there is to be international action to meet the developing country's problem of primary exports, it is desirable that this should, at the same time, provide the incentive and means for undergirding the priority of development in the country's domestic policy. It is therefore a decided advantage to interrelate—as this scheme does—domestic performance, external factors, and development assistance.

9. Although the foregoing proposals are essentially variations on the long-standing complaint of primary producing countries, the proposals of UNCTAD, with respect to manufactured exports, give a new perspective to the trade problems of developing countries. The demand for tariff preferences on the exports of semimanufactured and manufactured goods from the developing countries has been the most provocative and controversial of UNCTAD's recommendations.

It is readily understandable why there is now so much interest in the potential for industrialization through export of manufactures. Even if international and national policies were adopted to increase and stabilize the earnings from primary exports, most of the less developed countries would still remain pessimistic about their opportunities for development through primary exports. It is believed that the "widening trade gap" can only be narrowed by taking advantage of new export possibilities for manufactured goods.[33] Some countries that confront growing population pressure also foresee an inevitable need to become net importers of agricultural products and net exporters of manufactures. Even more significantly, one country after another has come to realize the severe limitations that it eventually encounters in attempting to industrialize through import-substitution. A strategy of industrialization through export of manufactures has therefore become increasingly favored.

To this end, the developing countries in UNCTAD agreed in principle that two types of preferential arrangements should be negotiated: (1) some form of general preferential system by which developed countries would grant preferences to less developed countries on manufactures and semimanufactures, without requiring preferences from the less developed countries in return (an exception to Article I of GATT), and (2) regional preferential systems among the less developed countries by which they would be allowed to discriminate in favor of one another without having to enter into a full-fledged customs union or free trade area comprising substantially all the commerce of the member nations (an exception to Article XXIV of GATT).[34]

[33] Manufactured exports from the less developed countries amounted to less than 5 percent of world exports of manufactures in 1965. Only Hong Kong, India, Israel, and Mexico export more than \$100 million of manufactures to developed countries; and together these countries account for more than one-half of industrial exports from developing countries.

It has, however, been estimated that, to support a 3 percent increase in per capita income, manufactured exports from the less developed countries would have to increase at least sevenfold between 1961 and 1980: Economic Commission for Europe, *Economic Survey of Europe in 1960*, United Nations, 1961, chap. V.

[34] The pertinent UNCTAD recommendations are contained in *Final Act*, *op. cit.*, Annex A.III.5 (general preferences), p. 39; Annex A.III.8 (re-

As between general and regional preferential arrangements, a stronger economic case can be advanced for a preferential tariff association among developing countries, even though the developing countries place greater emphasis on their receiving of preferences from the developed countries.

Contrary to GATT's insistence on zero tariffs within a customs union or free trade area, the theory of "second-best" would support a partial customs union or preferential tariff association among developing countries. When tariffs exist outside a customs union, and the customs union maintains an external tariff, it is not necessarily true that the complete removal of tariffs among members of the union will raise welfare; all that we can really conclude is that the constrained, or "second-best," optimum for the tariffs among the members will be something greater than zero and less than the tariffs on outside imports. If only some tariffs are to be changed by the formation of a preferential trading group, and trade diversion results as the degree of discrimination within the preferential trade area continues to increase, then a partial reduction of duties among the trading partners is more likely to raise welfare than would a complete removal of tariffs within the preference area.[35] There is therefore no economic justification in maintaining, as GATT does, that members of a regional trading group should be allowed to grant only 100 percent preferences to each other.

---

gional preferences), p. 41; Annex A.II.1 (phased abolition of existing preferential arrangements between developed countries and developing countries which involve discrimination against other developing countries), p. 30.

[35] See James E. Meade, *The Theory of Customs Union*, North-Holland Pub. Co., 1955, pp. 110–111; R. G. Lipsey, "The Theory of Customs Unions: A General Survey," *Economic Journal*, September, 1960, pp. 506–507; W. M. Corden, *Recent Developments in the Theory of International Trade*, Princeton Univ. Press, 1965, p. 54; Jaroslav Vanek, *General Equilibrium of International Discrimination*, Harvard Univ. Press, 1965, chap. I.

Moreover, once we compare a preferential tariff association with the existing situation in which the less developed countries are using trade restrictions to promote import-replacement industries, the real alternative now is obviously not between free trade and import substitution in a preferential tariff association, but rather between the present practice of import substitution within each developing country or within the proposed preference area. There is then considerable force to the argument that import substitution on a regional basis can enable the member countries to protect a given amount of industry at a lower real cost in terms of income foregone than do the present policies of national import substitution and compartmentalized industrialization within the narrower market of each developing country.[36]

Considering how difficult it is to expand their exports of manufactures to developed countries, the developing countries should give particular emphasis to ways of increasing trade among themselves. Through a preferential tariff association, trade in manufactures among the less developed countries might become considerably greater, in view of the restrictions that these countries have imposed against one another's manufactures as well as those from the more developed countries. The manufactures produced in a less developed country are also likely to be more appropriate for marketing in another less developed country than in advanced industrial countries where considerations of quality, specifications, and design become decisive.

Although a preferential trading arrangement would have the merit of bringing about a more rational location of industry, with industry concentrated in the lowest-cost producing country, this is, at the same time, its main drawback for some prospective mem-

---

[36] See C. A. Cooper and B. F. Massell, "Toward a General Theory of Customs Unions for Developing Countries," *Journal of Political Economy*, October, 1965, pp. 461–476.

bers. For this implies, of course, that other member countries will have to forego some national industries. As in a full customs union,[37] the members in a preferential tariff association would not benefit equally with respect to the growth of their industries. The basic problem is that unless a regional preferential arrangement fosters competition among the local industries of the member countries, and allows industrial production among the members according to their comparative advantages, there is little to commend it; but to the extent that it succeeds in doing so, some members will undoubtedly prefer their own national policies of industrialization.

For this reason, and because an expansion of trade among the developing countries would neither raise the supply of foreign exchange from the more developed countries, nor offer the possibility of providing "aid," the developing countries have given only minor emphasis to regional preferences. Their prime demand is for the granting of general preferences by the advanced countries.

10. The strongest argument in favor of general preferences is that it may allow foreign aid to be increased in the disguised form of trade policy. Because of the preferential advantage, prices for imports from the less developed countries could be higher (prior to duty collection) than for imports from developed countries; but the total price, including duty, would be lower for imports from the preference-receiving countries than from the developed countries. Hence the imports would be supplied by the less developed countries. If trade preferences thus enabled the exporters of the developing countries to charge the importing country a price that is higher than the world market price, the effect would be to transfer resources from the richer to the poorer countries, just as

[37] Cf. Chapter 7, section 11.

under aid.[38] In effect, the import duties that would be foregone by the preference-granting country would now revert to the preference-receiving country.

This possibility of a resource transfer is what makes preferential tariff reductions so much more attractive to developing countries than a nondiscriminatory most-favored nation reduction in duties. If it is also assumed that foreign aid programs would not otherwise be increased, and that trade preferences might be politically easier for a developed country to accept than a direct increase in aid, then there is considerable appeal in seeking an increase in aid through trade policy. The criteria of aid allocation that we previously discussed would, however, no longer apply,[39] and both the "donors" and "recipients" under a policy of aid through preferences would tend to be quite different from those in a pro-

[38] Cf. Gardner Patterson, *Discrimination in International Trade*, Princeton Univ. Press, 1966, p. 379; Pincus, *op. cit.*, pp. 202–204, 225–230.

As an illustration, assume that initially a developed country can supply a manufactured commodity on world markets for a price of $100, and a less developed country can supply the same product at $110. If another developed country imposes a 20 percent ad valorem duty on the product, then the importer can buy the goods from the first developed country for $120, but the cost from the less developed country would be $132. If now the import duty is completely removed on imports from the less developed country (100 percent tariff preferences), while the duty is retained at 20 percent for imports from the developed country, the preference-granting country will then import from the less developed country and pay $110. In the initial situation, the country imported at $100 and paid the 20 percent duty to itself; after preferences are granted, the cost of the import rises from $100 to $110, and there is a transfer of resources of $10 to the preference-receiving country.

To be effective, preferences must obviously give sufficient advantage to suppliers from the less developed country over the nonpreferred suppliers from other developed countries; and domestic producers and exporters from the nonpreferred countries must also not reduce their prices to maintain their markets.

[39] Cf. Chapter 5, section 6.

gram of open aid. Further, the argument that preferences substitute for aid may just as readily cut the other way and provide the preference-granting country with an excuse for reducing its aid program. The net result might then be to leave the poor country with less of a transfer of real resources from the aid-giving country than would otherwise have occurred.

In the deliberations of UNCTAD, the most frequently advanced argument for preferences has been related to infant industry protection. It is widely believed that if there is to be any significant rise in their exports of manufactured products, the developing countries must be given some initial protection in individual developed countries' markets against competition from other developed countries. If only the developed countries would institute for a limited period of time a preferential tariff system that would favor imports of manufactures from the less developed countries, then—it is asserted—the infant export industries could enjoy the benefits of a larger market and eventually become sufficiently efficient to be competitive in developed markets even without preferences. Should not the provision of relatively low tariffs by developed countries on competing exports from developing countries be considered simply as a corollary to acceptance of relatively high tariffs on import-competing industries within developing countries?[40] If infant industry protection is now allowed by GATT and widely practiced by developing countries to protect industries producing for the domestic market, then why should not the principle be extended to world markets as well? In short, the argument for preferences is for the "internationalizing" of protection—a logical extension of the infant industry argument.

Although developing countries have not chosen to do so, it is similarly possible to extend other protectionist arguments, such

[40] *Proceedings of* UNCTAD, Vol. IV, *op. cit.*, p. 27.

as the "attraction of private foreign investment" or the "overcoming of wage differentials," into an argument for preferences—the internationally protected industry now being an export industry instead of an import-competing industry, as under national protection. The extension of the infant industry argument, however, has tactical appeal, since GATT now recognizes infant industry protection. But we should be clear on the implications of "internationalizing" the argument.

If the properly qualified case for infant industry protection depends essentially on external economies, it is difficult to comprehend its relevance when the externalities arise in the preference-receiving country but the governmental assistance is to be provided by the preference-granting country. There is also a difference in the argument insofar as national protection of an infant industry entails the subsidization of domestic producers by domestic consumers; but a preference-giving country would subsidize industrial imports from the less developed countries by transferring income from the consumers of the preference-giving country to producers in the preference-receiving country—a distinctly different matter. Moreover, if preferences are to be granted only to the products of industries that are selected as having the greatest infant-industry potentialities, then complex procedural and administrative problems arise. If, on the other hand, a system of common preference rates is applied, then preferences would be granted even to those industries that do not need the large world markets to realize economies of scale and a competitive position. Finally, it is question-begging to assert that preferences need be only temporary: if the external economies are reversible or the exporting industries do not become truly competitive, the preferences would have to be permanent. Even more to the point, the wrong question is being begged: as previously discussed, the infant industry situation is a case of domestic distortions that should be removed by domestic subsidies, not by commercial policy. A preferential arrangement is only "second-best," or even "third-best," if it leads to trade diversion in the preference-granting country, as it is most likely to do when preferences are given to the high-cost infant industries instead of to only those lower cost industries that have already demonstrated a capacity to export competitively.

Beyond these doubts about the infant industry and aid arguments for preferences, any final judgment on trade preferences must turn on two essential questions: Would preferences be of benefit to developing countries? And, if so, would this benefit outweigh the other unfavorable effects of such a policy?

Answers to these questions obviously depend on the particular type of preference system adopted. For the effects could differ significantly according to the range of commodities covered by preferences, the particular classification of countries into preference-giving and preference-receiving countries, the margin of preference granted, the provision of limitations and safeguards for the preference-granting countries, and the duration of the preferences. Combining these variables in different ways, various countries have proposed many alternative preference schemes.[41] It is clear that many difficult technical, procedural, and administrative questions would arise in settling upon any one of the possible arrangements.

In the absence of detailed empirical studies of a particular scheme, only a tentative conclusion can be hazarded on the potential efficacy of preferences. But we might at least raise some broad preliminary considerations with respect to the type of preferential system that has been most frequently discussed—namely, a general and automatic scheme whereby all "developed countries" would

[41] See, for example, *Proceedings of* UNCTAD, Vol. I, *op. cit.*, pp. 152–155; Vol. II, pp. 218–223; Vol. IV, pp. 26–35; Vol. VI, pp. 57–66.

grant the same degree of preferences (at least 50 percent of the existing most-favored-nation rate) on all exports of manufactures and semimanufactures from all "less developed countries," without requiring reciprocity, for a limited period of time (ten or fifteen years).

Considering the introduction of such a scheme within existing tariff structures, Professor Johnson has submitted that trade preferences, even if not at a 100 percent level, might provide powerful incentives for the expansion of industrial exports from developing countries.[42] Professor Johnson rightly observes that the protective effects of existing tariff schedules cannot be fully appreciated by looking only at averages of nominal tariff rates, as is sometimes done. Even though the average ad valorem tariff rate on the developed countries' imports of manufactures does not appear excessively high, this does not truly reflect the high incidence of the developed countries' tariff barriers. Some of the highest tariff rates are on imports of labor-intensive and technologically-simple products in which the poorer countries may have an actual or potential comparative advantage. Of far greater importance is the fact that implicit rates of protection of value added in the process of producing finished goods are considerably higher than the

[42] Harry G. Johnson, "Trade Preferences and Developing Countries," *Lloyds Bank Review*, April, 1966, pp. 15–18; Johnson, *Economic Policies toward Less Developed Countries, op. cit.*, pp. 170–180. Also, Pincus, *op. cit.*, chap. VI.

Professor Johnson is, however, careful to note that the developing countries must be able to respond effectively to such export opportunities; that their price and cost levels are now often well above world market levels, and frequently the excess is substantially greater than the tariff-created excess of domestic over world market prices in the developed countries; and that preferences would be of no avail unless they were accompanied by drastic reform of the currency-overvaluation and protectionist import-substitution policies that make the less developed countries unable to compete in world markets.

nominal tariff rates. The tariff rates of the developed countries escalate according to the stage of production, with rates being low or zero on raw materials and rising with the degree of processing, so that the effective rates of protection on value added in the domestic production process are higher than the nominal tariff rates on the finished goods.[43] According to some empirical studies, the effective protection rates on manufactures of export interest to the less developed countries are in the neighborhood of 25 to 50 percent, and in particular cases, even higher.[44] There is therefore considerably more scope for preferences to offset the developing country's cost disadvantages than would be suggested by simply considering the lower nominal tariff rates.

It is, however, unlikely that the industries which would benefit the most from a system of uniform preferences would actually be those with the greatest infant industry potentialities. If we take the present level of protection in the developing countries as indicative of how much support would have to be provided by preferences in order to make the developing country's infant industry competitive in world markets, it actually amounts, in most cases, to much more than preferences could reasonably provide—effective tariff rates notwithstanding. When some developing countries now find it necessary to protect their infant industries by tariffs that are as high as 100 percent ad valorem, or more, it is im-

[43] This has been explained previously; pp. 194–195.

[44] See Bela Balassa, "Tariff Protection in Industrial Countries: An Evaluation," *Journal of Political Economy*, December, 1965, pp. 573–594; Gerard Curzon, *Multilateral Commercial Diplomacy*, Michael Joseph, 1965, pp. 227–231; Giorgio Basevi, "The United States Tariff Structure: Estimates of Effective Rates of Protection of United States Industries and Industrial Labor," *Review of Economics and Statistics*, May, 1966, pp. 147–160. Basevi's calculations of the effective rate of protection on value added by *labor* are especially high, and this is most relevant for the potential labor-intensive exports from the developing countries. See also, D. S. Ball, "United States Effective Tariffs and Labor's Share," *Journal of Political Economy*, April, 1967, pp. 183–187.

probable that any level of preferences that can be realistically expected would be sufficient to allow these industries to meet foreign competition in export markets, unless domestic costs were at the same time reduced considerably, and the subsequent dynamic effects of receiving preferences were substantial. It is likely that a system of uniform preferences would be effective for only those relatively few manufactured exports in which some developing countries are already competitive.

11. Even if it is believed that preferences can be effective in providing assistance to the developing countries, the question still remains whether preferences might not involve substantial costs that would offset this gain.

We should first recognize that preferences intensify the difficulties of pursuing trade liberalization in other directions. Preferences will be more effective, the higher the nonpreferential tariffs on imports from other developed countries. In the process of making preferences effective for less developed countries, the preference-granting countries might thereby be led to maintain higher trade restrictions on imports from other developed countries. Having once granted preferences, the developed countries might also find it politically impossible to engage in additional trade liberalization with other countries. And with the erosion of the most-favored-nation principle, countries will become less willing to negotiate tariff reductions when they realize that a tariff reduction might be subsequently withdrawn through discriminatory preferential arrangements with other countries.[45]

Further, it must be noted that uniform preferences would confer on developing countries the greatest advantage over their competitors for those commodities on which the preference-giving country has the highest duties. When all developed countries

[45] Patterson, *op. cit.*, pp. 354, 395.

lower their tariffs by a given percentage on imports of manufactures from the developing countries, the developing countries
thereby enabled to export manufactures will export to those developed countries that have the highest duties on these exports, since
this yields the preference-receiving countries the highest prices
for their exports.[46] This result may, in turn, lead the preference-
giving country to seek some form of alternative protection
through quantitative restrictions or to impose import barriers on
grounds of "market disruption." For if the high duties are indicative of the importing country's desire for protection, then a
preferential reduction of these duties may well be accompanied
by pressures for some compensation through non-tariff barriers.
Thus, preferences may cause deviations from the free trade principle that extend beyond the granting of preferences.

Moreover, if preferences are effective in expanding the exports
of manufactured commodities from the developing countries, they
are likely to do so through trade diversion (replacing lower-cost
and nonpreferred suppliers). When the preference-giving country
imports from the preference-receiving country instead of from
another developed country that can produce the manufactured
commodity at lower cost, there is a loss of efficiency in international resource allocation. In contrast, a multilateral nonpreferential tariff reduction could not, of course, cause trade diversion.
If investment is also attracted from a preference-granting or nonpreferred country to a preference-receiving country, the misallocation is intensified *a fortiori*.

Another major difficulty of any preferential scheme is that it
raises complex questions of equity. Uniform preferences might
act quite inequitably in imposing the burden of additional imports
on only a few of the developed countries and in conferring the
benefits of expanding exports on only a few of the developing

[46] *Ibid.*, pp. 351–352.

countries. While exports will tend to be concentrated in the preference-giving countries with the highest duties, these countries are not necessarily those that have the greatest ability to pay the subsidy entailed by granting preferences. To overcome the inequality in the impact of imports, it would be necessary either to depart from uniform percentage preferences (and allow the higher-duty countries to give smaller preference margins), or else allow the country to impose some type of import quota in order to allocate the burden more equitably.

The benefits of preferences are also likely to be concentrated in only those few developing countries that already account for the bulk of manufactured exports from developing countries, or in those countries that are more readily capable of attaining a competitive cost advantage. If the benefits of preferences were to be more widely distributed among the developing countries, it would be necessary to give preferences on selected products to selected countries in order to distinguish among countries and industries according to their relative degree of development and "competitive need." But this would be tantamount to opening up the negotiations on preferences to a host of political influences and special interests. Once the application of a preferential scheme becomes dependent upon political, arbitrary, or variable judgments, it is bound to reinforce divisive elements in the international economy —not only as between the developing and the developed countries, but also among the countries within each group.

In a fundamental sense, all these undesirable consequences of preferences arise simply from the fact that a preferential scheme departs from the principle of nondiscrimination. After the discriminatory trade practices of the thirties, recognition of the unconditional most-favored-nation clause was a hard-won achievement. It has the great merit of ensuring that third parties will not be discriminated against, and that a multilaterally-negotiated trade agreement will not be undermined subsequently by a discriminatory arrangement between one of the partners to the agreement and other countries. In contrast, to be fully effective, the application of preferences really calls for a gradation of preferences that would provide highly selective discrimination, giving greater preferences to some products than others, to some countries rather than others, and for different periods of time. Even if initially the preferential scheme involves only uniform preferences, strong pressures are likely to emerge to make the preferential arrangement more selective in view of the resulting "inequalities."

In the last analysis, if a preferential scheme is to fulfill its objectives, it must discriminate according to the immediate results desired. This contrasts with the principle of nondiscrimination which places ultimate value on the generality and neutrality of commercial policy. In other words, the principle of nondiscrimination can be justified by reference to a standard that transcends the immediate result that is achieved and is capable of uniform application, whereas discrimination cannot be decided with reference to any standard that can be stated in terms more general than its own result. It was an accomplishment of GATT to take the longer view and attempt to establish commercial principles of enduring value. This should not be lightly dismissed.

12. Indeed, a more wholehearted pursuit of GATT's original objective of freer trade may be the most effective way to expand exports of manufactures from developing countries. Instead of supporting preferences which amount to an inversion of protection in favor of some developing countries,[47] we come back to an emphasis on

[47] The notion of "inverted protection" is a central theme in Johnson, *Economic Policies toward Less Developed Countries, op. cit.,* passim.

Even though Professor Johnson is among those who are most optimistic about the potential efficacy of preferences in stimulating exports, nonetheless he still concludes that the question of expanded opportunities

trade liberalization as the direction in which the developed and less developed countries alike should move. This is now the central task. And it would be unfortunate if by emphasizing preferences, the international community were to be diverted from this larger goal. Although the argument for preferences is strong in underscoring the objective of expanding export earnings, more appropriate measures can be advocated. Instead of a proliferation of preferences and additional restrictions on efficient resource allocation, it would be more desirable to concentrate on eliminating the barriers to trade in semimanufactures and manufactures.

To expand exports from developing countries, it is especially important now to emphasize the removal of protective measures imposed by the developed countries as well as the developing countries. Developing countries do have legitimate grievances against the high tariffs, tariff differentials, and non-tariff barriers that they confront in industrial markets.[48] If the advanced countries were willing to follow the dictates of the free trade doctrine, they would reduce their tariffs even unilaterally without awaiting the willingness of other countries to reduce their tariffs.[49] To ensure the favoring of exports from the less developed countries,

---

for industrial exports from the less developed countries "could be resolved far more rationally and efficiently, from a strictly economic point of view, by a substantial move towards genuinely free international trade, at least among the developed countries. The fundamental political choice for the United States and other developed countries lies between meeting the demands of the less developed countries along the protectionist lines they have proposed and initiating new actions along the lines of the free-trade alternative" (p. 240).

[48] For a survey of these trade restrictions, see GATT *Program for Expansion of International Trade—Trade of Less Developed Countries—Special Report of Committee III*, Geneva, 1962; *Proceedings of* UNCTAD, Vol. IV, *op. cit.*, pp. 112–134.

[49] See Johnson, *Economic Policies toward Less Developed Countries*, *op. cit.*, pp. 132–135.

the tariff-reducing country could reduce its tariffs on products of special interest to the less developed countries and concentrate its tariff reductions on those products in which the other developed countries have the least comparative advantage. Although such a nonreciprocated tariff reduction would not allow so rapid an expansion of export markets for the tariff-reducing country, it would nonetheless yield a net economic gain to that country by allowing it to enjoy the traditional gains in efficiency that result from the exploitation of comparative advantage. Together with a reduction or removal of the tariff discrimination caused by escalation in tariff rates, a unilateral cut in tariffs by the developed countries on products of particular export interest to the less developed countries would make a considerable contribution to the stimulation of exports from the less developed countries, without incurring the costs of preferences.[50]

Non-tariff barriers—witness the use of quantitative controls, internal taxes and revenue duties, practices of customs administration, and arrangements to avoid "market disruption"—also inhibit the developing countries' exports of manufactures. While preferences would not ease this problem—in fact, would tend to exacerbate it—a removal of non-tariff restrictions deserves as much attention as does tariff reduction.

To allow their export industries to become more competitive,

---

[50] If previous tariff negotiations under GATT have concentrated the reduction in tariffs on those commodities that are mainly of interest to the principal industrial suppliers, it follows that considerable scope must remain for the reduction of tariffs on commodities of particular interest to the less developed countries that have not shared in the previous reductions.

A policy of unilateral reduction of tariffs would not, however, pass the burden of adjustment on to other developed countries, and it might, therefore, require a liberalized domestic assistance program for the domestic industries that would confront greater competition from exports of the less developed countries.

the developing countries must also eliminate their costly policies of import substitution and reduce their own trade barriers. As would also be true for preferences, the efficacy of a reduction in trade restrictions by the developed countries will depend, in turn, on responsive measures by the developing countries to take advantage of trade liberalization.

Despite the widespread support that has been given to import-substitute industries, these industries have not been able to proceed to a point so efficient as to enter export markets—in contrast to the historical experience of some countries that are now advanced.[51] The historical evidence shows that the rise of industry through import-replacement in the presently advanced countries, and the subsequent decline in cost of tradeables relative to nontradeables as income rose, was in large part due to systematic changes in supply conditions, not simply to a change in the composition of demand with rising income.[52] The changes in factor supply—especially the growth in capital stock per worker and the increase in education and skills of all kinds—were instrumental in causing a systematic shift in comparative advantage as per capita income rose. But the favorable supply conditions that emerged in other countries have not yet appeared in underdeveloped countries that have only undertaken a policy of industrial protection. The basic problem with this indiscriminately broad-scale type of protection is that it has led to an extensive range of consumer goods industries, producing small quantities of a large variety of goods for the home market, instead of to the intensive specialization required for entry into the export market. The dispersed structure of production and overdiversification effected through

[51] Cf. H. B. Chenery, "Patterns of Industrial Growth," *American Economic Review*, September, 1960, pp. 624–651.
[52] *Ibid.*, pp. 624–625, 628–629, 644.

indiscriminate protection have actually inhibited the concentration of effort and the specialization that are of the very essence in the development of an export industry.[53]

It must be re-emphasized that devaluation and a reduction in import restrictions could be equivalent to a subsidy on exports; these measures constitute the most effective action that the less developed countries can immediately take to increase their exports. As additional support to these measures, the developing countries could promote their exports through disinflationary policies, the special encouragement of private foreign investment into the country's export sector, and through an expansion of mutual trade among themselves. A variety of governmental measures of assistance at the micro-level may also be necessary to overcome the special costs and disincentives of initially engaging in the export of manufactures.[54]

Even though we have not gone into the details, the foregoing policy suggestions should indicate that much can be done within the present framework of GATT to expand exports from the less developed countries.

13. To achieve an expansion of trade within the framework of GATT, it may now, however, also be necessary to reform the other cornerstone of the postwar international economy—the IMF. When the world economy is not only tariff-ridden but also subject to recurrent balance-of-payments crises that militate against a removal of trade restrictions and an increase in foreign aid, the acceleration of development may require an increase in interna-

[53] See David Felix, "Monetarists, Structuralists and Import-Substituting Industrialization: A Critical Appraisal," W. Baer and I. Kerstenetzky, eds., *Inflation and Growth in Latin America*, Richard D. Irwin, 1964, pp. 382–391.
[54] *Proceedings of* UNCTAD, Vol. IV, *op. cit.*, pp. 70–71, 94–100, 207–209.

tional liquidity and a more expansionary international monetary system.

The IMF was intended to complement GATT, and one of the Fund's major objectives (as stated in the Articles of Agreement) was "to facilitate the expansion and balanced growth of international trade and to contribute thereby to the promotion and maintenance of high levels of employment and real income and to the development of the productive resources of all members ..." But the Fund can supplement world monetary reserves to only a limited extent, and it was not intended to be a source of development finance.

In establishing the IMF, the Bretton Woods Agreements did not envisage that the greater part of the increase in international liquidity would have to be provided through a deficit in the United States balance of payments and the emergence of the dollar into a central position as a key reserve currency. At the same time as development problems have come to the forefront, the postwar gold-exchange standard has been subject to increasing strains. A large number of proposals for international monetary reform have therefore been suggested to provide an expansion in world monetary reserves other than through an increase in monetary gold stocks or the accumulation of reserve currencies. What interests us here are not the technical details of these various plans,[55] but the central point of contention common to all the plans, i.e., should participation in the creation and distribution of any new international reserve assets be universal or limited to the small

[55] For a survey of the numerous plans, see Fritz Machlup, *Plans for Reform of the International Monetary System*, rev. ed., International Finance Section, Princeton University, 1964; Herbert Grubel, ed., *World Monetary Reform: Plans and Issues*, Stanford Univ. Press, 1963; Robert Triffin, "International Monetary Reform," *Economic Bulletin for Latin America*, April, 1966, pp. 10–41.

group of major strong-currency countries? And should the creation of additional liquidity be linked to the granting of additional development aid?

Several proposals would give the less developed countries first access to additional international liquidity. The Stamp Plan, for instance, would have an "expanded-IMF" distribute certificates of deposit to less developed countries which could then use them to pay for imports from developed countries; or the certificates could represent 50-year loans to the International Develpment Association which would, in turn, lend them to the developing countries. The developed countries that acquired the certificates of IMF deposits would hold them as international reserves.[56]

The Hart-Kaldor-Tinbergen proposal is for the creation of an international commodity reserve currency, i.e., a system under which the new IMF would issue certificates ("Bancor") against a reserve that consisted partly of gold and partly of a composite bundle of the main primary commodities entering into world trade. This plan is ambitious in being designed not only to increase liquidity by "monetizing" commodity stocks but also to stabilize, in terms of gold, the aggregate value of the "commodity bundle" through buffer-stock operations by the IMF.[57]

[56] See Sir Maxwell Stamp, "The Stamp Plan—1962 Version," *Moorgate and Wall Street*, Autumn 1962; reprinted, in Grubel, *op. cit.*, pp. 80–89.   •

[57] See A. G. Hart, Nicholas Kaldor, Jan Tinbergen, "The Case for an International Commodity Reserve Currency," in *Proceedings of* UNCTAD, Vol. III, *op. cit.*, pp. 522–538; A. G. Hart, "The Case For and Against International Commodity Reserve Currency," *Oxford Economic Papers*, July, 1966, pp. 237–241. For criticisms of a commodity reserve currency system, see Johnson, *Economic Policies toward Less Developed Countries*, *op. cit.*, pp. 233–236; Herbert Grubel, "The Case Against a Commodity Reserve Currency," *Oxford Economic Papers*, March, 1965, pp. 130–135; Milton Friedman, "Commodity Reserve Currency," *Journal of Political Economy*, June, 1951, pp. 203–232.

Professor Scitovsky has also proposed a plan which would link the creation of international money to the financing of development. A reformed IMF would create international paper money (Fund Obligations) that would be made available to developed countries that are in deficit and have unemployed resources against their national currencies, to be held as security by the IMF, and against real resources to be given as grants to developing countries. If, for example, a developed country, in deficit and with unemployed resources, wishes to obtain additional reserves (without being forced to contract its economy or impose trade restrictions), it would make a budgetary appropriation for a grant-in-aid to developing countries and hand over this grant to the IMF in the form of its national currency. Against the security of the member's currency, the Fund would issue an equivalent amount of Fund Obligations, which would ultimately become part of the deficit country's external reserves acceptable and usable as equivalent to gold by all member countries of the Fund. The intervening mechanism would be for the newly created Fund Obligations to be turned over to the International Development Association, which would use them to finance investment projects of developing countries. While the Fund Obligations received by the developing country would not be repayable, they would be "tied grants" that could be spent only on imports from the originating country (the country against whose currency they were issued). After being received by the originating country, the Fund Obligations would become unrestricted reserves for that country, spendable and acceptable in all other member countries.[58]

Of most interest is the report of the Group of Experts ap-

[58] Tibor Scitovsky, "A New Approach to International Liquidity," *American Economic Review*, December, 1966, pp. 1212–1220; *Requirements of an International Reserve System*, International Finance Section, Princeton University, November, 1965, pp. 10–11.

pointed by UNCTAD.[59] This group agreed that any scheme of international monetary reform "should make a substantial contribution to a solution of the problems posed by present and prospective shortage of international liquidity including that of developing countries," and "the methods of monetary reform adopted should assist and promote to the fullest extent possible the efforts of both developed and developing countries to accelerate their rate of growth and should eliminate any contractionary bias which might come in the way of this objective." (par. 59).

To solve "the problems posed by present and prospective shortage of international liquidity," the UNCTAD expert group advocates that the IMF should periodically create new reserve assets— "Fund Units"—against national currencies deposited by member countries with the Fund.[60] The initial distribution of the Fund Units would be in accordance with the pattern of IMF quotas— and hence not confined to a limited group of developed countries. In addition, the Fund could provide finance for development by having the power to lend a sizable part, or even all, of the usable counterpart currencies deposited by member countries, against the issue of Fund Units, to the World Bank and its affiliates for investment in the developing countries, receiving World Bank bonds in exchange.

The most controversial aspect of this proposal is whether it is

[59] UNCTAD, *International Monetary Issues and the Developing Countries*, Report of the Group of Experts, United Nations, 1965. See also UNCTAD, *The International Monetary System, 1958–1965*, TD/B/31, November 10, 1965; UNCTAD, *Submissions by Governments to the Expert Group on International Monetary Issues*, TD/B/33, November 10, 1965.

[60] For shorter term contingencies, the Report also recommends the provision of larger short-term credit facilities within the existing framework by lengthening, for developing countries, the repayment period to the IMF (par. 48), an extension of unconditional drawing rights within the Fund (par. 51), and an increase in the amount allocated by the Fund to compensatory financing (par. 56).

desirable to combine the provision of development aid with the creation of international reserves. Should a scheme of international monetary reform be devised to fulfill both objectives, or are the two objectives so distinct that a combining of the two will militate against proper attention to either one?[61]

The UNCTAD group responds to this question by maintaining that it is "quite clear that the amount of any new reserve creation should be determined by the monetary requirements of the world economy and not by the need for development finance. But once the need for additional reserves has been demonstrated and the amount of the addition determined on the basis of monetary requirements, the introduction of a link with development finance is entirely proper and desirable." (par. 103). A critic of this proposal would argue, however, that there is no sense in giving the less developed countries any share in the newly created reserves, as opposed to conditional borrowing facilities or long-term development financing, since they will spend the increase in reserves, and the reserves will in effect be converted into development finance.

On the link to aid, orthodox financial opinion would insist that liquid reserves and long-term development aid should be kept separate. Given the difficulties of achieving agreement on any new liquidity-creating arrangements, the task may become well-nigh impossible if aid decisions must also be agreed upon. It would be a tactical mistake to insist on an "aid link" if this were to cause rejection of liquidity arrangements. Instead of too ambitious a scheme that would directly incorporate financial aid, it might be better to be sure of the indirect benefits that would stem simply from the creation of additional international liquidity.

The quality of the assets acquired by an international credit

[61] Cf. Fritz Machlup, "The Cloakroom Rule of International Reserves: Reserve Creation and Resource Transfer," *Quarterly Journal of Economics*, August, 1965, pp. 352–355.

institution in the process of creating additional reserves is of concern in any scheme. In the UNCTAD proposal, IBRD bonds would become the backing of the "Fund Units" when the national currencies of the developed countries were invested in IBRD bonds. As for this problem, the UNCTAD group states that the real issue is not the character of the backing of the "Fund Units" but rather the issue of their transferability or acceptability: "the question of this quality [of the assets 'backing' the Fund's liabilities] only arises in the event of the withdrawal of a member, the liquidation of the system, or a decision to cancel part of the outstanding total of Fund Units. These may be regarded as minor, remote, or catastrophic contingencies . . ." (par. 75).

Finally, if the link to aid is operating, a developed country that does not share proportionately in the additional exports to less developed countries that result from the World Bank investments would not retain all the additional Fund Units which were initially allotted to it. To do so, the country would have to secure a share of the additional exports resulting from the operation of the link equal to the share of its own currency in the Bank loan expenditure. But if it failed to do so, it might then tend to reduce other types of aid, or adopt other policies in order to strengthen its balance on current account by as much as the amount of its currency withdrawn from the backing for the Fund Units and used for development assistance.

Even if there are objections to incorporating development aid directly with international monetary reform, the case for reform is still very strong from the standpoint of contributing to development through the indirect benefits that would follow from an increase in international liquidity. It is extremely important to realize, as the UNCTAD report does, that it is "a symptom of inadequate liquidity if the developed world, taken as a whole, were maintaining restraints upon its rate of growth, upon its imports of goods and services, or upon its export of capital and other forms of development finance, that would not seem to be necessary in terms of the requirements of monetary stability alone." (par. 21). When advanced countries resort to policies to increase or restore their reserves at the expense of sacrificing the objectives of full employment, economic growth, or freedom of international trade, this can be interpreted as indicative of a shortage of international liquidity. Many of the trade and aid policies of the developed countries that impede the development of the less developed countries are the result of balance-of-payments pressures aggravated by the deficiencies of the present international monetary system.[62] International monetary reform is then needed so that balance-of-payments problems will not impair the developed countries' contribution to an acceleration of the rate of growth in the world economy, an increase in foreign aid, and the liberalization of trade.

By permitting the achievement of these other objectives, the reform of the international monetary system may have more beneficial indirect effects on developing countries than the specific attempts to provide development aid directly through a link with additional liquidity. If the demand for exports from the developing countries is to grow more rapidly, if the international environment is to be conducive to trade liberalization, and if foreign aid is not to be limited by deference to balance-of-payments considerations, there is certainly a need for a more expansionary international monetary system. Unless this is done, there is cause for concern that the gold-exchange standard will continue to exercise a drag on international development.

14. UNCTAD has clearly raised a number of provocative arguments for international economic reform that will continue to challenge the international trading system and the international monetary

---

[62] Cf. Johnson, *Economic Policies toward Less Developed Countries,* *op. cit.,* p. 213.

framework. Given the wide-ranging character of current international discussions, we have attempted in this chapter to clarify only some of the general controversial issues. More definitive judgments must await a narrowing of the international debate to particular proposals.

It is, however, apparent that the central principle in all of UNCTAD's contentions—whether with respect to international commodity agreements, preferences, or international monetary reform —is that the less developed countries must acquire additional foreign exchange and that there must be a greater transfer of resources from rich to poor countries. While not questioning these objectives, our discussion has attempted to present a more balanced view—one that would not locate the obstacles to development simply in an unfavorable external environment, but would also give due weight to the impediments created by the whole complex of policies entailed in import-substitution and protection by the developing countries. And while we have stressed the indirect benefits to be derived from international monetary reform, we have not been as receptive to the range of trade proposals suggested by UNCTAD. Within the existing framework of international economic institutions, much can still be accomplished by a retreat from the protectionism practiced by rich and poor countries alike.

Instead of attempting to achieve an increase in aid in the guise of commercial policy, we have considered it desirable not to confuse the objectives of international efficiency (the gains from trade liberalization), international stabilization of primary exports (compensatory financing and supplementary financial measures), and international redistribution (open aid from rich to poor countries). Each of these objectives may be best promoted through changes in the national policies of both developed and less developed countries, and by international economic policies that are more consistent with the original purposes of the Bretton Woods

Agreements and GATT. Just as the IMF and GATT originally attempted to give maneuverability for domestic full-employment policies, so too must they now promote policies for international development by providing a more expansive international monetary system and facilitating the removal of trade restrictions. In a growing and integrated world economy—free of any recession in international trade or foreign aid—lies a major hope for the amelioration of poverty among nations.

Bibliographical Survey

The following bibliographical notes provide some guidance to the reader who wants to pursue additional reading on the central issues discussed in this book. Although detailed references on specific points have already been offered in the numerous footnotes to the text, the following is a broader list of readings. A few of the readings are of a background character, but most supplement the text's discussion of major topics.

1. The extensive literature on the economics of development may best be approached by consulting the following bibliographies: Arthur Hazlewood, *The Economics of 'Under-Developed' Areas, An Annotated Reading List of Books, Articles, and Official Publications*, rev. ed. (New York: Oxford Univ. Press, 1964); *Selected Readings and Source Materials on Economic Development*, General Development Course of the Economic Development Institute,

1965–1966 (IBRD, 1966); Development Center of OECD, *Catalogue of Social and Economic Development Institutes and Programs, Research* (OECD, 1966); *Economics Library Selections, 7: The Economics of Development and Growth* (Johns Hopkins University, Winter 1962–1963).

Several of the economic development textbooks also contain useful bibliographies.

2. A comprehensive bibliography on international trade is contained in H. S. Ellis and Lloyd Metzler, eds., *Readings in Theory of International Trade* (New York: Blakiston Co., 1949). More recent and selective reading lists are furnished by Gottfried Haberler, *A Survey of International Trade Theory*, 2d ed. (International Finance Section, Princeton University, 1961); W. M. Corden, *Recent Developments in the Theory of International Trade*, (International Finance Section, Princeton University, March, 1965); J. Bhagwati, "The Pure Theory of International Trade," *Economic Journal*, March, 1964.

3. Of the several excellent expositions of the traditional theory of international trade, Jacob Viner, *Studies in the Theory of International Trade,* (New York: Harper & Row, 1937) is unrivalled for its scholarly treatment of the history of doctrine and for its statement of the classical theory of comparative costs and international values. Also noteworthy is J. S. Chipman, "A Survey of the Theory of International Trade: Part 1, The Classical Theory," *Econometrica*, July, 1965; and "Part 2, The Neo-Classical Theory," *Ibid.*, October, 1965.

Among the many studies of modern developments in the pure theory of international trade, particularly outstanding is J. Bhagwati, "The Pure Theory of International Trade: A Survey," *Eco-*

nomic Journal, March, 1964, reprinted in *Surveys of Economic Theory: Vol. II, Growth and Development,* (New York: St. Martin's Press, 1965).

The following also deserve special mention: W. W. Leontief, "The Use of Indifference Curves in the Analysis of Foreign Trade," *Quarterly Journal of Economics*, May, 1933 (reprinted in *Readings in Theory of International Trade,* chap. 10); Gottfried Haberler, "Some Problems in the Pure Theory of International Trade," *Economic Journal,* June, 1950; James E. Meade, *A Geometry of International Trade*, (London: Allen & Unwin, 1952); Meade, *Trade and Welfare,* (New York: Oxford Univ. Press, 1955); Kelvin Lancaster, "The Heckscher-Ohlin Trade Model: A Geometric Treatment," *Economica*, February, 1957; R. E. Caves, *Trade and Economic Structure,* (Cambridge: Harvard Univ. Press, 1960); R. A. Mundell, "The Pure Theory of International Trade," *American Economic Review,* March, 1960; Jacob Viner, "Relative Abundance of Factors and International Trade," *Indian Economic Journal*, January, 1962; J. S. Chipman, "A Survey of the Theory of International Trade: Part 3, The Modern Theory," *Econometrica*, January, 1966; J. Bhagwati, "The Proofs of the Theorems on Comparative Advantage," *Economic Journal,* March, 1967.

---

4. Although there is no single volume that provides a comprehensive analysis of the interrelations between trade and development, several writers have considered various aspects of international trade from the viewpoint of developing countries. Special attention should be called to R. F. Harrod and D. C. Hague, eds., *International Trade Theory in a Developing World,* Proceedings of a Conference held by the International Economic Association, (New York: St. Martin's Press, 1963). Important quantitative studies are: Simon Kuznets, "Quantitative Aspects of the Economic Growth of Nations: X. Level and Structure of Foreign Trade: Long-Term Trends," *Economic Development and Cultural Change,* Part II, January, 1967; P. Lamartine Yates, *Forty Years of Foreign Trade,* (London: Allen & Unwin, 1959); A. Maizels, *Industrial Growth and World Trade,* (New York: Cambridge Univ. Press, 1963); R. I. McKinnon, "Maizels on Industrial Growth and World Trade: Implications for Economic Development," *Economic Development and Cultural Change,* October, 1965; United Nations, *World Economic Survey 1962, I: The Developing Countries in World Trade,* (United Nations, 1963).

Some fundamental development problems are interpreted in the context of the international economy by the following: Jacob Viner, *International Trade and Economic Development,* (New York: Free Press, 1952); J. R. Hicks, *Essays in World Economics,* (New York: Oxford Univ. Press, 1959), chap. 8; Hicks, *International Trade: The Long View,* (Central Bank of Egypt Lectures, 1963). Analyses of a more formal character are presented by Staffan Burenstam Linder, *An Essay on Trade and Transformation,* (New York: John Wiley, 1961); *Trade and Trade Policy for Development* (New York: Praeger, 1967). An interesting perspective on the relation of classical theory to development problems is given by Hla Myint, "The 'Classical Theory' of International Trade and the Underdeveloped Countries," *Economic Journal,* June, 1958. Gottfried Haberler's Cairo lectures on *International Trade and Economic Development,* (National Bank of Egypt, 1959) are highly instructive in bringing the tools of traditional theory to bear upon the problem of the contribution which foreign trade can make to economic development. So too is Haberler's "An Assessment of the Current Relevance of the Theory of Comparative Advantage to Agricultural Production and Trade," *International Journal of Agrarian Affairs,* May, 1964.

The most extensive and provocative discussion of the relation of trade to development is to be found in the writings of Ragnar Nurkse: "Some International Aspects of the Problem of Economic Development," *American Economic Review, Papers and Proceedings,* May, 1952; *Problems of Capital Formation in Underdeveloped Countries,* (Oxford: Basil Blackwell, 1953), chaps. III–VI; "The Conflict between 'Balanced Growth' and International Specialization," in *Lectures on Economic Development,* (Istanbul, 1958); *Patterns of Trade and Development,* Wicksell Lectures, (Stockholm, Sweden: 1959); "International Trade Theory and Development Policy," H. S. Ellis, ed., *Economic Development for Latin America,* (New York: St. Martin's Press, 1961). The Istanbul lecture and Wicksell Lectures are reprinted in *Equilibrium and Growth in the World Economy, Economic Essays by Ragnar Nurkse,* (Cambridge: Harvard Univ. Press, 1961). A well-balanced appraisal of the arguments in Haberler's Cairo Lectures and Nurkse's Wicksell Lectures is contained in A. K. Cairncross' review article, "International Trade and Economic Development," *Kyklos,* Vol. XIII, No. 4 (1960). Cairncross also questions Nurkse's argument in his later article, "International Trade and Economic Development," *Economica,* August, 1961.

---

5. Several models have been presented for analyzing the forces affecting the structure of comparative costs and movements in the terms of trade between developing economies. An early model was set forth in J. R. Hicks' "Inaugural Lecture," *Oxford Economic Papers,* June, 1953. Hicks clarifies this model in his *Essays in World Economics,* Note B. The most thorough analysis is contained in Harry G. Johnson's "Economic Expansion and International Trade," *Manchester School of Economic and Social Studies,* May, 1955 [revised and extended as chap. III in his *International Trade and Economic Growth,* (Cambridge: Harvard

Univ. Press, 1958)]; also "Economic Development and International Trade," *Pakistan Economic Journal,* December, 1959. A good summary of Johnson's analysis is offered in the review article of Johnson's book by Jagdish Bhagwati, "The Theory of International Trade," *Indian Economic Journal,* July, 1960. A number of other articles relate to Johnson's model, and are helpful in clarifying the effects of a country's development on its pattern of trade and terms of trade. Especially illuminating are W. M. Corden, "Economic Expansion and International Trade: A Geometric Approach," *Oxford Economic Papers,* June, 1956; John Black and Paul Streeten, "La balance Commerciale les termes de l'échange et la croissance économique," *Economie Appliquée,* April–September, 1957 [an English version appears as Appendix 1 to Paul Streeten's *Economic Integration,* 2d ed., (A. W. Sythoff, 1964)]; Jagdish Bhagwati, "Immiserizing Growth: A Geometrical Note," *Review of Economic Studies,* June, 1958; Bhagwati, "International Trade and Economic Expansion," *American Economic Review,* December, 1958; Bhagwati, "Growth, Terms of Trade and Comparative Advantage," *Economia Internazionale,* August, 1959. An important article showing the effect of factor-endowment changes on trade is by T. M. Rybczynski, "Factor Endowment and Relative Commodity Prices," *Economica,* November, 1955. The relationships between technological progress and comparative costs are sorted out by R. Findlay and H. Grubert, "Factor Intensity, Technological Progress, and the Terms of Trade," *Oxford Economic Papers,* February, 1959; also, Harry G. Johnson, "Effects of Changes in Comparative Costs as Influenced by Technical Change," *Malayan Economic Review,* October, 1961; P. K. Bardhan, "A Short Note on Technical Progress and Terms of Trade," *Oxford Economic Papers,* March, 1963. A generalization of Rybczynski's theorem is provided by A. Amano, "Factor Endowment and Relative Prices," *Economica,* November, 1963; also, A. Guha, "Factor and Commodity Prices in an Expanding Economy," *Quarterly Journal of Economics,* February, 1963.

Illuminating analyses of the effects of capital formation on trade are presented in D. M. Bensusan-Butt, "A Model of Trade and Accumulation," *American Economic Review,* September, 1954; T. N. Srinivasan, "Foreign Trade and Economic Development," *Metroeconomica,* January–August, 1965; H. Oniki and H. Uzawa, "Patterns of Trade and Investment in a Dynamic Model of International Trade," *Review of Economic Studies,* January, 1965; P. K. Bardhan, "Optimum Accumulation and International Trade," *Review of Economic Studies,* July, 1965.

Special attention should also be called to Bo Södersten, *A Study of Economic Growth and International Trade,* (Stockholm, Sweden: Almqvist & Wiksell, 1964). This book provides a more mathematical approach to much of Johnson's analysis and our analysis in Chapter 2, as well as some interesting extensions of the analysis.

---

6. The terms of trade analysis of Chapter 3 can be supplemented by a number of studies. A more elaborate geometrical analysis, employing shifts in reciprocal demand curves, is presented by F. L. Pryor, "Economic Growth and the Terms of Trade," *Oxford Economic Papers,* March, 1966. Also instructive are M. C. Kemp, "The Relation between Changes in International Demand and the Terms of Trade," *Econometrica,* January, 1956; F. R. Oliver, "Shifting Demand Schedules and the Terms and Volume of Trade," *Metroeconomica,* April, 1960; J. Bhagwati and H. G. Johnson, "Notes on Some Controversies in the Theory of International Trade," *Economic Journal,* March, 1960.

A review of historical long-term movements in the terms of trade and some speculations about future trends are offered by M. L. Dantwala, "Commodity Terms of Trade of Primary Producing Countries," and H. M. A. Onitiri, "The Terms of Trade,"

E. A. G. Robinson, ed., *Problems of Economic Development,* (New York: St. Martin's Press, 1965). An excellent discussion is also provided by C. P. Kindleberger, "Terms of Trade for Primary Products," Marion Clawson, ed., *Natural Resources and International Development,* (Baltimore: Johns Hopkins Press, 1964).

On the allegedly adverse secular trend in the terms of trade of underdeveloped countries, the following are especially noteworthy: R. E. Baldwin, "Secular Movements in the Terms of Trade," *American Economic Review, Papers and Proceedings,* May, 1955; P. T. Ellsworth, "The Terms of Trade between Primary Producing and Industrial Countries," *Inter-American Economic Affairs,* Summer, 1956; Theodore Morgan, "Trends in Terms of Trade, and Their Repercussions on Primary Producers," R. F. Harrod and D. C. Hague, eds., *International Trade Theory in a Developing World,* (New York: St. Martin's Press, 1963); Gottfried Haberler, "Terms of Trade and Economic Development," H. S. Ellis, ed., *Economic Development for Latin America,* (New York: St. Martin's Press, 1961); Jagdish Bhagwati, "A Skeptical Note on the Adverse Secular Trend in the Terms of Trade of Underdeveloped Countries," *Pakistan Economic Journal,* December, 1960; W. Baer, "The Economics of Prebisch and ECLA," *Economic Development and Cultural Change,* January, 1962; Bo Södersten, *A Study of Economic Growth and International Trade,* (Stockholm, Sweden: Almqvist & Wiksell, 1964), pp. 150–170; H. G. Johnson, *Economic Policies toward Less Developed Countries,* (Washington, D.C.: Brookings Institution, 1967), Appendix A.

---

7. The principles of balance of payments analysis set forth in James E. Meade's *Balance of Payments,* (New York: Oxford Univ. Press, 1951), and H. G. Johnson's *International Trade and*

Economic Growth, (Cambridge: Harvard Univ. Press, 1958), chap. VI, provide a helpful background for understanding the balance of payments problems of developing countries. Also of special interest are the following: H. C. Wallich, "Underdeveloped Countries and the International Monetary Mechanism," *Money, Trade, and Economic Growth. Essays in Honor of J. H. Williams,* (New York: Macmillan Co., 1951); E. M. Bernstein and I. G. Patel, "Inflation in Relation to Economic Development," IMF *Staff Papers,* November, 1952; Felipe Pazos, "Economic Development and Financial Stability," *Ibid.,* October, 1953; E. M. Bernstein, *et al.,* "Economic Development with Stability," *Ibid.,* February, 1954; J. C. Ingram, "Capital Imports and the Balance of Payments," *Southern Economic Journal,* Vol. XXII, No. 4, and "Growth in Capacity and Canada's Balance of Payments," *American Economic Review,* March, 1957; K. K. Kurihara, "Economic Development and the Balance of Payments," *Metroeconomica,* March, 1958; H. G. Johnson, "Fiscal Policy and the Balance of Payments in a Growing Economy," *Malayan Economic Review,* April, 1964; C. Kennedy, "Keynesian Theory in an Open Economy," *Social and Economic Studies,* March, 1966; "Domar-Type Theory in an Open Economy," *Ibid.,* September, 1966.

---

8. Among the more significant general studies of international aid are F. Benham, *Economic Aid to Underdeveloped Countries,* (New York: Oxford Univ. Press, 1961); I. M. D. Little and J. M. Clifford, *International Aid,* (London: Allen & Unwin, 1965); Goran Ohlin, *Foreign Aid Policies Reconsidered,* (OECD, 1966); Barbara Ward and P. T. Bauer, *Two Views on Aid to Developing Countries,* (Institute of Economic Affairs, Occasional Paper No. 9, 1966); John Pincus, *Economic Aid and International Cost Sharing,* (Baltimore: Johns Hopkins Press, 1965); Wolfgang G. Friedmann, *et. al., International Financial Aid,* (New York: Columbia

Univ. Press, 1966); R. F. Mikesell, *Public International Lending for Development,* (New York: Random House, 1966); J. D. Montgomery, *Foreign Aid in International Politics,* (Englewood Cliffs, N.J.: Prentice-Hall, 1967).

Statistics on foreign aid and a review of current aid programs are available in the periodic reports of the United States Agency for International Development; United Kingdom Ministry of Overseas Development; OECD, Development Assistance Committee; International Bank for Reconstruction and Development. Statistics on trends in the flow of long-term external finance to the developing countries are also presented in *Proceedings of* UNCTAD, Vol. V (United Nations, 1965), chap. I; United Nations, *International Flow of Long-Term Capital and Official Donations, 1961–1965* (New York, 1966).

Some of the special issues discussed in Chapter 5 are covered more fully in the following: Richard Cooper, *A Note on Foreign Assistance and the Capital Requirements for Development,* (Santa Monica: RAND Corporation, February, 1965); Bela Balassa, "The Capital Needs of the Developing Countries," *Kyklos,* Vol. XIX, 1966; John H. Adler, *Absorptive Capacity: The Concept and Its Determinants,* (Washington, D.C.: Brookings Institution, June, 1965); J. Clifford, "The Tying of Aid and the Problem of 'Local Costs,'" *Journal of Development Studies,* January, 1966; Dragoslav Avramovic, *et. al., Economic Growth and External Debt,* (Baltimore: Johns Hopkins Press, 1964); Pieter Lieftinck, *External Debt and Debt-Bearing Capacity of Developing Countries,* (International Finance Section, Princeton University, March, 1966); *Proceedings of* UNCTAD, Vol. V, (United Nations, 1965), pp. 72–117; G. M. Alter, "The Servicing of Foreign Capital Inflows by Underdeveloped Countries," H. S. Ellis, ed., *Economic Development for Latin America,* (New York: St. Martin's Press, 1961); Douglas S. Paauw and Forrest E. Cookson, *Planning Capi-*

tal Inflows for Southeast Asia, (National Planning Association, 1966); H. B. Chenery and A. M. Strout, "Foreign Assistance and Economic Development," *American Economic Review,* September, 1966.

For a linear programming approach to the problem of determining an optimum pattern of aid and growth over time, see H. B. Chenery and Arthur MacEwan, "Optimal Patterns of Growth and Aid: The Case of Pakistan," *Pakistan Development Review,* Summer, 1966. Also of interest are the empirical models of J. Sandee, *A Long-Term Planning Model of India,* (United Nations, 1959); H. B. Chenery and M. Bruno, "Development Alternatives in an Open Economy: The Case of Israel," *Economic Journal,* March, 1962.

---

9. A broad survey of the role of foreign investment in poor countries is provided by C. Wolf and S. C. Sufrin, *Capital Formation and Foreign Investment in Underdeveloped Areas,* (Syracuse: Syracuse Univ. Press, 1955); an annotated bibliography is also appended. The most rigorous analysis of the benefits and costs of private foreign investment is to be found in Sir Donald Mac-Dougall's "The Benefits and Costs of Private Investment from Abroad: A Theoretical Approach," *Economic Record,* March, 1960 (reprinted in *Bulletin of the Oxford University Institute of Statistics,* August, 1960). Also highly illuminating are the discussions in H. W. Arndt's "A Suggestion for Simplifying the Theory of International Capital Movements," *Economia Internazionale,* August, 1954, and "Overseas Borrowing—the New Model," *Economic Record,* August, 1957; J. Knapp, "Capital Exports and Growth," *Economic Journal,* September, 1957; T. Balogh and P. P. Streeten, "Domestic versus Foreign Investment," *Bulletin of the Oxford University Institute of Statistics,* August, 1960 (revised as chap. 5 in Streeten's *Economic Integration*); A. K. Cairncross,

"The Contribution of Foreign and Domestic Capital to Economic Development," *International Journal of Agrarian Affairs,* April, 1961; Anthony Y. C. Koo, "A Short-Run Measure of the Relative Contribution of Direct Foreign Investment," *Review of Economics and Statistics,* August, 1961; Felipe Pazos, "Private versus Public Foreign Investment in Under-Developed Areas," H. S. Ellis, ed., *Economic Development for Latin America,* (New York: St. Martin's Press, 1961); R. F. Mikesell, ed., *U.S. Private and Government Investment Abroad,* (Univ. of Oregon Books, 1962); Chandler Morse, "Potentials and Hazards of Direct International Investment in Raw Materials," Marion Clawson, ed., *Natural Resources and International Development,* (Baltimore: Johns Hopkins Press, 1964); Raymond Vernon, "Foreign-Owned Enterprise in the Developing Countries", John D. Montgomery and Arthur Smithies, eds., *Public Policy,* (Cambridge: Harvard Univ. Press, 1966); W. M. Clarke, *Private Enterprise in Developing Countries,* (New York: Pergamon Press, 1966). Two major theoretical articles are: M. C. Kemp, "The Gain from International Trade and Investment," *American Economic Review,* September, 1966; R. W. Jones, "International Capital Movements and the Theory of Tariffs and Trade," *Quarterly Journal of Economics,* February, 1967.

Problems of the international migration of technology to developing countries are discussed by A. K. Cairncross, *Factors in Economic Development,* (London: Allen & Unwin, 1962), chap. 11; C. A. Anderson and Mary Jean Bowman, *Education and Economic Development,* (Chicago: Aldine Press, 1965), pp. 113–129; J. Baranson, "Transfer of Technical Knowledge by International Corporations to Developing Economies," *American Economic Review, Papers and Proceedings,* May, 1966; Peter P. Gabriel, *The International Transfer of Corporate Skills,* (Boston: Harvard Business School, 1967).

Other studies that extend or apply some of the analysis in Chapter 6 are Yair Aharoni, *The Foreign Investment Decision Process,* (Boston: Harvard Business School, 1966); W. G. Friedmann and G. Kalmanoff, eds., *Joint International Business Ventures,* (New York: Columbia Univ. Press, 1961); Peggy Brewer Richman, *Taxation of Foreign Investment Income,* (Baltimore: Johns Hopkins Press, 1963), chaps. IV, V; R. B. Lillich, *The Protection of Foreign Investment,* (Syracuse: Syracuse Univ. Press, 1965); E. I. Nwogugu, *The Legal Problems of Foreign Investment in Developing Countries,* (Manchester, England: Manchester Univ. Press, 1965).

For some country studies of the role of private foreign investment, see J. V. Levin, *The Export Economies,* (Cambridge: Harvard Univ. Press, 1960); Raymond Vernon, ed., *How Latin America Views the U.S. Investor,* (New York: Praeger, 1966); Marvin D. Bernstein, ed., *Foreign Investment in Latin America* (New York: Knopf, 1966); Michael Kidron, *Foreign Investments in India,* (New York: Oxford Univ. Press, 1965).

---

10. Several protectionist arguments are clearly stated by B. N. Ganguli, "Principles of Protection in the Context of Underdeveloped Countries," *Indian Economic Review,* February, 1952; Gunnar Myrdal, *An International Economy,* (New York: Harper & Row, 1956), chap. XIII; Raúl Prebisch, "Commercial Policy in the Underdeveloped Countries," *American Economic Review, Papers and Proceedings,* May, 1959; P. K. Bardhan, "External Economies, Economic Development, and the Theory of Protection," *Oxford Economic Papers,* March, 1964; Bardhan, "Factor Market Disequilibrium and the Theory of Protection," *Ibid.,* November, 1964.

An excellent review of the relevant arguments is presented by Margaret G. De Vries, "Trade and Exchange Policy and Economic Development: Two Decades of Evolving Views," *Oxford Economic Papers,* March, 1966 (with extensive bibliography). On the specific arguments propounded by Raúl Prebisch, see M. June Flanders, "Prebisch on Protectionism: An Evaluation," *Economic Journal,* June, 1964.

Of exceptional interest are J. Bhagwati, "The Development of Trade Theory in the Context of Underdeveloped Countries," A. K. Das Gupta, ed., *Trade Theory and Commercial Policy,* (New York: Asia Pub. House, 1965); H. G. Johnson, "Tariffs and Economic Development," *Journal of Development Studies,* October, 1964.

H. W. Arndt's "External Economies in Economic Growth," *Economic Record,* November, 1955, provides a useful background to the external economies argument. Also significant is Hla Myint, "Infant Industry Arguments for Assistance to Industries in the Setting of Dynamic Trade Theory," R. F. Harrod and D. C. Hague, eds., *International Trade Theory in a Developing World,* (New York: St. Martin's Press, 1963). Modern variants of the "Manoilesco-type" of argument for protection [Mihail Manoilesco, *The Theory of Protection and International Trade,* (London: P. S. King & Son, 1931)] are formulated by W. A. Lewis, "Economic Development with Unlimited Supplies of Labour," *Manchester School of Economic and Social Studies,* May, 1954, and E. E. Hagen, "An Economic Justification for Protection," *Quarterly Journal of Economics,* November, 1958.

Two important theoretical papers on the effects of a differentiated tariff structure are: H. G. Johnson, "The Theory of Tariff Structure, with Special Reference to World Trade and Development," in H. G. Johnson and P. B. Kenen, *Trade and Development,* (Librairie Droz, Geneva, 1965); R. I. McKinnon, "Intermediate Products, Differential Tariffs, and a Generalization of Lerner's Symmetry Theorem," *Quarterly Journal of Economics,* November, 1966. For illustrations of the effects of differential tariffs in practice, see Santiago Macario, "Protectionism and Industrialization in Latin America," *Economic Bulletin for Latin America,* March, 1964; G. M. Radhu, "The Rate Structure of Indirect Taxes in Pakistan," *Pakistan Development Review,* Autumn, 1964; R. Soligo and J. J. Stern, "Tariff Protection, Import Substitution, and Investment Efficiency," *Ibid.,* Summer, 1965; P. T. Ellsworth, "Import Substitution in Pakistan—Some Comments," *Ibid.,* Autumn, 1966.

An increasing number of country studies indicate the practical effects of using protection as an instrument for industrializing through import-substitution. Among the most significant studies are J. H. Power, "Industrialization in Pakistan: A Case of Frustrated Take-Off?," *Pakistan Development Review,* Summer, 1963; "The Growth and Decline of Import-Substitution in Brazil," *Economic Bulletin for Latin America,* March, 1964; Stephen R. Lewis, Jr. and S. Mushtaq Hussain, "Relative Price Changes and Industrialization in Pakistan: 1951–1964," *Pakistan Development Review,* Autumn, 1966. Members of the Center for Development Economics, Williams College, have prepared an outstanding series of research memoranda on protection and import-substitution policies in Pakistan, Colombia, and Brazil. An excellent general analysis is presented by J. H. Power, "Import Substitution: Barrier to Subsequent Growth," in *International Development 1966,* 8th World Conference of the Society for International Development, (Dobbs Ferry, N.Y.: Oceana Publications, 1967). Also of interest are N. Kaldor, "Dual Exchange Rates and Economic Development," *Economic Bulletin for Latin America,* September, 1964; Richard Goode, *et. al.,* "Role of Export Taxes in Developing Countries," IMF *Staff Papers,* November, 1966; C. P. Kindleberger, *Liberal Policies vs. Controls in The Foreign Trade of Developing Countries,* AID Discussion Paper No. 14, April, 1967.

Among the large number of studies of customs unions or other preferential trading arrangements, several deserve mention for their analytical content: Jacob Viner, *The Customs Union Issue,* (Carnegie Endowment for International Peace, 1950); J. E. Meade, *The Theory of Customs Unions,* (Amsterdam, Netherlands: North-Holland Publishing Co., 1955); R. G. Lipsey, "The Theory of Customs Unions: A General Survey," *Economic Journal,* September, 1960; H. G. Johnson, "The Economic Theory of Customs Union," *Pakistan Economic Journal,* March, 1960; R. L. Allen, "Integration in Less Developed Areas," *Kyklos,* Vol. XIV, No. 3, 1961; Hal B. Lary, "Economic Development and the Capacity to Import—International Policies," in *Lectures on Economic Development,* (Istanbul, 1958); T. Scitovsky, "International Trade and Economic Integration as a Means of Overcoming the Disadvantages of a Small Nation," E. A. G. Robinson, ed., *Economic Consequences of the Size of Nations,* (Macmillan Co., 1960); Bela Balassa, *The Theory of Economic Integration,* (Homewood, Ill.: Richard D. Irwin, 1961), with selected bibliography; Paul Streeten, *Economic Integration,* 2d ed., (A. W. Sythoff, 1964).

More applied studies are Bela Balassa, *Economic Development and Integration,* (Centro De Estudios Monetarios Latinoamericanos, Mexico, 1965); S. Dell, *A Latin American Common Market?,* (New York: Oxford Univ. Press, 1966); M. S. Wionczek, *Latin American Economic Integration,* (New York: Praeger, 1966). For an illustrative exercise in measuring the gains and losses from a common market, see W. T. Newlyn, "Gains and Losses in the East African Common Market," *Yorkshire Bulletin of Economic and Social Research,* November, 1965; A. J. Brown, "Economic Separatism versus a Common Market in Developing Countries," *Ibid.,* May, 1961 and November, 1961.

---

11. A diversity of conclusions are to be found on the argument that underdevelopment is due to forces of the international trading system. The most comprehensive statement of Raúl Prebisch's view appears in the Economic Commission for Latin America's *Economic Development of Latin America and Its Principal Problems,* (United Nations, 1950); *Economic Survey of Latin America, 1949,* (United Nations, 1950); and *Towards a New Trade Policy for Development,* (United Nations, 1964). The unequal distribution of gains from trade argument is also presented by H. W. Singer, "The Distribution of Gains between Investing and Borrowing Countries," *American Economic Review, Papers and Proceedings,* May, 1950. Gunnar Myrdal's criticism of the traditional view of "growth through trade" is stated in his *An International Economy* (New York: Harper & Row, 1956), *Rich Lands and Poor* (New York: Harper & Row, 1957), and in a condensed form in his *Development and Underdevelopment: A Note on the Mechanism of National and International Economic Inequality,* (National Bank of Egypt, 1956). In addition, some provocative arguments against the traditional view are to be found in T. Balogh, "Some Theoretical Problems of Post-War Foreign Investment," *Oxford Economic Papers,* March, 1945; Hla Myint, "An Interpretation of Economic Backwardness," *Oxford Economic Papers,* June, 1954; Folke Hilgerdt, "Uses and Limitations of International Trade in Overcoming Inequalities in World Distribution of Population and Resources," United Nations, *Proceedings of the World Population Conference* (1955); Paul A. Baran's "On the Political Economy of Backwardness," *Manchester School of Economic and Social Studies,* January, 1952, and *The Political Economy of Growth,* (New York: Monthly Review Press, 1957); Staffan Burenstam Linder, *An Essay on Trade and Transformation,* (New York: John Wiley, 1961), pp. 40–81. A more temperate, but still rather pessimistic view, is presented by Ragnar Nurkse in his Istanbul lecture and Wicksell Lectures (see section 4, above). On the other side, Gottfried Haberler's Cairo lectures and the two articles by A. K. Cairncross (see section 4, above) provide a substantial case for the contribution that trade can make to development.

The following also help to define the main issues: Hla Myint, "The Gains from International Trade and the Backward Countries," *Review of Economic Studies,* Vol. XXII (2), No. 58 (1954–55); Myint, "The 'Classical Theory' of International Trade and the Underdeveloped Countries," *Economic Journal,* June, 1958; Myint, *The Economics of the Developing Countries,* (Hutchinson, 1964), chaps. 2–5; D. C. North, "Location Theory and Regional Economic Growth," *Journal of Political Economy,* June, 1955; E. J. Chambers and D. F. Gordon, "Primary Products and Economic Growth: An Empirical Measurement," *Ibid.,* August, 1966; R. E. Baldwin, "Patterns of Development in Newly Settled Regions," *Manchester School of Economic and Social Studies,* May, 1956; Baldwin, "Export Technology and Development from a Subsistence Level," *Economic Journal,* March, 1963; Dudley Seers, "An Approach to the Short-Period Analysis of Primary-Producing Economies," *Oxford Economic Papers,* February, 1959; Boris C. Swerling, "Some Interrelationships between Agricultural Trade and Economic Development," *Kyklos,* Vol. XIV, No. 3 (1961); Eric Clayton, "A Note on the Alien Enclave," *East African Review of Development,* June, 1963; Shu-Chin Yang, "Foreign Trade Problems in Economic Development," *Scottish Journal of Political Economy,* June, 1964; Werner Baer, "The Economics of Prebisch and ECLA," *Economic Development and Cultural Change,* January, 1962; M. June Flanders, "Prebisch on Protectionism: An Evaluation," *Economic Journal,* June, 1964; G. L. Hyde, "A Critique of the Prebisch Thesis," *Economia Internazionale,* August, 1963; H. Kitamura, "Foreign Trade Problems in Planned Economic Development," K. E. Berrill, ed., *Economic Development wtih Special Reference to East Asia,* (Macmillan

Co., 1964); Austin Robinson, "Foreign Trade in a Developing Economy," *Ibid.*; W. A. Lewis, "Economic Development and World Trade," E. A. G. Robinson, ed., *Problems in Economic Development,* (New York: St. Martin's Press, 1965).

For some historical perspective on the developmental effects of the export sector, and for specific country analyses, it is useful to consult A. J. Youngson, *Possibilities of Economic Progress,* (New York: Cambridge Univ. Press, 1959); J. R. T. Hughes, "Foreign Trade and Balanced Growth: The Historical Framework," *American Economic Review, Papers and Proceedings,* May, 1959; J. V. Levin, *The Export Economies,* (Cambridge: Harvard Univ. Press, 1960); K. E. Berrill, "International Trade and the Rate of Economic Growth," *Economic History Review,* April, 1960; C. P. Kindleberger, *Economic Growth in France and Britain, 1851–1950,* (Cambridge: Harvard Univ. Press, 1964); M. Mamalakis and C. W. Reynolds, *Essays on the Chilean Economy,* (Homewood, Ill.: Richard D. Irwin, 1965), pp. 203–398; R. E. Baldwin, *Economic Development and Export Growth: A Study of Northern Rhodesia, 1920–1960,* (Berkeley: Univ. of California Press, 1966); R. W. Clower, *et al., Growth without Development,* (Evanston, Ill.: Northwestern Univ. Press, 1966); D. R. Snodgrass, *Ceylon: An Export Economy in Transition,* (Homewood, Ill.: Richard D. Irwin, 1966).

-----

12. It is difficult to circumscribe the voluminous literature pertaining to the issues of international economic reform discussed in Chapter 9; and that chapter has already been heavily footnoted. Aside from the eight-volume *Proceedings of* UNCTAD, (United Nations, 1964), the major work covering the subject matter of Chapter 9 is H. G. Johnson's *Economic Policies toward Less Developed Countries,* (Washington, D.C.: Brookings Institution, 1967). A stimulating treatment of some of the issues is also furnished by John Pincus, *Trade, Aid and Development*, (New York: McGraw-Hill, 1967).

Also of particular interest are Henry Simon Bloch, *The Challenge of the World Trade Conference*, (School of International Affairs, Columbia University, Occasional Papers 1964–1965); Sidney Weintraub, *The Foreign-Exchange Gap of the Developing Countries*, (International Finance Section, Princeton University, September, 1965); *New Directions for World Trade*, Proceedings of a Chatham House Conference, (New York: Oxford Univ. Press, 1964); Gerard Curzon, *Multilateral Commercial Diplomacy*, (Michael Joseph, 1965); Gardner Patterson, *Discrimination in International Trade*, (Princeton, N.J.: Princeton Univ. Press, 1966); A. I. MacBean, *Export Instability and Economic Development*, (Cambridge: Harvard Univ. Press, 1966); Staffan Burenstam Linder, *Trade and Trade Policy for Development* (New York: Praeger, 1967); N. T. Wang, *New Proposals for the International Finance of Development*, (International Finance Section, Princeton University, April, 1967).

The documents and studies continually being issued by the Secretariat of UNCTAD and the Trade and Development Board provide much material of fundamental as well as current interest.

Index